Cybersecurity

Cybersecurity

Politics, Governance and
Conflict in Cyberspace

Damien Van Puyvelde
Aaron F. Brantly

Polity

Copyright © Damien Van Puyvelde, Aaron F. Brantly 2019

The right of Damien Van Puyvelde, Aaron F. Brantly to be identified as Authors of this Work has been asserted in accordance with the UK Copyright, Designs and Patents Act 1988.

First published in 2019 by Polity Press

Polity Press
65 Bridge Street
Cambridge CB2 1UR, UK

Polity Press
101 Station Landing
Suite 300
Medford, MA 02155, USA

All rights reserved. Except for the quotation of short passages for the purpose of criticism and review, no part of this publication may be reproduced, stored in a retrieval system or transmitted, in any form or by any means, electronic, mechanical, photocopying, recording or otherwise, without the prior permission of the publisher.

ISBN-13: 978-1-5095-2809-7
ISBN-13: 978-1-5095-2810-3(pb)

A catalogue record for this book is available from the British Library.
Library of Congress Cataloging-in-Publication Data
Names: Van Puyvelde, Damien, author. | Brantly, Aaron Franklin, author.
Title: Cybersecurity : politics, governance and conflict in cyberspace / Damien Van Puyvelde, Aaron Brantly.
Description: Cambridge, UK ; Medford, MA, USA : Polity Press, 2019. | Includes bibliographical references and index.
Identifiers: LCCN 2018056638 (print) | LCCN 2018056905 (ebook) | ISBN 9781509528134 (Epub) | ISBN 9781509528097 | ISBN 9781509528103 (pb)
Subjects: LCSH: Internet--Security measures--Government policy. | Computer security--Government policy. | Internet governance. | Internet--Political aspects. | Computer crimes--Prevention. | Security, International.
Classification: LCC TK5105.59 (ebook) | LCC TK5105.59 .V358 2019 (print) | DDC 005.8--dc23
LC record available at https://lccn.loc.gov/2018056638

Typeset in 10.5 on 12 Sabon
by Fakenham Prepress Solutions, Fakenham, Norfolk NR21 8NL
Printed and bound in the UK by CPI Group (UK) Ltd, Croydon

The publisher has used its best endeavors to ensure that the URLs for external websites referred to in this book are correct and active at the time of going to press. However, the publisher has no responsibility for the websites and can make no guarantee that a site will remain live or that the content is or will remain appropriate.

Every effort has been made to trace all copyright holders, but if any have been overlooked, the publisher will be pleased to include any necessary credits in any subsequent reprint or edition.

For further information on Polity, visit our website: politybooks.com

Contents

Figures, Tables and Storyboxes	vi
Acknowledgments	viii
Abbreviations	ix
Introduction	1
1 The expanding scope of cybersecurity	6
2 What is cyberspace?	24
3 Governing cyberspace	41
4 Cyber capabilities and insecurity	57
5 National cybersecurity and strategy	76
6 Cyber war	91
7 Non-state threats: From cybercrime to terrorism	105
8 Organizing deterrence and defense in cyberspace	123
9 Cybersecurity and democracy	139
10 The futures of cybersecurity	152
Notes	160
Bibliography	186
Index	200

Figures, Tables and Storyboxes

Figures

1.1	ENIAC, *c.*1946	9
1.2	ARPANET in December 1969 and July 1977	12
1.3	Internet users since 1990	16
1.4	The growth of significant cyber incidents, 2006–2017	21
1.5	Geographic spread of significant cyber incidents by continent, 2006–2017	22
2.1	The electromagnetic spectrum	31
2.2	Packet-switched v. circuit-switched networks	33
2.3	OSI and DoD models compared	35
2.4	Heartbleed logo	37
4.1	Polymorphic malware sample	61
7.1	Phishing email example	109
7.2	Logo of the Tech of the Islamic State	110
7.3	A dark net weapons market	113

Tables

3.1	Major Internet governance entities	52
4.1	Malware types	59
4.2	Malware features	60
4.3	The Cyber Kill Chain	67
4.4	Kinetic v. cyber capabilities	73

Storyboxes

1.1	The ENIAC	8
2.1	The "spade-hacker"	29
3.1	Net neutrality	53
5.1	Russian interferences: Hit and miss	84
6.1	Cybotage: From Stuxnet to Operation Olympic Games	96
6.2	Ukrainian blackouts	99
6.3	Leveraging cyberattacks: The Russo-Georgian war of 2008	101
7.1	The ISIS hackers	118
8.1	The greatest transfer of wealth in human history	135
9.1	The global surveillance disclosures of 2013	142
9.2	The EuroMaidan movement	144
9.3	GhostNet	147
9.4	The Apple–FBI debate over digital privacy	149

Acknowledgments

Aaron would like to dedicate this book to his three sons, Andrew, Oliver and Daniel, who patiently waited for him to play or read books to them while he worked on various sections of it. Damien dedicates this book to his wife Ana. He would also like to thank Liam Mcvay for his helpful comments on several chapters.

We would both like to thank Louise Knight who encouraged us to write this book and who, together with Nekane Tanaka Galdos and Sophie Wright, provided valuable assistance throughout its preparation.

We hope this book inspires future cybersecurity scholars and practitioners in their efforts to address the many challenges ahead.

Abbreviations

ABC	Atanasoff–Berry Computer
AI	Artificial Intelligence
ANSSI	Agence Nationale de Sécurité des Systèmes d'Information (France)
APT	Advanced Persistent Threat
ARPA	Advanced Research Projects Agency (United States)
ARPANET	Advanced Research Projects Agency Network
BGP	Border Gateway Protocol
C2	Command and Control
CCD COE	Cooperative Cyber Defense Centre of Excellence (NATO)
CENTCOM	Central Command (United States)
CERN	European Council for Nuclear Research
CERT	Computer Emergency Response Team
CIA	Central Intelligence Agency (United States)
CIA triad	Confidentiality, Integrity and Availability
CPU	Central Processing Unit
CSIS	Center for Strategic and International Studies
DARPA	Defense Advanced Research Projects Agency (United States)
DDoS	Distributed Denial of Service
DHCP	Dynamic Host Configuration Protocol
DISA	Defense Information Systems Agency (United States)
DNC	Democratic National Committee (United States)
DNS	Domain Name System
DoD	Department of Defense (United States)
DoS	Denial of Service

DPRK	Democratic People's Republic of Korea (North Korea)
EFF	Electronic Frontier Foundation
ENIAC	Electronic Numerator, Integrator, Analyzer and Computer
EPO	Entry Point Obfuscator
EU	European Union
FBI	Federal Bureau of Investigation (United States)
FSB	Federal Security Service (Russia)
FTP	File Transfer Protocol
GDPR	General Data Protection Regulation (European Union)
GPU	Graphics Processing Unit
GRU	General Staff Main Intelligence Directorate (Russia)
GUI	Graphical User Interface
HTTP	Hypertext Transfer Protocol
IAEA	International Atomic Energy Agency
IANA	Internet Assigned Numbers Authority
IBM	International Business Machines
ICANN	Internet Corporation for Assigned Names and Numbers
IDPS	Intrusion Detection and Prevention System
IDS	Intrusion Detection System
IETF	Internet Engineering Task Force
IGF	Internet Governance Forum
IMP	Interface Message Processor
IoT	Internet of Things
IP	Internet Protocol
IPB	Intelligence Preparation of the Battlefield
IPS	Intrusion Prevention System
ISAC	Information Sharing and Analysis Center
ISAO	Information Sharing and Analysis Organization
ISP	Internet Service Provider
ITRs	International Telecommunications Regulations
ITU	International Telecommunications Union
JTF	Joint Task Force
KGB	Committee for State Security (Soviet Union)
LOIC	Low Orbit Ion Cannon
LOL	Laugh Out Loud
MAC	Media Access Control
MILNET	Military Network
MVD	Ministry of Internal Affairs (Russia)
NASA	National Aeronautics and Space Administration (United States)
NATO	North Atlantic Treaty Organization

Abbreviations

NCCIC	National Cybersecurity and Communications Integration Center (United States)
NGO	Non-Governmental Organization
NHS	National Health Service (United Kingdom)
NIPRnet	Non-Classified Internet Protocol Router Network
NIST	National Institute of Standards and Technology (United States)
NOG	Network Operators' Group
NORAD	North American Aerospace Defense Command (United States)
NSA	National Security Agency (United States)
NSDD	National Security Decision Directive
NSF	National Science Foundation (United States)
NSFNET	National Science Foundation Network
NSI	Network Solutions Inc.
NTIA	National Telecommunications and Information Administration (United States)
OSI	Open Systems Interconnection
PC	Personal Computer
PII	Personally Identifiable Information
PLA	People's Liberation Army (China)
RBN	Russian Business Network
RFC	Request for Comment
RUNET	Russian segment of the Internet
SCADA	Supervisory Control and Data Acquisition
SDL	Security Development Lifecycle
SIGINT	Signals Intelligence
SMTP	Simple Mail Transfer Protocol
SVR	Foreign Intelligence Service (Russia)
TCP	Transport Control Protocol
TLD	Top-Level Domain
TLS/SSL	Transit Layer Security / Secure Socket Layer
Tor	The Onion Router
UDP	User Datagram Protocol
UK	United Kingdom
UN	United Nations
UN GGE	United Nations Governmental Group of Experts
URL	Uniform Resource Locator
US	United States
W3C	World Wide Web Consortium
WSIS	World Summit on the Information Society
WWW	World Wide Web
XSS	Cross-site scripting

Introduction

Every day, people interact with hundreds, if not thousands, of different devices, each connected to the Internet, forming a massive network of networks that has broadly become known as cyberspace. Everything from coffeepots to cars, mobile phones to grocery stores and gas stations is increasingly connected and sharing information with the world around us. We have come to depend on this connected world in innumerable ways. We rely on the Internet to share information about our lives with friends and family, to check our bank accounts and to verify our purchases at stores.

Beyond the obvious devices we hold in our hands or interact with consciously, we depend on hundreds more that we are unaware of, but that keep us safe and facilitate modern life. Nearly every aspect of our daily lives is touched by computers and networks. For instance, cars rely on hundreds of computer chips to manage traction control, and environmental and braking systems. Connected computers at intersections manage the flow of traffic and prevent accidents. The natural resources our modern society depends on are managed by industrial control systems that regulate voltages between substations, or water pressure in city utilities. Every computer chip we come into contact with plays a role in the larger ecosystem of cyberspace. Each of these individual pieces fits within a broader puzzle that is deeply vulnerable to manipulation, misuse and error.

This book focuses on the interactions of individuals, groups and states in cyberspace, and walks the reader through the security challenges faced in an increasingly digital world. While many of the problems faced at the individual device level and in small networks are highly technical, the broader systemic implications of their use and misuse are inherently political. From relatively humble and hopeful beginnings, social scientific thought on issues related to cyberspace has been evolving for nearly 70 years.[1] Debates on the technological connectedness of human society have changed from prognostications on the future to analyses of the present.[2]

Cyberspace is a unique and often perplexing environment, one referred to by the United States Department of Defense (DoD) as a domain of operations on a par with the other combat domains of land, sea, air and space.[3] Cyberspace, unlike its counterpart domains, is entirely man-made and depends on physical, logical and human structures and organizations to operate. Some scholars even refer to cyberspace as a "substrate" that forms the foundation of much of modern life and permeates political, social, economic, technical and environmental sectors.[4]

Cyberspace, as a term, was first derived from a work of fiction in the 1980s and defined as a "consensual hallucination," referring to its ability to alter the perceived reality of those who engage one another through it in chat rooms or virtual environments such as Second Life.[5] Its importance in popular culture has been prevalent long before it was widely used and its impact on national security policy has been significant almost from its inception. Social and cultural commentary on computers, individuals and networks and much more has often outpaced technological reality and informed discussions of the moral and ethical, legal and policy ramifications of an ever-connected world.

Among the most discussed ramifications in the development of cyberspace is security. Security is not an isolated concept. Security failures in cyberspace can result in a wide range of challenges that plague actors from individuals to states. Cybersecurity is often presented as an afterthought in the design and development of the Internet and its related technologies.[6] Although this is partially true, the lack of systemic security in cyberspace is a function of a variety of complex processes that include social, political, technical and economic considerations. Social scientific analysis of these attributes of cyberspace and associated technologies helps to examine the pieces of the puzzle and provides insights on how various outcomes occur or might be avoided.

The significance of cyberspace, and in particular security within cyberspace, to social scientists is growing every year. At present, more than half the world's population is connected in some way to cyberspace. Those who are not presently connected are expected to come online in the years to come. At the close of 2017, by some estimates, more than 250,000 new pieces of malicious software (malware) were being released daily.[7] The growth and diversity of malware spreading within cyberspace are having a substantial impact on nation states, businesses and individuals. Global anti-virus firm Symantec estimated that 978 million people in 20 countries were affected by cybercrime, equating to a total of approximately $172 billion or $142 per person in 2017.[8] Other malicious activities in cyberspace – such as espionage, Distributed Denial of Service (DDoS) attacks, social engineering, information operations and a host of other activities – are challenging modern societies in new ways.

To respond to cybercrime, espionage and other malicious behavior in cyberspace, businesses are spending large sums of money to develop robust cybersecurity strategies, and are investing in global governance organizations and fighting for norms and other behaviors to constrain the proliferation of cybercrime, espionage and malfeasant behaviors by states.[9] Within the business community, technology companies are leading the fight against cybercrime through the implementation of more ubiquitous encryption within platforms, and they are fighting government policies and legal efforts to undermine encryption within their products.[10] Businesses' efforts to secure their products come with trade-offs for law-enforcement and intelligence agencies. More secure communications devices and online platforms have been used by transnational criminals and terrorist organizations to plan and engage in attacks against citizens of multiple countries.[11]

Beyond the proliferation of malware for criminal activities, countless cyberattacks have targeted nation states and their critical infrastructures – including hospitals, public transit, electric and water facilities and many more. Most of these attacks were undertaken with the intent of destroying, degrading or denying critical national capabilities. Many states are now opting to invest substantial resources in the development of civilian and military cyber programs for both offensive and defensive purposes. International organizations such as the North Atlantic Treaty Organization (NATO) have begun outlining military responses to cyberattacks. Some countries, such as the United States, are going as far as claiming the prerogative to respond to certain cyberattacks with nuclear weapons.[12]

It is increasingly difficult to deny the immense importance and impact of cyberspace on every aspect of life in many developed and developing nations. There are huge socio-economic benefits associated with the increased development and proliferation of cyberspace into communities never before connected to the global community. We are now able to share information with friends and family members around the world instantaneously. We can learn about other countries and cultures, engage in global commerce and support communities around the world affected by natural disasters or political repression in ways never before possible. The potential of cyberspace to achieve a great many benefits is limited only by the creativity of those who leverage the increasing range of technologies available to them. Yet, as cyberspace expands and becomes more vital to everyday life, the security challenges often found offline – crime, war, terrorism, cultural and political repression, among many others – must be addressed within cyberspace.

Our approach

This book is designed for readers with limited prior experience in cybersecurity, or as a refresher for those with more robust backgrounds. The combined work introduces a variety of concepts, practical problems and core policy debates necessary to understand security in and through computer networks. Each chapter is carefully constructed to provide our readers with a comprehensive introduction to the complexities and challenges of cybersecurity in an engaging and relevant fashion. The chapters include case studies presented in storyboxes to help our readers analyze the complexity of cybersecurity in practice, as well as discussion questions to hone critical thinking skills, and a brief list of suggested readings. Upon reading this book, readers will know the key attributes of, controversies surrounding, policies and laws regarding, and challenges posed by cybersecurity, and will be well positioned to continue to advance their knowledge, should they choose to do so.

We structured this book around ten chapters designed to introduce readers to a range of concepts associated with cybersecurity. The core argument bringing these chapters together presents cyberspace as a complex socio-technical-economic domain that achieves relevance and importance through human design and manipulation. Despite its technical specificities and unique character, cyberspace is a domain of human activity and interactions. Humans created cyberspace, and have used digital means to serve both beneficial and malicious purposes. The centrality of humans in cyberspace makes social scientific approaches imperative to the study of cybersecurity. An emphasis on human interactions in and through cyberspace allows us to approach cybersecurity from multiple perspectives, ranging from realism to liberalism and constructivism, as well as multiple levels of analysis from the individual to the organizational, the local to the national and international, where rising norms of governance are redefining human interactions. The interactions between the actors of cyberspace and the structure of cyberspace constitute the core of our analytical framework. Users of cyberspace have a unique opportunity to shape the structure of cyberspace and are in turn shaped by its structure.

Chapter 1 introduces readers to the history of cyberspace, and the evolution of security and economic issues that have arisen over the years as cyberspace has grown. Chapter 2 explores what cyberspace really is and how it works by examining the basic technical functions of the domain. Most importantly, chapter 2 introduces readers to the "layers" of cyberspace as a means of making what seems to be an overwhelmingly complex environment more intellectually manageable. Chapter 3 traces the development of governance in cyberspace and examines the political tensions between different models of governance. Chapter 4 dives into the details of how cyber capabilities are developed by state and non-state actors, and how the development of these capabilities generates insecurity. Chapter 5 provides an overview of the complex national security implications of an evolving man-made domain that has come to pervade modern life. Chapter 6 presents the challenges of waging war in cyberspace, and explores how war in cyberspace is both similar to and different from more conventional notions of war and conflict. Chapter 7 takes a step back from state-to-state interactions and shifts the level of analysis to non-state threats associated with cyberterrorism and cybercrime. Chapter 8 looks at how actors across all levels organize for defense and deterrence in response to a multitude of cyber threats. Chapter 9 probes how cybersecurity and democracy, once thought to be mutually reinforcing, have become increasingly uneasy bedfellows, by examining how cyberspace can be both a tool for the enhancement of democracy and damaging to it. Finally, the book concludes by examining what the future of cyberspace has to offer with the increasingly important Internet of Things (IoT), Artificial Intelligence (AI) and biotechnologies.

1

The expanding scope of cybersecurity

This chapter explores the history of cyberspace and related security concerns, from the creation of computers to the present day. The development of computers has been spurred on by human innovation, from mechanical tabulators to digital machines linked together in networks. Security concerns have played a central role in this history. The governments of the United States and the United Kingdom funded early research into computers during the Second World War to improve anti-aircraft defense and codebreaking. In the aftermath of the Second World War, the US Department of Defense (DoD) sponsored much of the early research into computing and the development of computer networks to advance US capabilities and power. This stream of government funding has allowed scientists, in government, academia and the industry, to develop computers and networking as a collaborative tool to share resources and information. Openness and transparency – two values that are essential to the scientific process – guided their work, and helped to shape the early development of what would become the Internet.

Growing access to computers spurred on a number of online communities, allowing humans to express themselves and interact in a new domain: cyberspace. Human activities such as commerce and entertainment, but also espionage and theft, found new expressions online. The 1990s witnessed a rise of cyber threats affecting all levels of society and government. Cyberspace became a cause of concern for governments who feared that the sensitive data they kept on computers could be stolen, manipulated and potentially weaponized, to damage national defense, the economy or even the social fabric of society. As human reliance on computers has expanded, cyberspace has provided new opportunities to exert power, and to threaten the domestic and international order.

Today, cyberspace is a complex socio-technical-economic environment embraced by 3 billion individuals, and millions of groups and communities. All these actors benefit from the opportunities, facilitated by cyberspace, to share resources and information. Yet digital networks host an ever-growing number of cyber threats, which can disrupt human activities, in the digital and physical world. Cyberspace is now a global security issue that transcends national, social and cultural boundaries. As a result, cybersecurity has begun to emerge as an important issue in the field of International Relations, where researchers and practitioners are only now starting to consider the nature of cyber threats, and the most appropriate frameworks for mitigating them.

A brief history of the computer

The history of the computer can be traced back to nineteenth-century England, when mathematics professor Charles Babbage designed his analytical engine. Machines like the analytical engine relied on mechanical components such as levers and gears to compute complex calculations. What distinguished Babbage's machine from others – at least on paper, since his engine never came close to being built – was that it was programmable. While machines could only perform a single function, computers like Babbage's could be programmed to perform multiple functions.[1] New applications for mechanical computers emerged in the following decades. American inventor Herman Hollerith developed a method of storing information as holes punched into cards. His machine was used to tabulate the 1890 US census.[2] The US military developed mechanical computers to improve the use of bombsights on military aircraft in the 1930s. An aimer would input parameters such as speed, altitude and direction, and the bombsight calculated the point at which to aim.[3] Human "computers" continued to direct the "program" for these machines. This dependence on humans limited the speed at which mechanical computers could support their activities.

The first generation of electronic computers emerged in the 1930s. This new technology used electric relays and switches to make calculations. The Atanasoff–Berry Computer (ABC), created by physics professor John Vincent Atanasoff and his graduate assistant Clifford Berry, is often considered to be the first electronic digital computer.

The ABC was designed to solve systems of linear equations using binary numbers. The first prototype of the ABC was built in 1939, with the final rendition weighing more than 700 pounds. The advent of the Second World War oriented research into electronic computers. In the United States, researchers working at the Bell Laboratories developed an anti-aircraft gun director, the M-9, that could direct itself without human interaction using data fed by radar tracking. On the other side of the Atlantic, British codebreakers built another set of electronic computers, called the Colossus, to decode text generated by the Lorenz cipher, which was used by the German army to protect high-level messages. The use of these computers was characterized by a high level of secrecy, which limited any subsequent transfer of knowledge to the research and commercial sectors.[4] Storybox 1.1 presents a brief history of the ENIAC (figure 1.1), one of the first electronic general-purpose computers ever made, which is sometimes presented as the prototype from which most modern computers evolved.

> **Storybox 1.1 The ENIAC**
>
> In the aftermath of the Second World War, the US government and a group of researchers at the University of Pennsylvania completed the Electronic Numerator, Integrator, Analyzer and Computer (ENIAC). Unlike the ABC or Colossus, the ENIAC ran calculations at electronic speed, without being slowed by any mechanical parts. The ENIAC was also the first general-purpose computer, able to solve a large set of numerical problems through re-programming. Despite its versatility, this new computer was primarily used to calculate artillery firing tables, taking over the work of hundreds of humans working on missile tables.[5] The development of the ENIAC inspired a number of similar projects seeking to develop programmable computers that could store information.[6]

The next generation of computers emerged in 1947 and was characterized by the use of transistors, which increased their reliability.[7] This second generation was the first to be used for commercial purposes, leading, most notably, to the success of International Business Machines (IBM), a company aiming to produce computers for all. By the end of the 1950s, dozen of companies contributed to an emerging computer industry in the United States and the United Kingdom, but also in continental Europe and Japan. The development of general-purpose computers required programs to give

Figure 1.1 ENIAC, c.1946 (University of Pennsylvania Archives)

them functionality. The development of computer programming languages (to facilitate the tasking of computers) and operating systems (to manage the flow of work of a computer), throughout the 1950s, eventually led to the distinction between hardware and software.[8] The US DoD maintained an essential role, sponsoring specific computer languages and operating systems, and indirectly driving the industry.[9] Computers remained extremely expensive, which limited the market for them and, by extension, their uses. By 1962, there were around 10,000 computers worldwide, most of them located in the United States.

The invention of the integrated circuit allowed for the development of a third generation of computers. The minicomputers that arose in the mid-1960s were smaller, more powerful and more reliable. A new digital (r)evolution was taking place. Computers moved from being a government machine, to an esoteric hobby and then, finally, to a household item. A number of inventions facilitated this evolution. Human–computer interactions improved following the invention of multiple tiled windows on computer screens, text-editing software, and the mouse.[10] New financial and manufacturing applications contributed to the emergence of a market for software and further expanded the uses of computers.[11] Developments in hardware, specifically the creation of affordable personal computers (PCs), significantly widened access to computers, inspired new uses and forged communities of practice. In 1975, Steve Wozniak and Steve Jobs announced the Apple II computer, an off-the-shelf computer targeted directly for the consumer and small businesses. A few years later, IBM introduced its first PC. At a cost of $1,565, this PC was not beyond the reach of small companies and hobbyists. The percentage of American households with computers more than doubled in the 1980s, and continued to expand exponentially in the 1990s, eventually exceeding 40%.[12] In 2014, 80% of adults in the United States, 78% in Russia, 59% in China, 55% in Brazil and (only) 11% in India had a working computer in their household.[13] In a little over half a century, government support and scientific innovation transformed the digital computer from an advanced research tool to a household item. The increasingly prominent role played by computers in modern society has opened up countless opportunities for individual pursuits.

An open network of networks

The convergence between computing and communication is a defining feature of the digital age. Networked communication over wires has existed since the telegraph (1844), and evolved with the creation of the telephone (1876) and the teletype writer (1914). These machines all rely on circuits to communicate signals, voice or written messages, from one point to another. Their development led to the installation of wired connections across continents, forming vast communication networks. In the aftermath of the Second World War, scientists established connections between two digital computers relying on a single line of communication. If the line between these computers broke down, the communication ended. The practice of time-sharing allowed multiple users to get access to a computer simultaneously to use its processing power. Only a limited number of powerful research computers existed in the United States, and many researchers, who were far removed from their locations, sought to gain access to them.[14] As a result, accessing computers typically required extensive organization and travel. One solution to this problem was to connect computers together as a part of a larger network. Such a network would allow users to access specific computers and data remotely, and would ensure greater reliability than a simple connection between two computers. If one computer stopped functioning properly, other computers could keep the network running.

Computer networking flourished in the United States thanks to a robust and open research culture and substantive government support.[15] Most of the support behind the development of early computer networks came from the US DoD and its Advanced Research Projects Agency (ARPA), an organization established in 1960 to fund high-risk high-gain research. ARPA was particularly keen to develop computer networking to facilitate the sharing of research findings at universities and other government-sponsored laboratories throughout the nation. In 1969, ARPA funding helped establish the first computer network and ancestor of the Internet: ARPANET. Reflecting on the role of the US military in the maturation of computer networking, national security scholar Derek Reveron notes that "there has always been an implicit national security purpose for the Internet."[16]

Networking digital computers created a new means for humans to communicate with each other. ARPANET first served as a platform for researchers to develop and refine networking technologies that linked a handful of universities and research centers. On 29 October 1969, researchers at the University of California in Los Angeles tried to log in to a computer at the Stanford Research Institute, and began typing the required "log in" command. Their computer crashed after the two first letters; the first message ever sent on the ARPANET was "lo." Figure 1.2 shows how the original ARPA network grew from 2 nodes in 1969, to 55 in 1977.[17] Each of these nodes represents a processor, which can be considered as a router. The two maps show the type of institutions hosting these nodes: research universities and institutes, national laboratories, military and intelligence agencies. The 1977 map shows the nascent complexity of a network that connected processors through both landlines and satellite connections. On the other side of the Atlantic, French and British researchers were developing similar networks (CYCLADES in France, and the Mark I project at the UK National Physical Laboratories), but funding difficulties limited their progress.[18]

In the United States, more and more universities and research centers joined or wanted to join ARPANET. To help users connect together, Vint Cerf, a researcher at Stanford University, and Robert Khan from ARPA, developed a common transmission protocol (Transmission Control Protocol or TCP) that explained how to establish a connection and transmit messages on their network. A separate protocol was then developed to couple existing networks together. This protocol, the Internet Protocol (IP), facilitated the internetworking of digital computers. The complete description of these two protocols and the rights to use them were freely available

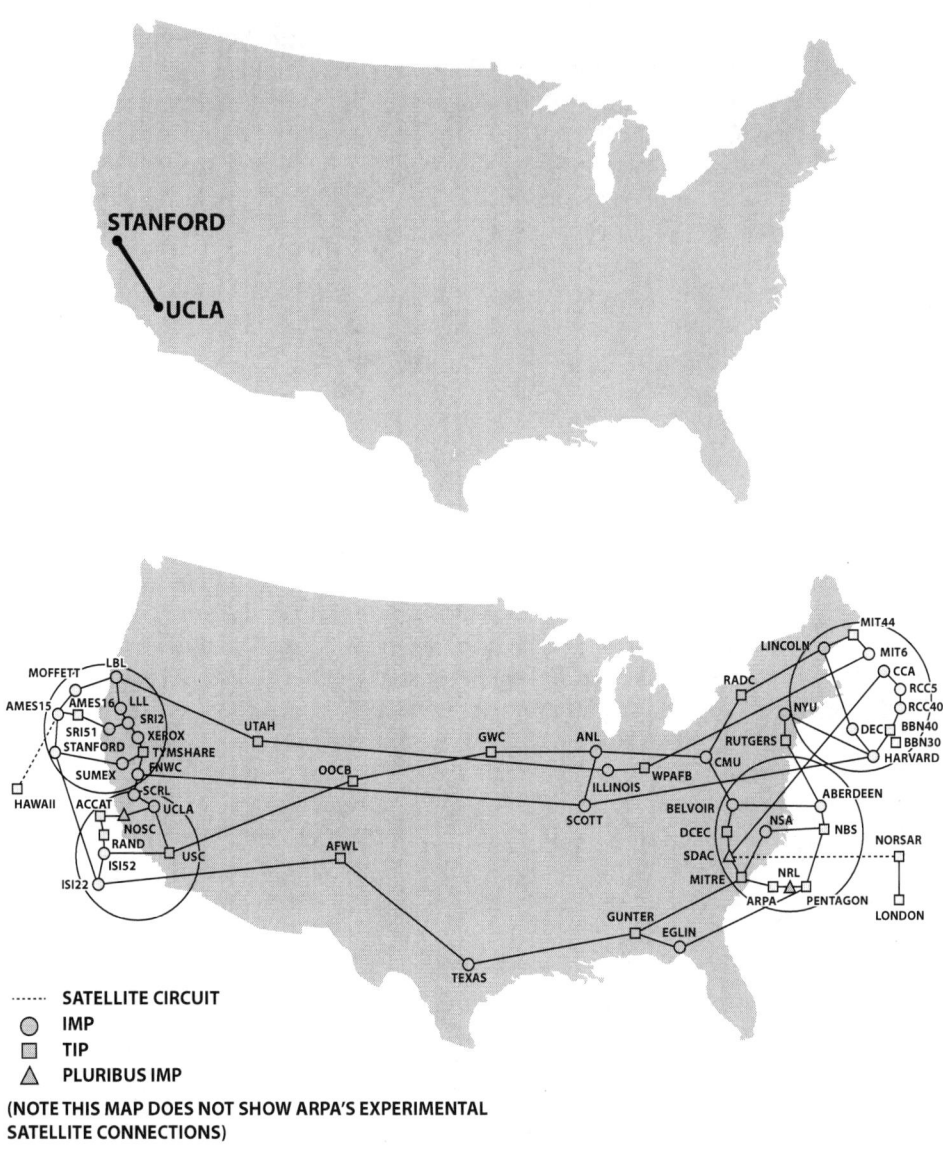

Figure 1.2 ARPANET in December 1969 (top) and July 1977 (bottom)

Source: Frank Heart, Alex McKenzie, John McQuillian and David Walden, *ARPANET Completion Report*, Bolt, Beranek and Newman Inc., Burlington, MA, January 4, 1978, III-79-III-89.

to all. Any network that wanted to join simply had to follow the Transport Control and Internet protocols. This open access policy – inspired by the academic practice of information sharing – defined the architecture of the early Internet and allowed the network to grow in scale.[19] Information technology pioneer and former ARPA employee Barry Leiner and his colleagues explained that the early Internet was developed as "a general infrastructure on which new applications could be conceived."[20] This approach stood in stark contrast to the way in which the US DoD (still the main funder of the Internet at the time) conceived of information sharing. In the defense and national security communities, the dissemination of information tends to be tightly controlled to prevent unauthorized disclosures. An important implication of the open architecture of the Internet is that no single entity could control access to and uses of the network. While this approach spurred a tremendous growth in network users, it would also pose a number of challenges. Malicious actors soon started to use the Internet to steal resources and information, and to mislead network users.

As networking became increasingly common, its value increased and researchers developed new applications, beyond sharing machines for their processing power. Initial Internet applications focused on communication means. Researchers started posting messages and replying to each other's comments on editable pages, or bulletin boards, accessible online. In 1972, computer programmer Ray Tomlinson wrote a program for reading, composing and sending messages from one computer to another. The electronic mail was born. Within a year, this new application generated 73 percent of all ARPANET traffic.[21] Soon the value of networked communication became clear to everyone involved, and an increasing number of universities and US government agencies joined the web of networks. Yet the early Internet continued to be mostly populated by researchers, supported by investment from the US government.

The spread of personal computers in the 1980s fed a growing interest in internetworking, and fostered a shift toward an increasingly social network, away from its previous principal application as a research hub. As well as a technological evolution, the growth of internetworking is a socio-cultural phenomenon. For Ceruzzi, social and cultural factors differentiate the Internet from previous networks. The emergence of PC hobbyists and communities of practices focusing on computers – for example, gamers – fostered internetworking from the bottom up in the 1980s.[22] It was in this context that science fiction writer William Gibson coined the term "cyberspace." Gibson imagined cyberspace as a virtual world of data linked by computer networks and accessible through consoles.[23]

The core infrastructure of the ARPANET had to expand to host new users. The network expanded beyond the United States, with new nodes established at University College London and then at the NORSAR research laboratory in Norway in 1982.[24] As more and more researchers, scientists and engineers joined the ARPANET, the military community developed its own network (MILNET) in 1983, to separate sensitive military from civilian traffic and implement stricter security requirements. ARPANET remained the preferred platform for industry, academia and government research. In 1985, the US National Science Foundation (NSF) launched its own network (NSFNET) to connect the supercomputing centers it funded across the country and promote advanced research and education on networking.[25] Any university receiving funding for an Internet connection was required to use NSFNET and provide access for users. In a few years' time NSFNET took over as the main hub for internetworking and ARPANET was decommissioned in 1990. The data routes developed for this scientific network eventually formed a major part of the Internet's backbone.[26] Growing commercial interest in ARPANET and then NSFNET changed the nature of internetworking, transforming the research hub into a popular communication platform. In 1994, the US government decided to turn over official control of the regional backbone connections of NSFNET to private interests. Commercial Internet Service Providers (ISPs) started offering their services to individual users, who could connect online using their phone landline.[27] As the Internet expanded, commercial providers of hardware (e.g. computers and modems) and software (e.g. browsers) multiplied.

The spread of the Internet

Internetworking became mainstream in the 1990s with the invention of the World Wide Web, which facilitated interpersonal communications in cyberspace. In 1990, a group of scientists based at the European Council for Nuclear Research (CERN) laboratory in Switzerland created a new document format to present information in a set of linked computer documents (Hypertext Transfer Protocol or HTTP). This protocol allowed users to link each document to another one through specific words, phrases or images. In 1991, these innovations spurred the creation of a new application which compiled and linked multimedia documents and made them available to any network user: the World Wide Web (WWW). An exponential number of interlinked HTTP documents became accessible online thanks to a system that identified them: the Uniform Resource Locator (URL), colloquially known as a web address. Subsequently, researchers at the University of Illinois developed a browser software named Mosaic, which simplified public access and ability to surf the web.[28]

Internet usage expanded dramatically in the following years, spurred by the convergence of increasingly cheap and powerful computers, the multiplication of modems facilitating Internet connection through phone lines, and new browsers like Internet Explorer and Netscape (1995).[29] At the dawn of the twenty-first century, further technological developments, such as the spread of wireless broadband technology, commonly known as Wi-Fi, and the rise of smartphones, facilitated further access to the Internet.[30] Figure 1.3 shows how the number of Internet users exploded from 2.6 million in 1990 to over 3.4 billion in 2016 (that is, roughly half of the world population). This rapid expansion has been matched by an exponential growth in the number of websites and applications. Amazon, Craigslist and eBay were all established in 1995, the Chinese e-commerce giant Alibaba was founded a few years later in 1999. Together, they have reshaped the way millions of humans shop and access consumer goods. In the last two decades, the Internet has become an increasingly social space, connecting individuals online through communities of interest. American companies such as LinkedIn (2002), Facebook (2004) and Twitter (2006) have provided new platforms for networks of "friends" to form. The Chinese Renren Network (2005) and Russian platform VKontakte (2006) developed similar services. The advent of these social media and other online applications empowered Internet users to shape and diversify the content of the "Web 2.0".[31]

The web has now become a central part of millions of lives across the globe. With the multiplication of social platforms and wearable technologies like smart phones and smart watches, cyberspace is now a central arena for life in the twenty-first century. Statistics reveal that more Internet users are now located in Asia (China and India account for more than 1.1 billion users) than in Europe and North America. Today, more than 70 percent of Internet users – some 2.5 billion people – interact on social media. The advent of the Internet has generated countless opportunities to learn from, and connect with, humans from across the globe. The borderless nature of this digital realm has opened space for millions of individuals to develop communities of interest and express their ideas and identity. Large

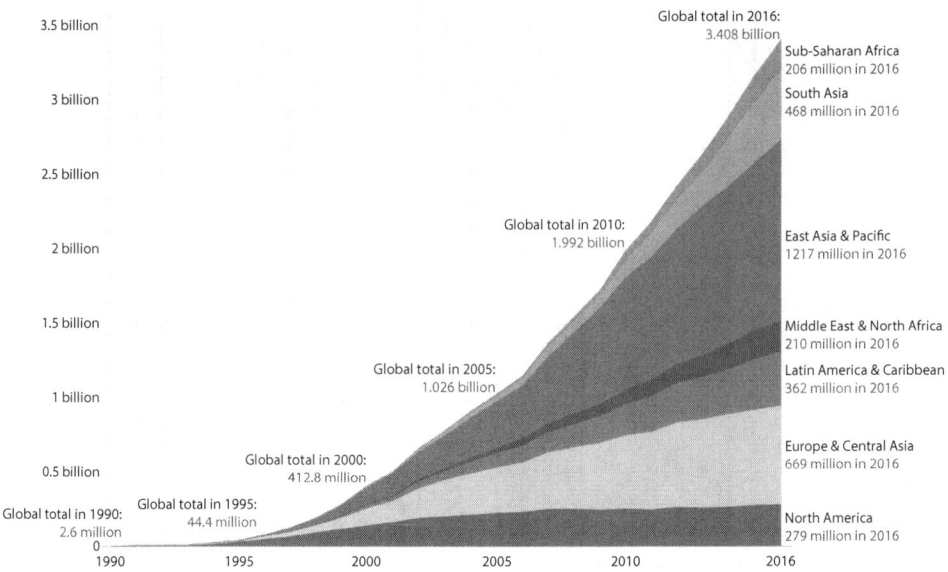

Figure 1.3   Internet users since 1990 (Max Roser, OurWorldinData.org)

Internet communities have formed around common interests like sports, cats and dogs, or environmental protection. The advent of the Internet is reshaping human lives, social bonds and politics, and challenging traditional, state-centric ideas about human interactions across the globe.[32] As the Internet and broader cyberspace become ever more prominent in the daily routines of billions of humans, vulnerability to cyberattacks and accidental disruptions has expanded dramatically.

The rise of cyber threats

The rise of cyber threats is directly linked to the growing complexity of computers and the scope of human activities in cyberspace, from research and military affairs to economic and social activities.[33] Given that the US government played a central role in the early development of computers and computer networks, the pre-history of cyber threats is American-oriented. Michael Warner, the historian of the US Cyber Command, distinguishes four successive insights that marked the history of national cybersecurity in the United States. Early US concerns about cyber threats can be traced back to the practice of multiprogramming, which broadened access to the information stored on computers. Warner finds that Congress started expressing concerns about this practice in the 1960s when government officials realized that computers could spill sensitive data (first insight). These concerns were relatively limited in the early days of networking when the overall number of ARPANET users was in the hundreds. In 1972, US intelligence agencies tested the security of their networks and found that a number of sensitive databases could be accessed from a single computer. The second key insight reached by the US government was that sensitive government data could be stolen, perhaps even manipulated, from a single point of access. The threats posed by such cyber intrusion rose to a new level when computers became essential to modern weapon systems and military decision-making. The networking of computers, and the open architecture that characterized internetworking, created vulnerabilities in government and military systems which could, for example, increase the risk that adversaries would disrupt military command and control systems used for missile warning. The threat of intrusion was sufficiently serious to push President Reagan to sign a National Security Decision Directive warning about the risk of "interception, unauthorized electronic access, and related forms of technical exploitation" to telecommunications and automated information processing systems. The directive put the National Security Agency (NSA) in charge of monitoring all "government telecommunications systems and automated information systems."[34]

A number of incidents confirmed growing US government concern in the following years. In 1986, a hacker penetrated sensitive systems connecting computers at the Lawrence Berkeley National Laboratory and MITRE Corporation. This remote attack relied on the ARPANET and MILNET to infiltrate dozens of computers at the Pentagon and a number of other military bases. Clifford Stoll, a systems administrator at Lawrence Berkeley Lab, first identified the attack and began to investigate its origins with the help of the Federal Bureau of Investigation (FBI) and the telecommunication company AT&T. The subsequent investigation revealed that hackers had sold the information they collected on the US networks to the Soviet Committee for State Security (the KGB). Stoll subsequently wrote a book that publicized what is often considered to be the first publicly known case of cyberespionage.[35] In 1988, a malicious code spread on the Internet and slowed thousands of computers used by US government and private organizations. This malware, nicknamed the Morris worm, demonstrated the inherent vulnerability of computer networks. The ability of cyber threats to spread across networks reinforced the need for cooperation between users. The effects of the Morris worm prompted the Defense Advanced Research Projects Agency (ARPA changed its name to DARPA in 1972) to establish a Computer Emergency Response Team (CERT) in order to coordinate information and responses to such computer vulnerabilities.

The public debate on cyber threats took a new turn in the early 1990s when experts started to discuss the military implications of cyberattacks. The public debate on cyber war, which we will examine in chapter 6, can be traced back to the early 1990s as analysts forecasted what war would look like in the twenty-first century.[36] At the time, cyber war was perceived as a form of information warfare, which sought to decapitate and exploit the command and control structure of the enemy forces. Cyberattacks provided new, electronic means to disrupt computer systems or corrupt the data they hosted. Computers, Warner notes, had become a weapon of war (third insight). The inclusion of computer attack in the US military arsenal would soon lead to a fourth insight: other countries may utilize computers for a similar purpose.[37]

In 1997, the US DoD ran an exercise codenamed ELIGIBLE RECEIVER, and found that a moderately sophisticated adversary could inflict considerable damage on sensitive US government networks. During this exercise, a small team of government hackers working at the NSA attacked the computer systems of multiple US military commands, gained administrative access to them, tampered with email messages, and disrupted operational systems. Government networks seemed wide open to electronic attacks. Shortly after this exercise, the US government suffered a series of real attacks that confirmed the existence of significant weaknesses. In February 1998, a series of cyberattacks targeted DoD unclassified computer networks at multiple Air Force bases, the National Aeronautics and Space Administration (NASA), and federal laboratories associated with the military. This operation, codenamed SOLAR SUNRISE, showed that the DoD detection systems were insufficient to protect government networks against unwanted cyber intrusions. Worse still, investigations into the attacks revealed that the attackers were not a foreign intelligence service, but two California teenagers who had been directed by Israeli hacker Ehud Tenenbaum.[38]

The rise of cyber threats has affected not only government networks and capabilities but also society. Originally, hackers were computer geeks motivated by curiosity and entertainment. The term "hacking" itself initially meant playing with machines, and hackers sought to demonstrate their aptitude for programming. A 1981 *New York Times* article describes how "skilled, often young, computer programmers" would "probe the defenses of a computer system, searching out the limits and the possibilities of the machine."[39] Computer industry pioneer Bill Gates, the founder of Microsoft, revealed on the BBC that he hacked into the computer system of his school as a teen so that he could attend all-girl classes.[40] Other hackers were driven by more nefarious purposes. In 1981, a hacker who used the nickname Captain Zap was convicted for breaking into AT&T computers and changing the company's billing system to create discounted rates during business hours.

The threat hackers posed to the corporate world, and by extension to the economy, generated increasing media coverage in the 1980s, eventually drawing the attention of legislators and entrepreneurs.[41] The US Congress passed the Federal Computer Fraud and Abuse Act in 1986 to prohibit unauthorized access to federal computers and traffic in computer passwords. A few years later, the Parliament of the United Kingdom passed the Computer Misuse Act in response to a 1988 court case targeting two hackers who gained unauthorized access to British Telecom's viewdata service (an early teletext network). This bill, and the growing scope of cyber threats, inspired a number of other countries, from Ireland to Canada, to draft legislation on cybercrime in the following years.[42]

In the 1990s, concern with cybersecurity deepened and became a security issue of societal proportions. Most of the cyber threats that are commonly known today – viruses, worms, trojans, denial of service (DOS) attacks – emerged at the same time that the Internet spread and computer networking became an increasingly prominent part of modern life. The rise of the World Wide Web diversified the uses of the Internet and expanded the scope of cyber threats. The growth of e-commerce, for example, created new opportunities for criminals to make profit online. The possibility to make online payments also led to new types of scam relying on emails, for example. Confronted with a rise in cyber threats, the corporate world developed new answers. The computer security company McAfee was established in 1987, and released its VirusScan the same year. An anti-virus software industry developed in the following years to serve not only the government and private sectors, but also users accessing the Internet from home.[43]

Critical infrastructure and key sectors of modern society such as agriculture, banking, healthcare, transportation, water and power rely on computer networks that control and supervise data streams (also called SCADA systems). In 2007, the Idaho National Laboratory ran an experiment, the Aurora Generator test, demonstrating that a computer program could disrupt a diesel generator used as a part of an electric grid, and cause it to explode.[44] Some experts fear that such an explosion could generate a cascading failure of an entire power grid. Growing concern about cyberattacks on critical infrastructure has pushed a number of governments to devise strategies to protect societal reliance on cyber infrastructure. The 2003 US "National Strategy to Secure Cyberspace" noted that "threats in cyberspace have risen dramatically" and emphasized the need for public–private engagement to secure cyberspace.[45] Since critical infrastructure is privately owned in most advanced countries, working across the public–private divide is essential to ensure national cybersecurity. As such, dozens of countries have adopted a similar approach to their national cyber security and developed specific organizations and strategies to counter cyber threats to the public and private sectors.[46]

A global security issue

The dawn of the twenty-first century saw the advent of increasingly sophisticated attacks and malware that spread around the world. The internationalization of cyberspace transformed cybersecurity into a global security issue. While most cyberattacks came from the United States and Europe in the 1990s, by the early 2000s they went international. In 2000, the Love Bug or "ILOVYOU" computer worm originated in the Philippines and spread across the World Wide Web (initially relying on an email attachment). The virus overwrote files hosted by tens of millions of computers causing an estimated loss of $10 billion in work hours.[47] The Zotob worm originated in Morocco in August 2005, and caused troubles at CNN, the *New York Times*, the US Senate, and the Centers for Disease Control and Prevention in the United States.[48]

Research shows the increasingly global character of cyber threats. The Center for Strategic and International Studies (CSIS), a renowned think tank based in Washington DC, has compiled a list of significant cyber incidents since 2006. While this list does not represent the whole spectrum of cyber threats, it illustrates their growing scope. The current list (2018) compiles 296 cyber incidents on government agencies, defense and high-tech companies, or economic crimes with losses of more than a million dollars. Figure 1.4 shows a rise in the number of significant cyber incidents since 2006, and figure 1.5 shows the diverse geographic spread of the attacks (by continent where victims are located). Most of the significant cyber incidents identified by CSIS researchers have targeted victims in North America, Europe and Asia. This should come as no surprise since the penetration rate of the Internet is highest on these three continents.

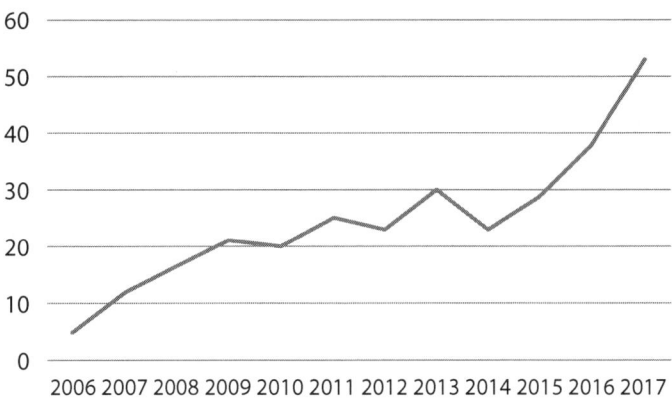

Figure 1.4 The growth of significant cyber incidents, 2006–2017 (CSIS)

In the last decade, most sophisticated threats, generally developed by well-resourced state actors, have affected computer systems across the public–private divide. A widely consulted report released in 2011 by cybersecurity company Mandiant exposed how one of China's cyber espionage units stole "hundreds of terabytes of data from at least 141 organizations across a diverse set of industries beginning as early as 2006".[49] This Advanced Persistent Threat (APT) targeted intellectual property – the bedrock of the modern economy – in a number of sectors, including information technology, financial services, construction and manufacturing, the chemical and energy industries, and aerospace, to name a few. Altogether, victims were located in 15 countries ranging from the United States and Canada, to Belgium, France and the United Kingdom, as well as Israel, the United Arab Emirates, India, Japan, Taiwan and South Africa. The fact that a company authored this widely discussed report further illustrates the development of a robust market for cybersecurity, which serves government as well as private-sector clients.

Given the global scope of cyberspace and cyber threats (see figure 1.5), social scientific research on cybersecurity should strive to consider cases beyond the United States. While the United States has historically played a leading role in the development of computers and internetworking, and thus continues to attract many cyberattacks,

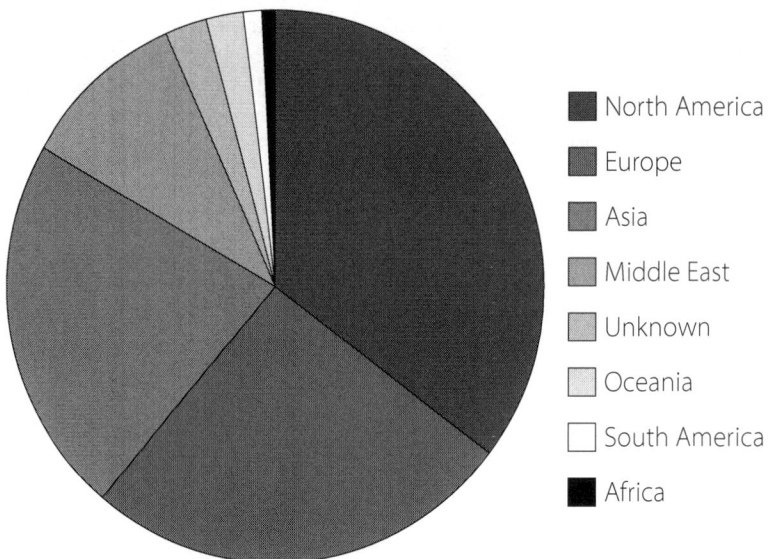

Figure 1.5 Geographic spread of significant cyber incidents by continent, 2006–2017 (CSIS)

cybersecurity is truly a global security concern. This book includes a number of case studies and examples from other countries, as well as non-state actors, to reflect this global scope. Cybersecurity is a global problem that requires a global approach. Yet, most of the physical layer of cyberspace and the governance of security threats takes place at the nation-state level, and national governments have developed the most advanced offensive and defensive capabilities in cyberspace. As a result, multiple levels of analysis (individual, organizational, societal, national and global) can help in understanding cybersecurity.

Discussion questions

1. In what ways has the development of cyberspace affected contemporary threats to cybersecurity?
2. What are the key turning points in the history of cybersecurity?
3. Read the latest CSIS list of significant cyber incidents and pick three events that caught your attention. What is the significance of these cyber incidents?

Further resources

Internet history timeline, see: www.computerhistory.org/internethistory.

Paul E. Ceruzzi, *Computing: A Concise History* (Cambridge, MA: MIT Press, 2012).

Werner Herzog, "Lo and Behold: Reveries of the Connected World," video documentary (available on Netflix).

Barry M. Leiner et al., "The Past and Future History of the Internet," *Communications of the ACM* 40/2 (1997): 102–8.

Michael Warner, "Cybersecurity: A Pre-history," *Intelligence and National Security* 27/5 (2012): 781–99.

2

What is cyberspace?

In 1983, President Reagan watched the blockbuster success *WarGames at Camp David*. The movie is a Cold War science-fiction film about a teenager, David Lightman, who hacks into a North American Aerospace Defense Command (NORAD) supercomputer, the WOPR – War Operations Plan Response – and pushes the United States to the brink of war. Nuclear Armageddon is thwarted when Lightman convinces the computer to play tic-tac-toe. The computer, leveraging artificial intelligence, learns that there is no optimal outcome between two experienced players and that all possible initiations of conflict result in mutually assured destruction. WOPR then calls off the nuclear launch realizing it was in a no-win situation. The movie had a profound impact on the President, who, in a meeting with the Chairman of the Joint Chiefs of Staff, questioned the plausibility of this scenario. The Chairman did not have an immediate answer and said he would look into it. A week later in a follow-up meeting, the Chairman explained to the President that not only was the plot of the science-fiction movie plausible, but reality was far worse than fiction.[1]

This banal event in the history and development of cyberspace triggered an important dialogue between the policy community at the highest levels and the technical community, about the implications of an increasingly connected world. The discussions of the possible ramifications of cybersecurity instigated by President Reagan led to a larger government conversation within the United States culminating in a National Security Decision Directive (NSDD-145) on "National Policy on Telecommunications and Automated Information Systems Security." The same conversation that President Reagan started continues today in an environment that has gone from well under a million connected users in the early 1980s – most of them Americans – to more than 4 billion users across the world in 2018.

The previous chapter provided insights into the history and development of cyberspace to set the stage for the diverse ways in which digital technologies have come to impact human society. Yet this cannot fully account for what cyberspace is and what it will become. The developers of IBM mainframes in the 1960s, or the designers of the navigation control systems on the Apollo missions, were not able to imagine a world in which teenagers would blithely carry mobile computers (iPhones) that are 120 million times more powerful than anything they could develop.[2] Moreover, computer pioneers could not foresee the ability of these same mobile computers to connect to nearly all of human knowledge, while still being used primarily to send emojis and watch cat and dog videos.

In tandem with substantial growth in the use of computers and networks, and increases in computing speed and information transmission, the problems first identified by a curious President after watching a science-fiction film have grown in scope and magnitude. What moved from ARPANET to NSFNET and MILNET to the Internet has now expanded to constitute an often-criticized term: cyberspace. The term "cyberspace" has its etymological roots in the Greek word *kubernētēs*, meaning "to steer." However, the modern use of the word "cyber" was picked up by World War II mathematician Norbert Wiener in his 1948 book *Cybernetics: Or, Control and Communication in the Animal and the Machine*. Wiener's use of the word "cyber" is in line with the Greek definition and implies the interface and interaction of the biological and mechanical. The field of cybernetics, which was established by Wiener, had strong proponents throughout academia and the government, yet the timing of this movement which sought to integrate man and machine was not matched by the then-available technology and eventually the field fell out of favor.[3]

Although cyber fell out of favor within military and academic communities, it was picked up by science-fiction writers in the 1980s. The interplay of man and machine and the potential dystopian futures of connected societies provided ample ground for creative minds to explore. One such mind was William Gibson, who in 1984 wrote *Neuromancer*. In his work, Gibson explored the interactions of individuals within a global network, complete with Artificial Intelligence (AI), hackers and more. Despite the dystopian nature of the novel, the book also eloquently describes the interconnection of humans and machines, and terms this interplay "cyberspace."

Gibson defines cyberspace broadly as a "consensual hallucination" – that is to say, a virtual environment in which humans engage one another and machines interactively.[4]

The term "cyberspace" expands beyond the conventional concepts of networks and encompasses both physical and virtual realities that constitute the problem set for the current volume. In the more than three decades since its use by Gibson, the word "cyber" has become a universal prefix to describe a variety of phenomena from cybercrime to cyberbullying and cyber war. The prefix "cyber" is often criticized for its universality, but, as noted by some scholars, the term is largely here to stay.[5] The focus in this chapter is on the function and structure of the environment encompassed by the term "cyberspace." Understanding the basic technical underpinnings of the environment provides students, scholars and policy-makers with a starting point upon which to base subsequent theoretical and policy debates. Absent an understanding of the technical, policy and scholarly communities are often disconnected from the technical communities that build and maintain what has come to be defined as cyberspace.

Defining cyberspace

Before turning our attention to the structural attributes of cyberspace and how they work, it is helpful to examine some of the definitions of the term under consideration. Defining the term establishes what is and what is not under consideration. Over the course of the last 30 years, the number of definitions of cyberspace has grown substantially.[6] In this book, we use two of the more encompassing definitions of cyberspace to provide intellectual and analytical space in which to understand and evaluate a variety of complex and related phenomena.

In 2009, in a seminal volume on cyberpower, Daniel Kuehl, a professor at the US National Defense University, defined cyberspace as "an operational domain framed by the use of electronics and the electromagnetic spectrum to create, store, modify, exchange, and exploit information via interconnected and Internetted information systems and their associated infrastructures."[7] Kuehl's expansive definition is packed with terms and concepts that begin to outline the borders of what the US DoD refers to as a domain. Before moving forward to the second definition of cyberspace as outlined by the DoD, it is helpful to pull apart these combined terms.

First, Kuehl introduces the concept of electronics, a class of physical devices dependent on the use of electrical energy for operation.[8] Electronic devices can include toasters, circuits, telephones, computers, or anything else that requires electricity to function. Second, he identifies the use of the electromagnetic spectrum, a range of frequencies and radiation, wavelengths and photonic energies.[9] The electromagnetic spectrum includes everything from WiFi and radio received on a car stereo to infrared remote controls for TVs, and much more. Third, he implies that cyberspace is neither the use of electronics nor the electromagnetic spectrum in isolation but their ability to work in tandem to create, store, modify, exchange and exploit information. Fourth, it is not simply the attributes of information – creation, storage, modification and exchange within a single system – but the ability to transmit information across connected systems and their associated infrastructures that constitute cyberspace. Kuehl's definition of cyberspace is a far cry from that William Gibson's hallucination. He emphasizes the physical and informational nature of cyberspace, and does not address the impact or value of the information that circulates in this space. We will return to the physical nature of cyberspace further down. But first it is helpful to contrast this definition with the current operational definition from the US DoD, which provides a simplified structural framework within which to conceptualize cyberspace.

Department of Defense Joint Publication 3-12 defines cyberspace as follows:

> Cyberspace consists of many different and often overlapping networks, as well as the nodes (any device or logical location with an Internet protocol address or other analogous identifier) on those networks, and the system data (such as routing tables) that support them. Cyberspace can be described in terms of three layers: physical network, logical network, and cyber-persona. The physical network layer of cyberspace is comprised of the geographic component and the physical network components. It is the medium where the data travel. The logical network layer consists of those elements of the network that are related to one another in a way that is abstracted from the physical network, i.e., the form or relationships are not tied to an individual, specific path, or node. A simple example is any Web site that is hosted on servers in multiple physical locations where all content can be accessed through a single uniform resource locator. The cyber-persona layer represents yet a higher level of abstraction of the logical network in cyberspace; it uses the rules that apply in the logical network layer to develop a digital representation of an individual or entity identity in cyberspace. The cyber-persona layer consists of the people actually on the network.[10]

This definition of cyberspace builds on Kuehl's more physical and informational definition and adds in the concepts of logic and persona. Both definitions are helpful because they frame the possible actions and policies that can and do impact the digital domain. However useful these definitions are, they have not settled the debate on the definition of cyberspace. Researchers should always consider the uses and limits of the definition they choose. Definitions are often suited to a particular field of study. Computer scientists focus on the logical layers more intently than computer engineers, who focus on the physical layers. Policy-makers and social scientists tend to place their emphasis on the cyber-persona layer of cyberspace, and most users interact within the persona layer also. Yet the reality is that the physical, logical and persona attributes of cyberspace are deeply intertwined. How the layers interact and their value to one another form the basis of what cyberspace is. Cyberspace is a physical and virtual domain. It is the product of human creation and ingenuity. It is a domain that, while man-made, is still impacted by its interactions within other domains, such as land, sea, air and space. The remainder of this chapter breaks apart the layers of cyberspace – physical, logical and persona – to develop a more detailed understanding of its complexities.

Physical-network layer

Scholars of international relations often study cyberspace exclusively on the logical or persona layers of cyberspace.[11] These works privilege the transnational nature of data flows made possible by computers connected into networks, and subsequent networks connected in an ever-widening structure. Emphasis is largely placed on how the logical and persona layers are able to be manipulated with code or other forms of information. These accounts leave off the very physical and tangible nature of cyberspace, the geographic and spatial relationships that impact the way in which cyberspace functions. The physical-network layer constitutes the closest approximation to other traditional domains of interaction: air, land, sea and space. All of the physical-network layer aspects of cyberspace are located in one of these domains.

If cyberspace is the connection of billions of networked devices, then the physical unit of the network layer starts at the node itself. A node can be anything that uses electronics and the electromagnetic spectrum to store, create, modify and exchange data. A node is not the exchange of data itself, it is the physical system that makes exchange possible. For the purpose of conceptualization, nodes can be construed as any device connected to a network that has a Central Processing Unit (CPU) and would be commonly referred to as a computer. The number and types of nodes within cyberspace is diverse and grows every year. As of 2018, there are an estimated 17–19 billion devices (nodes) connected to the Internet and making up cyberspace.[12] Within this physical device structure, there are some nodes that constitute the core and some that form an ever-widening periphery. Core nodes are comprised of servers and core routers. Servers are used for a wide variety of functions from managing and keeping track of where various nodes are within the network structure to specific network services, such as storing information, and managing various services found within the logical and cyber-persona layers of cyberspace. Routers direct packets of data around the backbone – a central nervous system for the Internet – and manage the efficiency of the network. The average speed of the core routers is around 100 gigabits per second (Gbit/s) with some exceeding 400 Gbit/s and they function much faster than your typical home or business network.[13]

Core nodes are connected by backbone lines that function similarly to the central nervous system in the human body. Backbone lines are long-haul fiber-optic lines that carry bits (one of the most basic units of information used in computing) in the form of photons between core routers and servers. In the United States, these long-haul lines almost mirror the US interstate highway infrastructure system.[14] They spread out like capillaries as they enter more densely populated areas. Each branch is managed by a router that directs the flow of traffic. These capillaries of fiber lines typically connect back to the core or trunk lines at other locations to provide resilience in the face of potential network failure or network isolation of a single line. Storybox 2.1 tells a brief story of the physical nature of these lines and how vulnerable they are.

Storybox 2.1 The "spade-hacker"

On March 28, 2011, just three years after a swift and decisive war between the Republic of Georgia and the Russian Federation, Armenia fell off the global Internet. Armenia received 90 percent of its Internet access through a series of core Internet lines that run through the Republic of Georgia. When the Internet went down, many in the region feared the worst and thought another conflict between Russia and Georgia was imminent. However, upon closer examination, the culprit was identified as a 75-year-old Georgian woman digging for copper to sell for scrap. The woman was dubbed by local news sources as "the spade-hacker."[15]

Branching away from the trunk lines, the diversity of devices increases. Regional and local ISPs for Internet access usually manage networks at the local and hyperlocal level. These providers service overlapping lines of infrastructure that include routers and switches, domain name servers (the Internet's equivalent of a phonebook) and many more nodes that make it possible for the Internet to function. Often each region of a municipality is controlled by centralized routers that connect different networks. Switches connect nodes within networks and hubs forward network traffic (packets of information) to all the nodes within a network. ISPs typically route traffic all the way to the customer or neighborhood where they use another node to manage the flow of traffic to a house, to a modem. The modem itself is then either both a modem and a Wi-Fi router or connects to a Wi-Fi router that creates a local area network for all the connected devices within a home.

Although walking around in a house using Wi-Fi might seem as though the Internet is everywhere and enveloping, the reality is that from any Wi-Fi hotspot to the hard line that feeds it back out to the global network, there is often less than 100ft of physical distance. The same is true of mobile phone towers that use the electromagnetic spectrum to send and receive data from mobile devices. Although the range on these devices is substantially greater than Wi-Fi, the principle of information flowing within hard-wired networks remains the same.

Despite the lack of cables associated with Wi-Fi or mobile radios that use 3G or LTE technologies, the use of the electromagnetic spectrum is itself physical and comes in the form of radio waves, or radiation used to transmit and receive data. Whether radio waves are used to communicate between cellular towers and a mobile phone, or originate from a satellite used to broadcast the Internet from space, they are physical structures susceptible to a variety of manipulations and degradations, both natural and man-made. Figure 2.1 highlights the electromagnetic spectrum, with its different radiation types, their wavelength, approximate scale and frequency. Whereas, in the story above, Armenia fell victim to a rogue spade on a trunk line, wireless networks are susceptible to a variety of forms of interference, including those beyond our planet caused by solar flares.[16]

Despite the use of satellites as orbital assets or nodes, the overwhelming majority of data in cyberspace flows through physical fiber-optic lines that traverse the oceans around the world or across continents. Large ships lay thousands of miles of fiber lines with traffic repeaters to boost the speed and range of the signals traveling through them across the oceans and back to nodes on land. Transoceanic fiber-optic lines

Figure 2.1 The electromagnetic spectrum (Jonathan S. Urie [CC BY-SA 3.0] via Wikimedia Commons)

are vulnerable to a wide variety of hazards including – but not limited to – sharks, which like to eat the casings around non-Kevlar wrapped fiber-optic lines;[17] earthquakes, which cause displacement or pinching of the lines; anchors dropped from ships, which on occasion sever the fiber-optic lines; and nation-state sabotage.[18]

Each of the physical-network layer attributes of cyberspace – computers, modems, routers, cables, etc. – uses light and/or electricity to function. Without electricity, the physical layer of cyberspace, upon which the other two layers depend for their operation, becomes useless. A computer without electricity is a box. To reverse the argument, light and electrons used on lines can in certain instances themselves become physical instruments that degrade or damage the physical-network layer. Just as attaching a firehose to a home plumbing system will burst all the pipes in a house, running too much Internet traffic clogs the network. This can happen with Distributed Denial of Service (DDoS) attacks that overwhelm the ability of a node – usually a server – to handle requests to transfer packets of data; it can also happen when all Internet traffic within a given area is rerouted due to a cut fiber-optic line. In 2008, a ship dropped anchor and cut the FALCON cable partially severing several nations from the Internet and causing the traffic on those lines to be rerouted.[19]

To summarize, despite a great deal of rhetoric focused on impacts occurring at the logical and persona layers of cyberspace, the domain remains tied to a deeply physical framework. Each of the physical attributes of cyberspace falls within a legal jurisdiction or within a legal framework developed through international, national or local law and regulation. These physical points are readily locatable on maps. Although cyberspace has many virtual characteristics, its underlying infrastructure is physical. From this perspective, cyberspace is not unique and many of the traditional scholarly frameworks developed to discuss politics and international relations in the physical world, from realism to constructivism, can help us understand security in cyberspace.

Logical-network layer

The logical layer of cyberspace comprises those attributes that use sets of rules or code, written instructions – often broken into categories of protocols – firmware (code that enables the hardware of a computer or device to function) and software (code that allows you to interact with and accomplish novel tasks or provide instructions to the computer). These categories break down into more nuanced structures, each with responsibility for the management and control of information within networks or on nodes. At their most basic, each of these categories is composed of a series of instructions that tell various nodes within networks how to process and transmit data. In many ways, the logical layer forms the DNA of cyberspace in that it tells physical components how to operate. Each set of instructions influences the interaction of nodes within cyberspace. At its core, the Internet functions as a packet-switched network. The concept of packet switching was developed and confirmed independently by Paul Baran of the RAND Corporation and Donald Davies at the National Physical Laboratory in the United Kingdom.[20] Packet switching differs from circuit switching in that it allows fault tolerance. Figure 2.2 illustrates the differences between packet- and circuit-switched networks. While circuit-switched networks require a dedicated channel of communications and can only be used for one transmission at a time, packet-switched networks route traffic through a variety of nodes within a network which both is fault tolerant and allows for multiple simultaneous transmissions. Although one of the founding myths of the Internet is that it was created to provide resilience for military communications in the event of a nuclear attack, the truth is that this resilience was initially only considered with regard to telephone or voice communications.[21] By contrast, the development of ARPANET discussed in the previous chapter was largely to facilitate decentralized usage of expensive computing resources.[22]

Packet switching describes the method by which information (packets of data) transits networks. Beyond this method, a set of rules or protocols manage the interaction of computers (nodes)

Figure 2.2 Packet-switched v. circuit-switched networks

that generate and transmit information in cyberspace. In the early days of ARPANET, these interactions were managed by Interface Message Processors (IMPs), steel-encased specialized computers the size of a small Volkswagen that sat in front of the computers on the network and took the data from different machines (computers) on the Internet and translated it for use. The best way to think of these is as two translators who sit with two diplomats who speak different languages. Diplomat 1 says something which is then translated by his translator into a second language. Translator 2 then translates the message from translator 1 into the language that diplomat 2 can understand. IMPs were expensive, difficult to maintain and inefficient in facilitating network communications.

The inefficiencies of the IMP were finally resolved thanks to the Transmission Control Protocol / Internet Protocol, one of the primary protocol suites for Internet operation.[23] The TCP/IP specifies how data on hosts (computers) is to be broken down into packets with information headers. These information headers function much like the image on a puzzle box but with more specificity, and provide the ordering information for packets. These packets are subsequently transmitted with IP address information across the network. Finally, when the file that has been broken into packets, each with information headers, arrives at its final destination, it is reconstituted using the information headers as a map. If any given packet is missing or corrupted, the recipient computer can request the sending computer to resend the missing or corrupted information.

Within cyberspace, there are a variety of protocols that set rules for how computers and networks communicate and operate. At the most basic level, protocols must address issues regarding how different data formats are exchanged, how their addresses are formatted and mapped, how information is to be efficiently routed across networks, when transmission errors occur, how to acknowledge receipt of packets, how to signal loss of information, and how information flows.[24] All of these component pieces form the basic logical rules for how cyberspace functions. Different types of services within cyberspace utilize different protocols. Some of the most common protocols include FTP (File Transfer Protocol), UDP (User Datagram Protocol), DNS (Domain Name Service), TLS/SSL (Transit Layer Security / Secure Socket Layer), DHCP (Dynamic Host Configuration Protocol), SMTP (Simple Mail Transfer Protocol) and HTTP (Hypertext Transfer Protocol). There are hundreds of other protocols, some of which are proprietary and owned by patent holders, while others are public and available for general use, free of charge. Protocols operate within their own set of layers with what is

What is cyberspace? 35

Systems Interconnection Model (OSI Model). The OSI model has seven layers that range from everything down to the physical-network layer in the previous section up to the highest logical layer called the application layer. Figure 2.3 shows the OSI Model in comparison to the US DoD model discussed above.

Visiting websites is an example of the first two layers working together. When a user queries a website such as Facebook.com on their computer, it sends a request which is pushed down from the browser application layer all the way to the physical layer. This initial request goes to the most efficient DNS, typically located at an individual's local ISP. This DNS server maintains a database that is regularly updated and syncs through the Internet back through various DNS servers to the Root DNS server managed by the Internet Corporation for Assigned Names and Numbers (ICANN), which will be discussed in the next chapter. This database functions in much the same way

Figure 2.3 OSI and DoD models compared

as a foreign-language dictionary does. Facebook.com equates to IP address 31.13.71.36. Each block in the address corresponds to a network location somewhere in the world. The DNS server sends this address back to the requesting browser which then uses the address to connect to Facebook.com. When the Internet was first being developed the common standard was a four-block set of numbers called an IPv4 Address. There are 4,294,967,296 possible IPV4 addresses comprised of 32 bits. This number of addresses has already been surpassed and the Internet Engineering Task Force (IETF) and its constituent bodies have begun replacing the IPv4 standard with IPv6, which contains 340,282,366,920,938,463,463,374,607,431,768,211, 456 possible addresses comprised on 128 bits, giving the logical layer of cyberspace ample room to grow in the coming decades.

The logical layer of cyberspace is susceptible to a large variety of manipulations, exploitations and degradations, many of which will be examined in subsequent chapters. One example in recent years of a serious vulnerability in a protocol was the Heartbleed security bug released in 2014. Heartbleed manipulated a popular implementation of TLS called OpenSSL and allowed for attackers to intercept and reinitiate encrypted web sessions for users. For example, when a customer accesses his bank's website to check his account balance, his computer and the bank's computer connect and authenticate over OpenSSL. Heartbleed would allow an attacker to follow behind him, much like someone sneaking past a metro turnstile without paying. The hacker would not have to reinitiate the connection and would gain access to his account. Although the fundamental nature of the protocol itself was unaffected, the faulty implementation of the protocol led to potential exploitation.[25] Figure 2.4 displays the Heartbleed logo designed by security company Codenomicon. With thousands of different protocols and implementations, the probability of vulnerabilities and exploitations of the logical layer of cyberspace remains large. Many of these protocols serve as the entry points for a variety of exploits and attacks against computers.

Beyond the logical-network layer of cyberspace used in the transmission of data between computers is the implementation of firmware and software on the computer itself. While firmware and software can engage network protocols, they can also be primarily host-based, meaning they stay on the computer. These programs are also part of the logical layer of cyberspace, although they are not necessarily involved in data transmission. Vulnerabilities (flaws in the code or its implementation) within these logical structures can have substantial ramifications. Whether it is the firmware that controls a specific piece of hardware, or software – a broader category than

What is cyberspace? 37

Figure 2.4 Heartbleed logo

firmware that provides data instructions to a computer – many famous cyberattacks originate and occur somewhere in the nexus between the logical-network layer and the firmware and software. Examples of such attacks include: the 2015 Ashley Madison breach that spilled the details of more than 37 million users of a site that facilitated infidelity between people in relationships;[26] the Conficker worm, a piece of malware that provides hackers with remote access into victims' computer systems;[27] the Home Depot and Target hacks in 2013–14 that resulted in the theft of the details of more than 120 million credit cards from the point-of-sale systems.[28]

The logical layer of cyberspace defined by protocols and code, both within networks and on hosts, is extremely vulnerable to manipulation, exploitation and degradation. Minimizing such vulnerabilities is an essential part of the software development process. Software companies such as Microsoft and Accenture, and public organizations such as the US National Institute of Standards, develop manuals and tools for examining and minimizing the number of bugs (vulnerabilities) within various software programs prior to their release.[29] As the number of lines of code used to create software increases, so too does the difficulty in auditing that code. Some experts estimate that software that does not go through a secure development lifecycle process averages between 15 and 50 bugs per 1,000 lines of code.[30] The most recent Ford F-150 truck, for instance, has approximately 150 million lines of code, and a Mercedes has more lines of code than an Airbus A380, the largest passenger plane in the world.[31] If the Ford F-150 adheres to industry standards, it has between 2.25

million and 7.5 million bugs or vulnerabilities that should be identified and patched. The diversity of the ecosystem within the logical layer of cyberspace and the speed with which that ecosystem of protocols, firmware and software evolves, combined with the challenge of eliminating vulnerabilities, make cyberspace highly susceptible to security threats.

Persona layer

The cyber-persona layer, in contrast to the physical-network and logical-network layers described above, moves the definition of cyberspace away from the technical attributes to a higher level of abstraction. In 1995, the *New Yorker* published a Peter Steiner cartoon with two dogs looking at a computer screen. The caption under the cartoon was "On the Internet, nobody knows you're a dog." In many ways, this cartoon encapsulates the nature of the persona level of cyberspace. This layer consists of the people interacting and utilizing the networks themselves. The abstraction of this level is important and well articulated in the cartoon because it serves as one of the defining generalized characteristics of cyberspace, in which the representation of any given entity can be flexible. It is often difficult to discern between various persons, entities such as businesses or corporations or even bots (computer programs designed to simulate human behaviors) online.

Cyber personas do not need to reflect actual persons and can often be hybrids or complete falsifications. In November of 2017, the *Daily Beast*, an online news publication, reported that @Jenn_Abrams – a twitter username that had garnered more than 70,000 followers, many of them from the Alt-Right movement – a strong supporter of President Donald Trump's 2016 election campaign, was a fake account run out of the Internet Research Agency in St. Petersburg, Russia.[32] Famous diplomats and celebrities argued with this twitter personality, all the while oblivious to the reality that the person with whom they were arguing was not American, was not a woman, and was not real.

Few technical discussions on cyberspace include the cyber-persona layer, yet it is in this layer where individuals operate and interact. Since cyberspace was created by and for humans, a comprehensive analysis of cyberspace requires engagement with the persona layer. By changing their persona, by masking their location, IP address or Media Access Control (MAC) Address, by obfuscating their online behavior, humans are able to utilize cyberspace in ways that actors in the other domains of land, sea, air and space cannot. Spies operating outside of cyberspace can forge documents, use disguises, safe houses or other obfuscation techniques, but the degree to which they may alter their fundamental nature is constrained by physical laws. Such constraints are largely absent in cyberspace. The creation of false cyber personas has multiple uses, many of which are mundane. Entire virtual communities such as Second Life or World of Warcraft allow individuals to live out their lives virtually, playing games, socializing with others around the world and even engaging in commerce in virtual worlds.[33]

The manipulation of cyber personas can be a life-or-death matter in repressive countries around the world, and some organizations such as the National Democratic Institute, Open Technology Institute, Electronic Frontier Foundation, Reporters Without Borders, Tactical Technology Collective and others focus on building tools that enable users to more effectively hide who they are within cyberspace.[34] Programs such as Tails Boum, The Onion Router (Tor) and others use anonymization techniques to protect individuals' online personas. Interestingly, many of these programs have been developed with the support of, or within, government research organizations, such as the Naval Research Laboratories in the United States.[35] I2P, Freenet, Orbot, ASL19, Psiphon and hundreds of other platforms have been developed within open source communities around the world to facilitate anonymization. The ability to manage and control online personas is, and will continue to be, a substantial issue for journalists, human rights activists and political dissidents around the world. At this level, cyberspace is a deeply political tool, which some activists have considered to be a "liberation technology."

The ability to manipulate who, what and where individuals are in cyberspace does come with a parallel dark side. Anonymity and low probabilities of attribution allow for states to engage in espionage and attacks.[36] In cyberspace, malicious actors are able to change who and what they look like to a potential adversary or victim, and even to reroute traffic to create the impression that an attack is coming from a third-party nation, in what is called a "false flag operation."[37] Beyond nation states, other categories of actors regularly manipulate the persona layer. Criminals including paedophiles and drug traffickers, as well as terrorists, each manipulate the cyber-persona level to the detriment of their victims.[38] Many of the threats to the logical and physical layers of cyberspace originate within the persona layer.[39] Data indicate that over 95 percent of all cyberattacks that result in the compromise of computer systems succeed because of something the human user has done.[40]

Understanding cyberspace: The technical value

To understand how states and non-state and individual actors interact and create cyber insecurity, it is necessary to first gain a foundational understanding of what cyberspace is and how it functions. This chapter has touched on a widely used model of cyberspace, emphasizing three overarching physical, logical and persona layers. While it is often convenient to focus on one layer at the expense of the others, together they form a synergistic entity that comprises cyberspace. Considering the complexity of these various layers can add much-needed nuance to debates on cybersecurity. Very often, war fighters, policy-makers, computer scientists, network engineers and the broader public talk across one another with limited mutual understanding. Further examining the physical, technical, logical and human underpinnings of cyberspace breaks down communication barriers and allows for progress to be made across disciplines. Studying cybersecurity is an interdisciplinary endeavor.

Discussion questions

1. How do the various layers of cyberspace impact cybersecurity policy decisions?
2. How do the layers of cyberspace interact to create a global network that we rely on daily for work, entertainment and more?
3. Are there borders in cyberspace? What are the implications for physical borders in a virtual domain?

Further resources

YouTube videos by Code.org:
- "Introducing How Computers Work," https://youtu.be/OAx_6-wdslM
- "The Internet: Packets, Routing and Reliability," https://youtu.be/AYdF7b3nMto
- "The Internet: Wires, Cables & Wifi," https://youtu.be/ZhEf7e4kopM
- "What is the Internet?" https://youtu.be/Dxcc6ycZ73M

Rus Shuler, "How Does the Internet Work?" 2002, https://web.stanford.edu/class/msande91si/www-spr04/readings/week1/InternetWhitepaper.htm.

3

Governing cyberspace

Substantial governance challenges lie beyond the physical and virtual characteristics of cyberspace. This chapter emphasizes the unique governance and legal regimes within and surrounding the digital domain. Although most users do not give Internet governance even a passing thought, their daily use of the Internet and its associated technologies is dependent on complex regimes that form the foundation for how cyberspace functions. The World Summit on the Information Society (WSIS) 2003–5 defines Internet Governance as "the development and application by governments, the private sector, and civil society, in their respective roles, of shared principles, norms, rules, decision-making procedures, and programs that shape the evolution and use of the Internet."[1] This definition shows well the variety of actors and processes involved in the management of cyberspace. Research on the management of the Internet and the broader cyberspace often centers on the role multiple actors play. On the one hand, the notion of multistakeholderism favors a model that brings together a variety of public and private "stakeholders" – individuals or groups of interest – into a single governance regime. On the other hand, multilateralism posits that nation states are, or should be, the only important parties to governance regimes.

Governance in cyberspace dates back to the early days of ARPANET. ARPANET users posted "Request for Comment" (RFC), which became a venue for discussions on the technical and social attributes of the nascent network. The first request (RFC 1) was first published by Steve Crocker on April 7, 1969. Crocker's first

RFC suggested changes and improvements to host software on the IMPs that enabled communications on the early Internet. The RFC process, which continues to this day, now includes more than 8,000 RFCs on nearly as many topics. Each RFC is open for comment and facilitates a decentralized governance process initiated by the original ARPANET designers.

Governance in cyberspace is a contentious and difficult issue that can be examined through various lenses. The disaggregation of governance across categories facilitates a more nuanced understanding of the contentious politics associated with the complexity of a continually evolving domain. First, cyberspace governance in its oldest form originates in its technical nature and function. A multitude of institutions and actors have a stake in how cyberspace operates and seek to influence its form and functions. Initial governance mechanisms such as the RFC system were sufficient to manage growing network complexity in its early days, but as the network expanded beyond the Advanced Research Projects Agency (ARPA) and the National Science Foundation (NSF) to encompass more functions and users, it quickly became apparent that political and technical issues were arising that challenged the existing status quo.[2] Many of the early technical organizations, such as the Internet Engineering Task Force (IETF), adapted and became increasingly complex institutions tasked with managing various aspects of the Internet. Second, many of the institutions that facilitate the functional aspects of cyberspace also began to have a stake in the social and political attributes that inform not merely the technical nature of the domain, but also the implications for how individuals, groups, businesses and governments utilize the domain to achieve various outcomes. Arguments in this second category broadly balance the sovereign concerns of states against the functional concerns of engineers, the daily usage concerns of individuals, and the financial and economic concerns of firms. Third, at the highest level of abstraction and often separated from much of the Internet governance literature for practical reasons, are the laws and policies of states and international bodies in relation to their interactions within and through cyberspace. This chapter examines each of these three categories to provide the reader with a more nuanced understanding of governance in cyberspace. Although each of the issues is examined in isolation, the reality is that the three views of cyberspace are intimately intertwined and often mutually inform, reinforce or – as is often the case – contradict one another. From this perspective, the study of cyberspace, just like other domains of human activity, reflects the complexity of social interactions.

Technical governance of cyberspace

The history of governance in cyberspace is largely a technical story of innovation and adaptation to practical challenges faced in the development of a network of networks. The history of computers and computational machines dates at least to 1911 with the establishment of the Computing–Tabulating Recording Company, which would later become IBM. The conceptualization of modern governance structures on the Internet can be traced back to a more contemporary example. In 1958, Peter Samson, a freshman at MIT, stumbled across the Model Railroad Club in a room filled with model trains and an environment made of papier-mâché. The club broke down into two groups interested in working on the ever-evolving project. One group focused on the user-interface of the environment and how the trains, the mountains, towns and other attributes looked and were perceived; the other group focused on how the circuits and signals under the table served to make the world above function.[3] Many of the participants in the second group would become some of the first hackers. These individuals, and the attitude of early governance on ARPANET and other similar projects, were oriented toward functional problem-solving. They adopted an engineering-centric approach focused on issues that made the visual world function.

In tracing the history of the Internet, Janet Abbate, Katie Hafner and Mark Lyon discuss the value of both working groups, and the development of the RFC process that in many ways fostered something not dissimilar from the MIT Model Railroad Club of Peter Samson.[4] Although, in the early days of ARPANET, governance decisions over the nascent networks were controlled by program managers, they often did so following substantial consultation with engineers.

Governance efforts have been around since the very inception of the Internet. RFCs 2 and 3 introduced governance structures for how individuals involved in the network should suggest and work toward improvements.[5] RFC 3 specified the structure of RFCs, their content requirements and the initial distribution list.[6] The process was standardized with the intent of providing a forum for development.

During early development of the Internet, governance discussions focused on interoperability and efficiency, not on the core political issues that dominate more contemporary debates. Issues such as sovereignty, data localization, IP address allocations and Domain Names had not yet arisen in a network populated by small university and government research communities. The number of countries involved in the network grew but remained confined to liberal democracies. The primary early governance goal was not to achieve a robust governing body to solve political problems related to the network's growth and use, but the development of the network itself. To facilitate governance, RFCs served a vital role in the process of documenting and validating protocols for use within the network.

One particularly fascinating subset of governance discussions centers on the management of Internet resources. When Robert Kahn and Viton Cerf began to push TCP/IP as a protocol for communications between computers, initial corporate pushback from the original network managers at the American company BBN Technologies – who managed and built early IMPs – was overcome. In the early days of ARPANET, the community of users allowed enough room for failure within engineering projects for novel protocols to be proposed, challenged and accepted or rejected on their technical merits and ability to improve the network. The best technical solutions could prevail over less efficient ones.

On March 26, 1972, Cerf and Jon Postel authored an RFC that made the first foray into the systematic management of network resources.[7] In RFC 322, the two Internet pioneers requested that all Host Technical Liaisons submit their socket numbers to the Network Measurement Group. This initial registry of numbers predates the IANA (Internet Assigned Numbers Authority), which would be established by Jon Postel in RFC 1083 in 1988 under contract from the United States DoD.[8] From 1972 until his death in 1998, for all intents and purposes, Jon Postel was the manager of all Internet Names and Numbers. He controlled both the registration and mapping of all website domain names (e.g. google.com or facebook.com) to Internet Protocol addresses, and the allocation of IP Addresses (e.g. 216.58.219.206 and 31.13.71.36) to all entities globally. He was also responsible for arbitrating domain name disputes, and disputes on the allocation of address space.

In 1994, the NSF subcontracted the registration of Domain Names to a single private company, Network Solutions Inc (NSI). This move by the NSF sparked a heated debate among states, international and national non-governmental organizations (NGOs), and within the private sector, over who should control the Internet and how. The result was a conflict often referred to as the "DNS War."[9] NSI, under contract from the NSF, was able to charge for the registration of domain names and used this money to support the costs of maintaining and running the network. The centralization of management and securement of financial resources in a US corporation was controversial. Both nation states and private businesses launched legal actions to challenge the contractual agreement and the cost of registering websites. Legal actions eventually decreased until the overall control of NSI was limited with the subsequent creation of ICANN and the expansion of domain name registrars.

In February 1998, a green paper (used for rule-making proposals) was put forward proposing the creation of a new organization, to be constituted under the National Telecommunications and Information Administration (NTIA), an agency within the US Department of Commerce. The paper, written in response to a 1997 request from President Clinton, suggested the development of a new organization capable of improving the technical management of Internet names and addresses.[10] ICANN was formally approved on September 18, 1998, and incorporated as a non-profit under California Law 12 days later. As a non-profit, ICANN is designed to support charitable or public purposes. Although ICANN was under contract with the NTIA, governance over domain names and IP addresses was fostered via an agreement with the IETF, the main technical organization overseeing the functioning of the Internet. In 2016, ICANN became a fully independent multistakeholder NGO when its contractual obligations to NTIA were allowed to expire.

The technical governance of the Internet, while rooted in the RFC process and still heavily dependent on RFCs, has evolved since the late 1960s. The current structure of this technical governance follows a long line of committees, sub-groups and organizations created primarily by scientists and engineers. Many of the original groups were small and technically focused. The expansion of the Internet and its increasing complexity have resulted in a present breakdown of Internet governance structures into three broad categories. The first, originating out of technical standards and development, are multistakeholder institutions. The second, originating out of the political, social, economic and societal concerns brought on by the development and expansion of the Internet, are multilateral institutions. The third category is composed of private entities such as network operators, service creators and vendors, Internet Exchange Points, and other types of businesses who build, develop, manage and utilize network infrastructures. Generally, all three groups interact within multistakeholder processes to develop and manage the core functional attributes of the Internet.

Currently, the major multistakeholder organizations that focus on the fundamental technical functions of the Internet fall under one of three broad institutional structures. The IETF, the Internet Architecture Board and the Internet Research Taskforce are part of the Internet Society and emphasize the technical function of the global Internet. The World Wide Web Consortium (W3C) manages the development of the protocols associated with the World Wide Web – often accessed via a computer browser such as Chrome, Internet Explorer, FireFox or Safari. ICANN manages IANA and the Domain Name functions of the Internet. Each of these organizations is open to public membership and reserves space in their governance structures for actors of all types while attempting not to privilege any one actor at the expense of the others. Engagement with these multistakeholder organizations is difficult due to the cost in time and expertise required to participate and exert influence.

States and private-sector organizations tend to work within and through the multistakeholder processes of the core institutions listed above. While the trend has been to work within the multistakeholder institutions currently established, many states would like to begin shifting much of the governance of the Internet away from a multistakeholder to a multilateral structure. In a multilateral structure, the needs and wants of states are negotiated and sub-state actors such as NGOs, businesses, individuals, engineers and others must seek representation via their respective state. This structure substantially weakens the influence of traditional actors over how the Internet is developed and managed.

Thus far, multistakeholder organizations, many liberal democracies and technology firms have rejected attempts to shift these core governance functions away from their current structures. Their primary argument is that exclusive state involvement in how the Internet functions would impact its ability to develop, innovate and adapt in the future. Their arguments are not without precedent. France created an independent network for online services – the Minitel – in the 1980s, and Iran is currently trying to create a "Halal" Internet. While the reasoning behind these two attempts to create independent networks is different, they highlight some of the fundamental political, social and economic issues that the more technical governance approaches to the Internet tend to overlook.

The political, social and economic governance of cyberspace

"Governments of the Industrial World, you weary giants of flesh and steel, I come from Cyberspace, the new home of Mind. On behalf of the future, I ask you of the past to leave us alone. You are not welcome among us. You have no sovereignty where we gather." This extract from the *Declaration of the Independence of Cyberspace*, authored by American poet, essayist and cyber-libertarian John Perry Barlow in 1996, served as an early rallying cry for many Internet users. However, Barlow's declaration does not account for the variety of issues that have arisen that make the absence of sovereignty in cyberspace both impractical and potentially damaging to the very ideals his declaration sought to uphold. In writing on the development and current state of Internet governance, scholar Laura DeNardis provocatively claims that there is an ongoing "global war for Internet governance."[11] Hyperbole aside, the conflict over Internet governance is one taking place across multiple venues, between and within nations. To understand why Internet governance has taken on and continues to grow in importance, it is first necessary to disaggregate some of the many issues in contention.

From the sidelines, as a user of the Internet, governance issues might seem trivial. Yet the issues in contention within the Internet are anything but trivial. The Internet – now often broadly seen as cyberspace – facilitates social, political and economic actions globally. Issues including the control over generic Top-Level Domains (TLDs) ranging from .com and .org to .cn and .ru, and the distribution and allocation of IP addresses globally, are some challenges facing governments around the world. Countries are given control over their TLD, the .nation part of the URLs used to access and locate just about everything on the Internet. But with the expansion of TLDs into new areas such as .Amazon, .Patagonia, .wine and untold others, who should be able to control sites that arise from their use? Should the countries where the Amazon river flows or the US Corporation Amazon.com be in control of a given domain? How should IP addresses – the fundamental routing numbers that make the Internet function – be distributed?

Misappropriation of these addresses or the misuse of IP addresses and domain names by one nation can have global ramifications. In 2008, in an attempt to prevent Pakistanis from accessing the video-sharing site YouTube, which featured anti-Islamic videos, a Pakistani ISP was ordered to censor the site. The ISP responded by modifying the Border Gateway Protocol (BGP) for YouTube, which accidentally resulted in the global redirection of YouTube to Pakistan.[12] The provider could not deal with the amount of traffic it received as a result of this "hijacking" and many users around the world were unable to access YouTube for a couple of hours. Pakistan's YouTube mistake is not an isolated incident, but the tip of a coming change in domestic laws that have global ramifications. National and regional laws such as the European General Data Protection Regulation (GDPR), which came into effect in May of 2018, change the way in which firms may use the Internet within sovereign jurisdictions and affect users' ability to surf the web. The GDPR focuses on data rights of European citizens, but its implications are technical, political and financial, and visible at a global level due to the inherent connectivity of cyberspace and its transnational nature.[13] Laws such as the GDPR challenge the technical mechanisms that foster the efficient transmission of data and create costs for online service providers that rely on data storage servers located in nations adhering to the GDPR.

Internet governance is expansive and includes a variety of challenging questions on the utilization of information, the freedom of information and many more. Some of the questions include whether smaller nations should have to pay higher Internet prices because they cannot offer symmetrical peering (data transfer) agreements with large Internet providers. Cost structures of peering agreements can and do impact potential access of impoverished nations to the modern global economy. Other questions that are addressed by Internet governance include: How should data transit between and amongst nations be managed, regulated, stored? Should traffic on the Internet be neutral, or is it acceptable to privilege some traffic at the expense of others (a question we will examine more below)? Should ISPs be required to monitor Internet traffic for illegal or immoral behaviors or even the activities of journalists or human rights activists?[14]

States have long held jurisdiction over their territory and citizenry. International law recognizes two forms of sovereignty, *de jure* (legal control) and *de facto* (physical control), over that which occurs within their borders. The Internet challenges the sovereign rights of states. Nations have pursued increases in their sovereign rights over the Internet through a variety of fora. The International Telecommunications Union (ITU), a specialized United Nations agency, has served as one of the primary vehicles for states to press for their increased role in governing the Internet.

Internet governance at this international level rose to prominence following two United Nations summits entitled the WSIS, in 2003 in Geneva and 2005 in Tunis. Although organized within a multilateral organization, the United Nations, the summits were multistakeholder in participation and engagement. The 2003 WSIS resulted in the creation of the Working Group on Internet Governance and eventually led to the further creation of the Internet Governance Forum (IGF) as a multistakeholder body under the UN Secretary-General.

Further contention arose in 2006 with the renewal of contractual agreements between ICANN and the US Department of Commerce's NTIA. Some stakeholders expressed concern that this contract gave the

United States too much influence over the Internet. To overcome these criticisms, the 2006 contract renewal opened the door for the potential internationalization of ICANN at a future, unspecified date. ICANN and its management of the DNS root zone and IANA functions ran into controversy in 2007 when a debate arose over whether to create a .xxx top-level domain. The TLD question sparked debate on the control of critical internet resources and was central to IGF meetings held later that year in Brazil. Also, in 2006, the ITU began to more formally involve itself in discussions of Internet governance.

From 2006 to 2012, the importance of the Internet grew substantially, in tandem with marked increases in numbers of global Internet users. The role and prominence of the Internet in global journalism, protest movements and political movements in the United States and elsewhere further highlighted ways in which the Internet was not only a technical but also an inherently political domain. Decisions made about how the Internet functioned, what protocols were adopted, and how information should be treated within it became points of contention for various stakeholders.

During her tenure, US Secretary of State Hillary Clinton became instrumental in pursuing a multi-million-dollar effort to promote Internet freedom and human rights at various international conferences, and through the funding of a variety of technologies for human rights activists, journalists and dissidents around the world.[15] Secretary Clinton famously intervened with technology companies during the 2009 Green Revolution in Iran by asking social media platform Twitter, used by Iranian activists, to delay a scheduled update so as to continue to provide a means for information dissemination and protest organization.[16] While these actions were seen within the Western liberal democracies as enhancing the fundamental tenets of freedom and democracy, many non-Western democracies saw these efforts as a direct attack via the newly evolving and expanding medium of cyberspace, and as a threat to their sovereignty.

The advancement of democratic norms within cyberspace did not occur in isolation. In 2012 in Dubai, the ITU published the International Telecommunications Regulations (ITRs). The opening lines of the regulations affirm the sovereign rights of states, and declare the ITRs as an effort to foster the development and harmonization of worldwide telecommunications. The opening lines of the documents establishing the ITU, emphasizing the sovereign rights of states, highlight the challenges confronted by engineers, businesses, individuals and NGOs in the face of state Internet governance efforts. As the Internet became an increasingly political tool in the 2000s, multiple stakeholders started to wrestle for its control.

The revelations orchestrated by former NSA contractor Edward Snowden about the global reach of the United States within cyberspace provided fodder for renewed calls for the internationalization of the core responsibilities associated with the Internet. Critics wondered how the United States could be trusted with the governance of key Internet assets if they were using them to spy on the world. The global outcry in response to the Snowden revelations was swift and boosted the positions of many stakeholders emphasizing issues such as the need for sovereignty within multilateral Internet governance frameworks and the Internet freedom agenda.

On April 14, 2014, in the wake of the Snowden revelations, ICANN and the Brazilian government organized NetMundial, a large global multistakeholder meeting on the future of Internet governance. The conference produced a non-binding document on Internet governance principles emphasizing multistakeholderism: open and participative, consensus-driven governance that is transparent, accountable, inclusive and equitable, distributed, collaborative, and emphasizes access and the lowering of barriers.[17] Controversies arose regarding the structure and organization of the permanent 25-member representative committee for governance of NetMundial when the organizing nations attempted to secure permanent representation. This attempt at buttressing multistakeholderism within the Internet governance agenda, while admirable, faced substantial criticism.[18]

Internet governance is one of the most rapidly evolving areas of governance globally. The continual development of technologies and the variety of state and non-state approaches to these technologies have provided a fertile testing ground for scholars and practitioners. Governance on the Internet most closely aligns with theories associated with liberal institutionalism and constructivism. Both schools of thought help to explain how and why so many divergent interests are coalescing into various organizational structures. Liberal institutionalism indicates that organizations and shared government institutions can increase and aid in the cooperation between states and thereby reduce conflicts.[19] By contrast, constructivism posits that relations between states are the result of historical or social patterns that are developed (constructed) over time rather than the result of structural or essential human or political characteristics.[20] Internet governance is characterized by both the creation of institutions and the managing of interests from very divergent social and historical contexts. These two theoretical lenses provide vantage points from which to view the role and development of Internet governance and its subsequent diffusion and impact on cyberspace.

The concept of multistakeholderism best explains the convergence of multiple actors concerned with the management of Internet resources. Mark Raymond and Laura DeNardis define multistakeholderism as "two or more classes of actors engaged in a common governance enterprise concerning issues they regard as public in nature and characterized by polyarchic authority relations constituted by procedural rules." The multiple stakeholders involved in cyberspace have established a complex and ongoing flux of governance regimes.[21] The Internet is global. Its roots are based in technical solutions that have evolved and created political, social and economic implications.

The approach states take toward governance in cyberspace is often a function of their domestic regime type and position within international politics. States such as China, Russia and Iran seek multilateral solutions to governance challenges while the United States and its allies seek multistakeholder solutions.[22] This divergence of approach sets the stage for conflict, and pits organizations such as the ITU against ICANN. While the balance still largely favors multistakeholder institutions, this might not be a permanent state of affairs. Some scholars contend that the current status quo of Internet governance might lead to a fragmentation of the Internet between states that favor control through multilateral institutions and those that favor multistakeholder ones.[23] Table 3.1 identifies the wide number of organizations that play a role in the governance of the Internet, and the diversity of their functions.

ISPs and telecommunications providers (Telcos) also play a major role in the governance of cyberspace. ISPs and Telcos provide for and maintain the delivery infrastructure of the Internet. In 2012, all large US ISPs committed to tackling three areas of substantial concern in cyberspace: botnets, domain name fraud and Internet route hijacking. The ability of ISPs and Telcos to address cybersecurity challenges differs significantly from country to country. Yet, as the maintainers and providers of the Internet, these actors have a substantial role to play in governance and security. Many ISPs and Telcos have joined together in both formal and informal groups called Internet Network Operators' Groups (NOGs). NOGs provide a forum within which network operators can discuss issues of interest and establish best practices in the implementation of protocols and new technologies. Storybox 3.1 introduces the debate on net neutrality in the United States. This debate directly concerns ISPs, which, under the principle of net neutrality, are asked to treat all data on the Internet equally.

Table 3.1 Major Internet governance entities

Entity	Role	Functions
Certificate Authority (CA)	Issues digital certificates and certifies the ownership of a public key by the named subject of a certificate	Operations, services
Internet Architecture Board (IAB)	Oversees the technical and engineering development of the IETF and IRTF	Advice, community engagement, policy, standards, research
Internet Corporation for Assigned Names and Numbers (ICANN)	Coordinates the Internet's systems of unique identifiers, including IP addresses, Protocol-Parameter Registries and TLD space	Community engagement, operations, policy, services
Internet Engineering Task Force (IETF)	Develops and promotes standards for the Internet Protocols	Community engagement, policy, standards
Internet Exchange Points (IXPs)	Provides the physical infrastructure through which ISPs and Content Delivery Networks (CDNs) exchange Internet traffic	Operations, services
Internet Governance Forum (IGF)	A multistakeholder open forum for debate on Internet governance issues	Advice, community engagement, policy
Internet Network Operators' Group	Discusses and influences matters related to Internet operations and regulation within informal fora comprised of ISPs, IXPs and other stakeholders	Advice, operations, services
Internet Research Task Force (IRTF)	Promotes research on the evolution of the Internet, creates focused long-term research groups working on topics related to protocols, applications, architecture and technology	Research
Internet Service Providers (ISPs)	An organization, public or private, that provides services for participating in, accessing or using the Internet	Operations, services
Internet Society (ISOC)	Assures the open development, evolution and use of the Internet for the benefit of all people	Community engagement, education, policy, services
Regional Internet Registries (RIRs)	Five regional Internet registries manage the allocation and registration of Internet number resources within geographic regions	Operations, policy, services
World Wide Web Consortium (W3C)	Creates standards for the World Wide Web that enable an open web platform	Standards

Storybox 3.1 Net neutrality

One of the most important issues to arise in recent debates on Internet governance within the United States and many other countries around the world is the concept of net neutrality. Net neutrality is the idea that all traffic that transits the Internet should be given equal priority. Think of the Internet as a highway, where all cars with access to the road may travel at the same speed without any one car being given special privileges. In a non-neutral Internet, a priority lane is provided that allows for some cars to travel in "fast lanes" for a fee, while cars that do not pay that fee are relegated to the "slow lanes."

While some Internet firms, such as Google, Facebook, Twitter, Amazon.com and other actors with deep pockets, might be able to pay substantial sums to be provided faster access to customers, the majority of smaller Internet retailers and service and entertainment providers would be unduly slowed and therefore lose potential markets. A non-neutral Internet could privilege existing large firms at the expense of small firms that are unable to compete and new firms that are unable to break out with new, potentially more innovative products.

In countries where net-neutrality laws have been rescinded or limited, ISPs have fragmented consumer access to specific applications or services and thereby limited their exposure to other platforms, products and services. For instance, in Portugal, a mobile phone subscriber can purchase a data plan with limited data access to the general public Internet but unlimited data access to Facebook and Snapchat.[24]

Under the administration of President Donald Trump, the United States revoked its net-neutrality rules, a move widely rebuked by most experts and industries except ISPs. The rule on the revocation of net neutrality in the United States garnered such substantial opposition that it crashed the US Federal Communications Commission public commenting service after comedian John Oliver spoke out about the proposed rule on his popular television show *Last Week Tonight*.[25] The public outcry against the government's decision also inspired satirical opposition advertisements by fast-food company Burger King.[26]

Internet governance is not only about how the Internet runs and who controls what aspects of how it runs. The next and final section addresses legal regimes and norms of state behavior that have developed, and continue to develop, in cyberspace. Discussions about legal regimes in cyberspace emphasize concerns over behaviors of states and their citizens. These issues of governance typically arise through purely multilateral organizations and institutions, often with input from non-state actors such as private corporations and NGOs.

The laws and norms of cyberspace

For a variety of issues outside of cyberspace, governments have developed a robust body of international law or focused on the establishment of norms (standards of behavior) to manage the interactions between states. Although the distinction between laws and norms is in many ways arbitrary, this section focuses on the development of laws and norms pertaining to cyberspace in an effort to facilitate a more robust understanding of how states manage their interactions within this evolving domain. The scope of international law is extremely broad and extends well beyond discussions of the technical management of cyberspace. Issues such as espionage, criminal extradition and the laws of armed conflict are most often dealt with between nations in a multilateral fashion.

The establishment of the Convention on Cybercrime in 2001, and its subsequent ratification by fifty-seven nations, serves as a good starting point for discussions on international law and cyberspace. In the late 1990s, as the Internet was expanding, so too were digital crimes. The violation of digital systems and the impact of criminal activities on the confidentiality, integrity and availability of computer systems steadily rose within the international consciousness. Dozens of nations gathered in Budapest to begin devising a multilateral strategy for addressing cybercrime. The Budapest Convention on Cybercrime sought to harmonize national laws within each of the signatory countries, enhance investigative techniques and facilitate communication and cooperation.[27] The convention serves as an example of one of the first major treaties between nations to address issues arising in cyberspace.

The Convention on Cybercrime was a strong first step toward developing international consensus around issues impacting all states. Starting in 2004 and convening periodically until 2017, a United Nations Governmental Group of Experts (UN GGE) has met to discuss and develop norms and laws relating to cyberspace.[28] The group releases periodic reports to the UN General Assembly providing updates on discussions and advances in the field. UN GGE discussions and reports serve as the foundation for consensus upon which potential laws or norms might be established in the future. By working in multilateral discussion groups, nations are able to enhance their understanding of how they perceive various changes and actions in cyberspace.

Following the 2007 coordinated cyberattacks against Estonia, NATO established the Cooperative Cyber Defense Centre of Excellence (CCD

COE) in Tallinn in 2008. NATO's CCD COE served as a central location for NATO partners to work together and address problems arising in and through cyberspace. Two of the more impactful outcomes of this effort have been the Tallinn Manuals released in 2013 and 2017 and produced through a deliberative process between international lawyers and legal scholars. These manuals systematically interpret, and apply international law to, actions occurring in and through cyberspace.[29] The manuals are not legally binding and do not formally establish norms, but they are the most robust collection of legal analysis on the issues related to cyber conflict between states to date.

International interactions in cyberspace at the legal and normative levels are still in flux. Despite the lack of concrete rules of the road for states within cyberspace, general normative behaviors and legal precedents are being worked toward.[30] For countries such as the United States and many of its allies, the Laws of War and many of the norms of international behavior still broadly apply to cyberspace.[31] Much work remains in developing norms and laws in cyberspace, but continued efforts offer the possibility of more stable interactions.[32]

Internet governance is a complicated mess

As should be apparent, there is a substantial lack of consensus on just about every issue relating to the governance of the Internet, and cyberspace more broadly. Although this chapter divided governance between the technical multistakeholder organizations, the more multilateral international governmental organizations and interstate laws and norms, issues of importance for the maintenance of the Internet and the interactions of states, economies, societies and individuals converge and mingle at every level and across almost all issues. Internet governance is complex, messy and incredibly important to everything that touches cyberspace. The fight over what the future of the Internet will look like is ongoing, highly political, and will continue to proceed as new technologies are developed and new policy challenges are encountered.

Discussion questions

1. Why is Internet governance important to cybersecurity?
2. What is the difference between a multilateral and a multistakeholder institution?
3. How do technical changes to the core protocols of the Internet impact policies in states?

Further resources

Center for International Governance Innovation, "A Universal Internet in a Bordered World: Research on Fragmentation, Openness and Interoperability," www.cigionline.org/publications/universal-internet-bordered-world-research-fragmentation-openness-and-interoperability.

Center for International Governance Innovation, "Who Runs the Internet? The Global Multi-stakeholder Model of Internet Governance," www.cigionline.org/publications/who-runs-internet-global-multi-stakeholder-model-internet-governance.

Jovan Kurbalija, *An Introduction to Internet Governance*, 7th edn. (Geneva: DiploFoundation, 2016), www.diplomacy.edu/resources/books/introduction-internet-governance.

4

Cyber capabilities and insecurity

On land, soldiers use tanks, armored personnel carriers, rifles and artillery, among a variety of other weapon systems; the same is true in the air, on the sea, and might one day be true in space. Many of the weapon systems used in the more conventional domains of war revolve around explosives and projectiles designed to use impact or force to render harm. As states begin to leverage cyberspace for military operations, what types of weapons will they use? And what types of weapons will they encounter? US military doctrine as of June 2018 simply refers to the ability to leverage cyber means as a "cyberspace capability."[1] This chapter examines what cyberspace capabilities constitute, and how they are developed, managed, maintained and utilized by a range of actors. Examining these capabilities sheds some light on how they facilitate or obfuscate attribution, and enhance or degrade cybersecurity. As humans invest more time and resources in the development of cyber capabilities, the dynamics of cyber insecurity become more complex.

Cyber capabilities are often directed against one of three core areas associated with the security of computers and networks. These core areas are the confidentiality, integrity and availability of computers, networks and their resident data or data in transit. These three targets are collectively referred to as the CIA triad. Capabilities targeting the confidentiality of a device seek to violate the privacy of data either in transit within networks or at rest on a computer. Capabilities targeting the integrity of computers, networks or data seek to violate the intended state of data or systems. Capabilities that target the availability of computers, networks or data seek to prevent the utilization of these devices or data when desired by the intended user. All cyberattacks, whether they take the form of espionage, sabotage or theft focus on one or more of these three attributes.

To begin, it is helpful to take a step back and reemphasize some of the core concepts from chapter 2 on what cyberspace is and how it works. Unlike land, air, sea and space, cyberspace constitutes a substrate that facilitates many of the weapon systems used in other domains. Cyberspace does have physical attributes in the same way as the other domains of conflict, but it is also a virtual domain with both logical and persona layers of interaction. A warfighter, spy or criminal seeking to utilize cyber capabilities to achieve an effect in cyberspace must think across and within the layers of cyberspace. Very often an attacker may use a capability to exploit one layer of the domain (e.g. a scam targeting a persona) to gain access to other layers (e.g. sensitive data hosted on a server). In many ways, the development and utilization of a cyber capability across these layers is an intellectual exercise that requires strategic, operational and tactical skills.

Historical examples of strategy help to elucidate some of the more contemporary concepts behind the development of cyberspace capabilities. For instance, during World War II, in an effort to reach the ultimate target of the Japanese home islands, General Douglas McArthur and Admiral Chester Nimitz devised an intricate "island-hopping" and "leap-frogging" strategy to stress enemy supply lines and reduce Allied casualties.[2] These hops and leaps strategically positioned Allied forces for a potential invasion of Japan. By contrast, President Kennedy in 1962 employed a quarantine (blockade) of Cuba to prevent the delivery of nuclear missiles by the Soviet Union.[3] Finally, Odysseus in Homer's *The Iliad* concocted a ploy to build a massive hollow wooden horse for the people of Troy. He and his men hid inside the horse until the unsuspecting Trojans, believing they had won the war, took the horse inside their city gates. That night the Achaeans (Greeks) climbed out of the horse, opened the gates and sacked the city.[4]

Each of these strategies approximates strategies in cyberspace. It is possible to "island-hop," "leap-frog," blockade and covertly infiltrate in the digital realm. To employ these strategies, cyber capabilities can increase or decrease in complexity in relation to the effect being sought. Average cyber capabilities are quite simple and typically constitute only about 125 lines of code,[5] while more complicated and robust malware originating from nation states can exceed more than 15,000 lines. Understanding what cyber capabilities are, and how they are developed, maintained and utilized, sheds light on their intent, and can facilitate attribution in some instances. Before delving into the development of cyber capabilities, it is helpful to start with a general taxonomy of capabilities available.

The arsenal of possibilities

Many of the capabilities used for attacks, espionage or theft in cyberspace fall within a taxonomy not dissimilar from that of epidemiology or public health.[6] Software-based forms of cyber capabilities for malicious use are termed malware. malware is a type of software designed to alter the intended purpose of a computer or its resident data. Malware falls within specific typologies of that range from viruses and worms to Trojans and rootkits.

Table 4.1 Malware types

Backdoor	Exploit within existing or installed code that allows unauthorized access to affected computers.
Bot	Software programs that leverage computers to engage in activities, often against the will of the computer's user or administrator.
Exploit	Software vulnerabilities often originating within a software "bug" that allow for unauthorized access to affected computers.
HackTool	Exploitative, attacking and/or scanning tools used to penetrate and access a computer.
Rootkit	Software tools that enable unauthorized access to a computer system without user knowledge.
Spyware/Adware	Software that invades a computer user's privacy and transfers data to a third party.
Trojan	Non-replicating software often installed via user interaction with hidden functions with the intent of manipulating or providing access to a computer system.
Virus	Self-replicating malicious software often hidden within a file and requiring a user to initiate infection. Viruses often attach to files enabling their spread.
Worm	Self-replicating malicious software that does not necessarily require any user actions.

Table 4.1 highlights various types of malware. Malware types can be used independently or combined in a multitude of different ways to achieve varying effects. Most malware is specifically targeted to particular types of operating system (Windows, Linux or Mac OSX, Android or iOS).

Unlike in conventional conflict domains, the ability to both create and utilize many forms of malware is not limited to state actors. Actors ranging from individual hackers to criminals and terrorists can also create, reuse or purchase capabilities. There is significant variation in their capability levels. While the most complex forms of malware often originate at the state level, these capabilities rapidly disperse to lower levels of actors. Beyond the different types of malware highlighted above, the diversity and complexity of malware varies substantially within each type. Table 4.2 presents some additional layers of complexity that can be found within malware.

Table 4.2 Malware features

Entry Point Obfuscator (EPO)	Malware that denies forensic analysis of how malware arrived on a computer.
Metamorphic	Malware that alters its code beyond its encapsulation or encryption designed to bypass malware detection, based on pattern matching, in the same way that it might be possible one day to change the genetic make-up of a person to avoid detection.
Multi-part	Malware comprised of multiple components that work together to achieve an outcome.
Multi-partite	Malware designed to infect more than one object within a system.
Polymorphic	Malware that changes its encapsulation or encryption to continuously obfuscate its appearance in order to avoid malware detection based on coding signatures, in the same way an individual might change their appearance using wigs or make-up.
Resident	Malware that resides within the active memory of a computer.
Stealth	Active concealment of presence to avoid detection.

Figure 4.1 is a screen capture of a polymorphic malware sample that assesses what anti-virus programs are running on a computer in an attempt to re-encapsulate itself and avoid future detection. The increasing complexity of malware with features designed to evade common defensive measures challenges users and organizations at all levels. As malware displays more and more functionalities, it is used more frequently and contributes to a wider array of attacks, from espionage activities to criminal behaviors.

```
1 Public Function Sspyg{} As Varient
2
3 Sspyg= Array {"Amazon","Anonymous","Bitdefender", "Blue Coat","Cisco
  Systems","Cloud","Data
  Center","Dedicated","ESET,spol","FireEye","Forcepoint","Fortinet","Hetz
  ner","Hosted","Hosting","LeaseWeb","Microsoft","nForce","OVH
  SAS","Proofpoint","Security","Server","Strong Technologies","Trend
  Micro","Trustwave","blackoakcomputers","mimecast",}
4
5 End Function
```

Figure 4.1 Polymorphic malware sample

There is a diversity of weapon types, functions and uses in cyber conflict, just as in conventional forms of conflict. In 2014, IBM estimated human error was a contributing factor in more than 95 percent of all computer security incidents.[7] Human error, arising at any level from the configuration of the physical and logical layers to human persona activities within a system, provides a robust vector for the utilization of cyber capabilities. Within this 95 percent figure, the vast majority of security incidents occurs through user interaction with malicious links in emails or on websites. In an effort to combat this human vulnerability, the US DoD began stripping all active HTML links from DoD emails and placed additional text in the subject line of emails originating outside of the Department stating "Non-DoD Source" in 2015. The commander of the Defense Information Systems Agency (DISA), Vice Admiral Nancy A. Norton, indicated the result of these actions has been a dramatic reduction in the number of successful penetrations of DoD networks, but not a reduction in the number of overall attempts to penetrate the network.[8]

Although the complexity and sophistication of malware continues to advance, the primary beachhead into systems and networks remains the human user. Concurrently, while human users remain increasingly vulnerable, the number of lines of code within systems continues to grow resulting in a general increase in the number of bugs (vulnerabilities) within a given set of code. Each new bug offers a new potentially exploitable vector for an attacker. The industry average in 2012 was between 15 and 50 bugs per 1,000 lines of code (a measure known as KLOC).[9] However, this ratio is not exact, because many bugs go undiscovered. The increasing complexity and length of codes hide potential avenues through which attackers can manipulate systems and networks.

As the arsenal of cyber capabilities is growing in complexity and volume, the number of potential new vulnerabilities available to exploit grows. The relationship between new and old vulnerabilities and exploits is not linear. Cyber capabilities are developed to exploit vulnerabilities, patches that fix these vulnerabilities are released, new software and hardware platforms are deployed, and new defensive measures are developed. The patching of computer systems within and across organizations is not uniform, meaning that the mere fact that a vendor releases a fix for a software vulnerability does not mean that all computers with that vulnerability are immune to potential exploits. Often individuals fail to update or patch their systems regularly, leaving them vulnerable to exploitation long after fixes have been released.

In 2017, North Korea utilized EternalBlue, an exploit developed by the NSA and subsequently stolen by the hacker group called Shadow Brokers, to create a destructive ransomware attack: WannaCry.[10] Although Microsoft released a patch for the stolen vulnerability two months prior to its use by North Korea, millions of computers around the world had not yet implemented the patch.[11] The National Health Service (NHS) in the United Kingdom was hit particularly hard in its electronic medical records systems and legacy systems.[12] The challenge of keeping systems up to date becomes more complex, the more specialized a system is. NHS systems, and similar systems that run critical infrastructures or large manufacturing processes, are often tailored software and hardware collections that are unable to implement generic patches without customization to prevent the fixes themselves from rendering existing systems inoperable.

Cyber capabilities for both offensive and defensive actions are in constant flux. On the defensive side, users are constantly required to update, upgrade and secure their systems and networks, changing the vulnerabilities at both the logical and physical network layers, and attempting to minimize vulnerabilities at the human persona layer. By contrast, on the offensive side, actors attempt to quickly develop, and if necessary utilize, cyber capabilities before they are no longer effective. For instance, a worm, virus or trojan developed to exploit Windows XP is unlikely to impact Windows 10. While there are similar analogies in conventional conflict, the rifle has remained a resilient tool of combat for more than 200 years and is unlikely to be defeated as an instrument of warfare anytime soon. The lifespan of malware is limited and decreases in value as targets upgrade and patch their systems. The constraints on the arsenal of cyber capabilities impacts how and why such capabilities are developed. The next section explores how offensive cyber capabilities are developed.

Developing offensive cyber capabilities

Developing an offensive cyber capability varies based on the effect being sought. The more complicated the effect, the more complex the development process. Criminal exploits such as ransomware are often overt and do not seek to hide their effects. Overt malware can be utilized more quickly than more complex exploits such as Flame or Buckshot Yankee, which seek to establish remote access and pose an Advanced Persistent Threat (APT) within a network or system. Both forms of malware can be damaging. Whereas ransomware attacks seek to extort victims, more covert malware exploits are often used to exfiltrate intellectual property. Both forms of attack impact individuals, businesses, critical infrastructures and governments. Researchers have identified a trend in the history of malware development, from a single developer working for a month or two to more complex teams that take much longer.[13] This trend would indicate that the aggregate level of complexity of malware is likely to increase over time.

Growing complexity is also apparent when considering cyber criminality. In Russia and Ukraine, criminals posed as reputable software manufacturers and developed software packages designed to mimic anti-virus programs in an effort to gain access to unsuspecting users.[14] Users in the United States and Europe attempting to do due diligence to protect their computers against malware purchased subscriptions to these fake anti-virus programs. These fake programs subsequently began to slowly extort the user for more money, asking for upgrades or fixes to malware, or simply provided criminals access to the user's computer. This type of attack is extremely difficult to overcome and requires a high level of due diligence from users who often lack the requisite computer skills necessary to make informed judgments.

By contrast, exploits such as fake anti-virus programs are not effective at penetrating most medium to large businesses or governments who use verified vendors. Targeting large businesses and governments requires more sophisticated capabilities that nearly always begin by targeting human users within hardened network infrastructures. These capabilities tend to be multifaceted and often require both user error and technical vulnerabilities.

The trend in malware development continues toward ever more complex organizational structures for criminal purposes, as will be examined in chapter 7. Similarly, states are relying on increasingly complex assemblages of military, civilian and proxy organizations to develop their offensive cyber capabilities. The publication of national cyber strategies and leaks to the press provide a window into the development of cyber capabilities. At present, all European countries, the United States, Canada and dozens of others have created cyber strategies, many of which include provisions for the development of offensive capabilities as well as defensive ones. These documents signal a state's intent to defend its networks, while warning potential adversaries that it too has offensive capabilities. The development of these capabilities also communicates the level of importance that states give to cyberspace and its potential impact on security. The rest of this section examines two different directions in the development and use of cyber capabilities: the development of criminal networks, and powerful state-sponsored cyber actors.

Criminal cyber-capability development

Within the criminal world, the Russian Business Network (RBN) is one of the most famous – or infamous – organizations. Throughout the mid-2000s, RBN both developed and provided a variety of services for criminal activities in cyberspace.[15] At its peak, it is estimated that the RBN was earning over $150 million per year.[16] Criminal activities within RBN infrastructure were as diverse as child pornography, phishing, spam, and malware distribution.[17] RBN is also famous for providing resources for patriotic Russian hackers to launch Distributed Denial of Service (DDoS) and cross-site scripting attacks against government websites in the Republic of Georgia, both during and prior to Russia's 2008 invasion of South Ossetia and Abkhazia.[18] The RBN denies its complicity with criminal activities, but forensic data indicate a sophisticated web of connections between ISPs and BGPs designed to obfuscate traffic and facilitate criminal activities.[19] The RBN spanned over 24 networks and utilized dozens of different malware varieties.[20] Collective organizations like the RBN allow for the consolidated development of malware within ecosystems conducive to criminal behaviors. The organizational structure of the RBN, while centralized in its root infrastructure, was highly decentralized in the development and utilization of malware. The RBN's efforts were entirely profit seeking, although it was susceptible to state influence by the Russian Federation. Current research on the status of the RBN has largely fallen by the wayside as Russian intelligence services – such as the Foreign Intelligence Service, the SVR (Sluzhba Vneshney Razvedki), and the General Staff Main Intelligence Directorate, the GRU (Glavnoye Razvedyvatel'noye Upravleniye) – have risen in prominence. Russian criminal hacking networks are thought to be still quite prolific, but by most accounts the RBN as an independent entity no longer exists.[21]

The RBN is by no means unique. There are a plethora of criminal organizations ranging from Mexican drug cartels to individual criminal hackers who both generate novel exploits and utilize existing malware through available libraries such as Metasploit. Cyber capabilities added a dimension to criminal theft that has in many ways made criminal behavior easier in terms of time and energy, and less risky for the criminal. Whereas a bank robber used to have to leverage the threat of violence to compel a teller to hand over money, a modern bank robber accesses the financial information of the bank via the Internet through anonymous routing services such as Virtual Private Networks (VPN) or The Onion Router (Tor) to steal substantially more money in less time, with greater anonymity.

State cyber-capability development

The efforts of RBN and similar criminal enterprises, while organized, are less focused on specific targets and are not centrally controlled. By contrast, the People's Liberation Army (PLA) Unit 61398, a military hacking unit accused by the US Department of Justice of engaging in substantial intellectual property theft from US commercial firms, is centrally organized, funded and controlled.[22] In 2013, Mandiant (now FireEye) released a comprehensive report detailing the espionage efforts of this unit.[23] PLA Unit 61398 constituted a highly organized military unit within the 2nd Bureau of the 3rd department of the PLA General Staff.[24] Analysts estimate this unit compromised more than 141 companies across 20 industries as of 2013.[25] Mandiant deemed the unit APT1 (Advanced Persistent

Threat 1) because of its immense reach and scale. APT1 maintained persistent access on target systems in excess of 1,764 days.[26] The unit leveraged more than 40 different malware families or subtypes of cyber capabilities identified above. Each of the targets selected was exploited for intelligence gain. Unit 61398 must have had substantial staffing and resources with annualized budgets to stage such an operation. Mandiant assesses that the unit had been in existence since at least 2006 and had stolen in excess of 6.5 terabytes of data (for comparison, the US Library of Congress is comprised in its entirety of 15 terabytes).[27] The scale and organizational complexity of Unit 61398 far outpaces that of the RBN. While the RBN was profit seeking, Unit 61398 was focused on national security and economic espionage.

Externalities associated with the proliferating nature of cyber capabilities include a diffusion of malware away from state actors down to sub-state and criminal elements. Robust malware libraries are available both through open source collections and through profit-seeking ventures. The diffuse nature of mid- to low-tier cyber capabilities has facilitated criminal activities in and through cyberspace. The malware and skills that facilitate espionage are equally relevant to the theft of information from corporate databases, which is often initiated via emails leveraging social engineering. Cybersecurity breaches in the private sector have resulted in the availability of personally identifiable information (PII) markets, resulting in credit card fraud and identity theft.

The production and distribution of malware is not entirely democratized, with many of the most complex malware types remaining at the state level, due to the time and specificity required for their creation. However, the volume of malware available below the state level fosters strategic challenges for economies around the globe. The creation of malware by states, criminal organizations, corporations such as the Hacking Team, and individuals indicates an increasingly contested and potentially risky environment.

There is no single approach to developing effective malware and each actor, state or criminal must tailor their efforts to the resources available to them and the targets they seek to attack or exploit. There are dozens of different software development models used globally in the development of software for commercial and non-commercial use. However, as a means of assessing the general processes for developing malware, US defense company Lockheed Martin created the "Cyber Kill Chain," a useful model for examining how actors develop and utilize offensive cyber capabilities. Table 4.3 provides a detailed walk through the Cyber Kill Chain.

Table 4.3 The Cyber Kill Chain[28]

Step 1: Reconnaissance	The attacker gathers information on the target before the actual attack starts. He can do it by looking for publicly available information on the Internet.
Step 2: Weaponization	The attacker uses an exploit and creates a malicious payload to send to the victim. This step happens on the attacker's side, without contact with the victim.
Step 3: Delivery	The attacker sends the malicious payload to the victim by email or other means, which represents one of many intrusion methods the attacker can use.
Step 4: Exploitation	The attacker gains access to the victim via a software, hardware or human vulnerability.
Step 5: Installation	Installing malware on the infected computer is relevant only if the attacker used malware as part of the attack, and even when there is malware involved, the installation is a point in time within a much more elaborate attack process that takes months to operate.
Step 6: Command and control	The attacker creates or maintains a command and control channel in order to continue to operate his internal assets remotely. This step is relatively generic and relevant throughout the attack, not only when malware is installed.
Step 7: Action on objectives	The attacker performs the steps to achieve his actual goals inside the victim's network. This is the elaborate active attack process that takes months, and thousands of small steps, in order to achieve.

The Cyber Kill Chain provides a good procedural model for how offensive cyber activities are undertaken, but it does not explicitly outline what resources, skills, strategies, operations and tactics are needed to both develop and utilize cyberspace capabilities for offensive actions. Criminal organizations such as the RBN are likely to do the minimum *reconnaissance* necessary to prepare for a cyber operation. If they are engaged in spamming or other forms of social engineering, they might conduct a basic search on the Internet or write emails that are generic enough to work for dozens of individuals. By contrast, Unit 61398 probably engages in substantial reconnaissance of its targets. It leverages all-source intelligence to develop a picture of a target and assesses which vulnerabilities are most likely to be successfully exploited. Reconnaissance activities for both criminal and state organizations are ongoing, but we can reasonably assume that states devote substantially more resources to understanding a target to develop tailored malware and ensure success. The RBN and similar criminal organizations are more likely to engage in criminal activities that yield greater profits by attacking more broadly and with fewer upfront costs devoted to reconnaissance.

In the *weaponization* phase of the Kill Chain, both criminal and state actors take the information or intelligence gained from the reconnaissance phase and begin the process of creating a payload that can be delivered to the target. As in the island-hopping strategy, states are likely to want payloads to be delivered to specific targets, and therefore more carefully craft weaponized code. Criminal organizations seeking profit do not need to expend time or money on highly specialized targeting and therefore can avoid such strategies to focus on the exploit requiring the least effort.

The craft with which code is weaponized can provide substantial forensic clues as to its authorship. Many states are beholden to international law, and their weaponized code attempts to conform to these legal standards. For instance, the Stuxnet worm that attacked Iran's nuclear enrichment facilities appears to have been written in close consultation with lawyers.[29] The code targeted specific configurations of Siemens controllers that were designed to manage centrifuge arrays in specific configurations known through International Atomic Energy Agency (IAEA) reporting to have been used in Iranian nuclear enrichment processes. The code also verified the date on the systems to ensure that it was operating within its specified timeframe. How code is weaponized and what its constraints and limitations are can and often do provide indications regarding the actor who developed the code, and the strategy and tactics it employed. The weaponization phase often requires expertise well beyond that of hackers, and can necessitate engineers, physicists or a variety of technical, legal and policy specialists. Stealing data might not be that difficult, but changing the enrichment levels of a centrifuge array will probably require a nuclear engineer.[30]

Once code has been weaponized, its *delivery* can be as simple as emailing an infected PDF or Microsoft Word file to an unsuspecting recipient, or it can involve leaving dozens of infected USB drives outside of a US military facility in Iraq, as was the case for Buckshot Yankee.[31] Delivery techniques can be direct or indirect, they can be complex or remarkably simple. Delivery methods are predicated on the target(s) being sought after, and the capabilities of the attacker to leverage a diverse set of delivery tactics. Sometimes, as in the case of the Natanz nuclear facility in Iran, a human insider, either knowingly or unknowingly, transports the malicious code into a facility. At times, it is possible to draw targets out so that they go onto a specific website or an IP address – this approach is known as a watering-hole attack. In Ukraine, the Russian military has used cellular tower spoofing to hijack soldiers' mobile communications and send infected attachments purporting to be from family or friends, via MMS or SMS.[32]

Delivering a weapon often requires access into the system being targeted. This access constitutes the *exploitation* phase of an attack. At its most basic, exploitation is the culmination of the delivery phase of an attack and links delivery and installation as well as subsequent functions within the Kill Chain. Exploitation can target any of the three layers of cyberspace. Exploitations of the physical network and logical network layers often require the use of a 0-Day vulnerability (a previously undiscovered or unpatched vulnerability). Exploitation at the human persona layer often involves social engineering a human user to click on a link or visit a website. The overwhelming majority of exploits occur through human interactions. Kevin Mitnick, one of the most famous hackers of the 1990s, was moderately skilled on the technical side but excelled at social engineering. He was arrested by the FBI in 1995 and charged with computer hacking and wire fraud.[33] Social engineering remains one of the most effective means of exploitation. This is largely due to the human nature of cyberspace, but also to the substantial investments most organizations put into defensive tools to secure the more technical attributes of networks and systems.

Following the delivery and exploitation of a target, malware frequently needs to be *installed*. If malware is being installed, then it must be directed against systems it can infect. Malware designed to run on Windows is unlikely to work on machines running MacOS or Linux. Even within specific versions of operating systems, malware must account for updates and patches so that it can be installed and function as intended. Not all cyberattacks require installation. DDoS attacks can overwhelm an adversary's ability to handle large volumes of traffic without installation. This was the case of the Mirai DDoS attacks in 2016, which disabled a major Domain Name Server that provided services to companies such as Netflix, GitHub, Twitter, Reddit and Airbnb.[34] The installation phase can be difficult and, if improperly done, might alert system users or network administrators, or trigger system defenses such as anti-virus software or intrusion detection and prevention systems (IDPSs). If these defenses identify a malware, they will seek to limit its potential effects. The installation of malware can trigger prompts to users or administrators that might alert them to the attackers' intentions or degrade system resources temporarily so as to indicate that a system's functioning state is changed. Indications of installation must be managed for an attack to be successful. Crafting malware for successful installation often requires in-depth knowledge of how systems are managed and what privileges various user accounts have with systems and networks, to overcome cyber defenses.

Attacks that seek to gain a foothold – in a similar way to the island-hopping strategy – often require *command and control* (C2) capabilities. Some attacks can be run from a single C2 server, or, for instance, Unit 61398 attackers established 937 C2 servers spread across 849 IP addresses in 13 countries.[35] The resources available to the attacker and the attributes of the target itself determine the development and maintenance of C2 for the purpose of attacking an adversary. Criminal organizations are unlikely to have the capability to manage large-scale C2 in the same way a state might, but with moderate resources they can still achieve robust C2. More complex C2 facilitates increasingly robust and resilient offensive cyber actions. However, the establishment of C2 is resource intensive and can require substantial time and coordination. C2 capabilities are typically established in advance of malware installation. First, if malware needs to be directly installed by the attacker, C2 establishes the communications link that allows for installation. Second, if malware is self-propagating or user-installed, and exfiltrates data or executes commands at the direction of the attacker, it requires a place to call home for directions or the reception of data. The management of C2 over time is difficult and can expose an attack if done improperly.

One early case that has become legend is the tale of Clifford Stoll's tracking of KGB-funded hacker Markus Hess as he stole information from Lawrence Berkeley National Laboratory.[36] C2 requires the transmission of data from one system to another. Anomalies in traffic usage, where the data originates and where it goes, and even the electrical consumption of devices can raise red flags among systems administrators. Clifford Stoll worked as a system administrator at the Lawrence Berkeley National Laboratory when he traced a $0.75 accounting error to the unauthorized use of 9 seconds of laboratory computer time. Stoll eventually realized that a hacker had acquired access to the Laboratory system, and contacted intelligence and law-enforcement agencies. His meticulous forensic analysis resulted in a surprising find, a KGB penetration. His investigation illustrates the difficulty of maintaining long-term presence on a target system.

To achieve such a presence on a target system requires substantial C2 capabilities. Often, C2 capabilities are routed through proxy states or organizations to obfuscate their origin or intention and to prevent attribution. In the case of DDoS attacks, C2 can function like a conductor of an orchestra, calling on different bots (infected computers) within its network to launch an attack at different times, or using all of them simultaneously.

Finally, after all the previous steps have been implemented, the final step in the development and utilization of an offensive cyber capability is an *action on objectives*. In this final stage of the Cyber Kill Chain, effects are actuated. Actions span a spectrum from exploitation and exfiltration of data, passwords or other credentials, to the manipulation of data to violate its integrity within a system, the degradation of a system to slow it down or minimize its efficiency, and the destruction of the system or device it is running. The majority of offensive cyber actions focus on the theft (exploitation and exfiltration) of data. Both the RBN's criminal endeavors and those of Unit 61938 were primarily interested in the theft of data. While RBN sought profit, Unit 61938 sought intelligence for both national security and national economic gain. The majority of malware seeks to steal data for profit or intelligence, but new forms of malware such as CryptoLocker are now being used for extortion, via the threat of data destruction and the degradation of systems. Whereas previous attacks made money from the data itself, by engaging in credit card fraud and identity theft, attacks using CryptoLocker extort the computer's or system's owner to pay a fee to unlock their data. In sum, cyber actions can take multiple forms and be used to achieve different objectives. Unlike many conventional weapons – such as bullets or bombs – which result in first-order effects, the impact of cyber capabilities is necessarily indirect.

The effects and characteristics of cyber capabilities

Bullets fired from a gun achieve first-order effects through their impact with a given target. Bombs dropped from a plane cause first-order effects through their explosive blasts. Beyond the theft of data for espionage or criminal purposes, there are few first-order effects achieved through offensive cyber operations. The apparent absence of first-order effects is one of the main reasons why some scholars have been reluctant to use the expression "cyber war." Below is a comparison of eight key attributes of cyber capabilities and kinetic weapons. Understanding these attributes helps decision-makers choose the most applicable tool in a given situation.

First, effects in cyberspace differ in their key characteristics from kinetic effects. Kinetic weapons privilege direct effects over indirect effects; by contrast, cyberattacks privilege indirect effects, or what Herb Lin refers to as second- and third-order effects.[37] The second attribute is that of reversibility. The effects of most kinetic weapons are difficult and often costly to reverse. It takes time to rebuild an area that has been destroyed by a bomb, to heal from a gunshot wound. Cyberattacks are in many cases reversible with limited cost to either the attacker or the target, particularly within short time horizons. For instance, a CryptoLocker attack on a victim can be reversed if the victim pays a fee to the hacker, thereby releasing (decrypting) the data. Third, cyber capabilities are often costly to research and develop, but inexpensive to maintain. Kinetic weapons, however, have costs extending from research and development through procurement and maintenance. Once an exploit is available for a given vulnerability, it will remain effective until that vulnerability is patched. Fourth, kinetic weapons often are limited in both number and complexity based on the wealth of a state, whereas the capacity to build cyber weapons can be relatively democratized as the resources (i.e. coding skills, hardware and software) necessary for their creation are widespread and inexpensive. Fifth, the intelligence requirements necessary for successful deployment of both cyber and kinetic weapons are high. Both types of weapon require strategic intelligence to understand the adversary's capabilities. The utilization of both types of weapon also requires substantial intelligence preparation of the battlefield (IPB). Sixth, both kinetic and cyber capabilities involve uncertainties in planning and execution – however, the process of conducting battle damage assessments after use can be very complex in the case of cyber capabilities, in contrast to kinetic weapons. Since cyber effects are indirect, it is often difficult to discern whether the cause of a problem with a computer is the result of a cyberattack, an error or some other malfunction. In 2016–17, when North Korea experienced a series of ballistic missile test failures, some observers hinted that these failures might be the result of US "left of launch" cyberattacks against the missiles themselves. However, as noted by David Sanger, while many "cyber experts" claimed these test failures were due to cyberattacks, aeronautical engineers specializing in missiles indicated that the probable source of the failure was mechanical and not cyber related.[38]

Seventh – and often overlooked – is the returnability of cyber capabilities upon use. Once a bomb explodes or a bullet is fired, it generally cannot be re-exploded or re-fired. A cyber capability once used, if not properly deleted from the target system, can be forensically reconstituted and repurposed as a new capability for the adversary or other actors who might gain access to the code or vulnerabilities it exploited. The returnability of cyber capabilities against the attacker or other actors eliminates the concept of fire and forget. In cyberspace, if you fire, you also need to protect your own systems against the weapon being used. Eighth, proliferation is a challenge for both kinetic weapons and cyber capabilities. However, transporting tanks, bombs, missiles and even guns is substantially more difficult than emailing or file-transferring malicious software with the click of a mouse. Tracking, maintaining security of, and accounting for an arsenal of cyber capabilities over time poses substantial challenges to many states, as evidenced by the NSA's loss of numerous exploits to the hacker group the Shadow Brokers. Table 4.4 provides an overview of the major differences between kinetic and cyber capabilities.

Table 4.4 Kinetic v. cyber capabilities

Kinetic capabilities	Cyber capabilities
Direct effects	Indirect effects
Difficult and costly to reverse	More easily reversible
Costly to maintain	Easy to maintain
Costly to develop	Relatively easy to develop
Substantial intelligence requirements	Substantial intelligence requirements
Relatively simple damage assessment	Very complex damage assessment
Not returnable	Returnable
Physical burden of proliferation	Easy proliferation

Although characteristics diverge between kinetic and cyber capabilities, substantial effects can be achieved by both. Both types of capabilities are capable of achieving violence either against large populations or targeted against individuals.[39] The predictability of effects achieved through kinetic weapons remains more easily understood by policy-makers, warfighters and criminals. And, although effects of cyber capabilities are difficult to assess in the current forms of use, this might not always be the case as new weapons are developed and more and more systems connect to cyberspace and increase the potential for violence. The continued development of ever more advanced cyber capabilities is likely to create new effects that might more closely approximate those of kinetic weapons. While, in the near term, prognostications of a "Cyber Pearl Harbor" remain unfulfilled, as the number and importance of computers and cyberspace expand, the effects that are able to be achieved in and through cyberspace with cyber capabilities are likely to increase.[40]

Cyber capabilities: A weapon?

There remains a substantial debate within the field of international relations as to whether cyber capabilities constitute a weapon at all. While Lucas Kello identifies cyber capabilities as "virtual weapons," other scholars such as Thomas Rid, Erik Gartzke and Jon Lindsay push back on the application of the term "weapon."[41] This chapter deliberately uses the muted term "cyber capability" as opposed to a more aggressive term – "cyber weapon." Removing hyperbole from the debate allows us to focus on what it is that states and criminal actors seek to achieve via cyber means and how they go about doing so. There is often a desire to leverage common terminology across domains – however, as was seen in 2016, the use of conventional language to describe "cyber bombs" hitting the Islamic State is not really applicable. Talking about "cyber bombs" obfuscates the true nature of cyber capabilities and their inherent complexity, and establishes false impressions of their effect.[42] Cyber capabilities are just that: capabilities. They can be developed, used and discarded and are wholly dependent on the target and objectives being sought. In cyberspace, unlike in conventional war, one cyber capability does not necessarily equate to another in the same way that one bullet is similar to other bullets. The organization, planning and management of capabilities in cyberspace have proven difficult. The continued expansion of cyberspace provides ample room for the development of new forms of capabilities in the years to come.

A continued focus on malware and the vulnerabilities of systems and networks often overlooks the largest security gap associated with cyber capabilities: the human user. The single greatest weapon a hacker, state or criminal possesses is the user of the system they are targeting. While the emphasis of this chapter was on the development of capabilities in terms of malware, one of the most successful capabilities hackers deploy is a thorough understanding of human psychology. Social engineering against a user can substantially ease the technical requirements necessary for the development of most other cyber capabilities.

Discussion questions

1. Is malware a weapon or a capability? Discuss.
2. Are cyber capabilities developed by states or by criminal actors more dangerous? Why?
3. How does Lockheed's "Cyber Kill Chain" help in understanding cyberattacks?

Further resources

Robert Belk and Matthew Noyes, "On the Use of Offensive Cyber Capabilities: A Policy Analysis on Offensive US Cyber Policy," Belfer Center, March 20, 2012, www.belfercenter.org/sites/default/files/files/publication/cybersecurity-pae-belk-noyes.pdf.

Dennis Distler, "Malware Analysis: An Introduction," SANS Institute InfoSec Reading Room, December 14, 2007, at www.sans.org/reading-room/whitepapers/malicious/malware-analysis-introduction-2103.

Emily Goldman and John Arquilla, *Cyber Analogies* (Monterrey, CA: Naval Postgraduate School, 2014), https://calhoun.nps.edu/bitstream/handle/10945/40037/NPS-DA-14-001.pdf.

5

National cybersecurity and strategy

National cybersecurity is a complex endeavor, involving millions of actors and billions of devices. Cyberspace permeates so much of the critical social, economic and military infrastructure of modern nations that it forms a foundational substrate upon which national security relies. This chapter focuses on national efforts to achieve cybersecurity, and the continuing relevance of state actors in cyberspace. Although non-state actors – such as hackers, criminal organizations, non-profit organizations and companies – affect cybersecurity, states have unparallelled authority, legitimacy, expertise and access to resources.[1] Governmental and societal reliance on information technology infrastructure inevitably creates vulnerabilities that public authorities seek to mitigate. National decision-makers, and the processes they follow, shape cyberspace and the interactions that take place within it.

The need for national cybersecurity is now widely recognized, and the debate on the ends, ways and means necessary to achieve national cybersecurity has attracted increasing public and scholarly attention in the last decade.[2] The networked nature of cyberspace requires national cybersecurity to span multiple divides between public and private, and local, national and international organizations. The national cybersecurity strategies of major powers such as China, Russia and the United States all emphasize the need to coordinate multiple actors and approaches to security in and through the digital realm. Despite significant differences in national cyber strategies, nation states face a number of common challenges to achieving national cybersecurity.

Cyber power, national security and strategy

National security can be understood both in the objective sense of physical safety, and in a more subjective way, as the protection of national values.[3] While the physical safety of nations poses similar challenges across the globe, variation in national interests and values – specifically between liberal democracies and authoritarian regimes – produces different approaches in the pursuit of national security.

To maintain national security, governments wield power. In its simplest form, power is the ability to influence others. This ability rests on economic, demographic, political and socio-cultural resources, among others. States use a variety of instruments – diplomacy, information, military and economic capabilities (also known as DIME) – to leverage these resources and pursue goals they believe will have a positive impact on their regime or population. In democracies, governments are elected to formulate national interests through policy objectives and strategies that translate into action.[4] They sometimes opt to wield hard power, using or threatening to use military operations and economic sanctions to force other actors to change their behavior. At the softer end of the spectrum, policy-makers use information and diplomacy to influence actors through persuasion. One of the core challenges confronting high-level decision-makers is to effectively combine hard- and soft-power resources – what Joseph Nye calls a smart-power strategy – to achieve national security objectives.[5] Much of the contemporary debate about national cybersecurity explores how to leverage specific cyber capabilities to contribute to such a strategy.

The concept of cyber power provides a useful basis for discussing the role of cyber capabilities in the context of national security policy. Strategist John Sheldon defines cyber power as "the ability, in peace, crisis, and war to exert prompt and sustained influence in and from cyberspace."[6] With the distinction between "in" and "from" cyberspace, Sheldon suggests that cyber operations establish influence beyond cyberspace, in the physical world. For Daniel Kuehl, another strategist, cyber power is a dimension of the informational instrument of power that "links to, supports, and enables the creation and exercise of the other instruments" to create advantages and influence events.[7] Cyberspace is inherently linked to the economic performance of major nations. Digital goods and services accounted for 6.5 percent of the US economy in 2016 and over 30 percent of the Chinese GDP.[8] States also leverage cyber capabilities as a means of influencing opinions throughout the world and, increasingly, to exert military force. Cyber capabilities have come to permeate all elements of national power.

During the Cold War era, the information element of national power was focused on strategic communications and propaganda, two types of information-based influence operations meant to affect the perceptions and attitude of specific audiences. With the advent of cyberspace, the information domain has expanded significantly. All sorts of state and non-state actors can leverage cyberspace to advance their interests in and through the digital world. The Internet is sometimes referred to as the "great equalizer," reflecting the way in which easy access to cyberspace empowers actors that do not traditionally wield significant informational influence. In a realm where both state and non-state actors play a prominent role, power cannot simply be exerted over others to influence them, but must also be utilized co-operatively.[9] Wielding power in cyberspace and achieving national cybersecurity require public–private and international cooperation.

Leveraging instruments of power in a coordinated manner is essential to achieve national objectives. Strategy aims to align ends (objectives), ways (courses of action) and means (resources). Cyber strategy seeks to connect these elements to cyber power in the pursuit of national security objectives. In their seminal book, *Cyberpower and National Security*, Franklin Kramer, Stuart Starr and Larry Wentz define cyber strategy as "the development and employment of strategic capabilities to operate in cyberspace, integrated and coordinated with the other operational domains, to achieve or support the achievement of objectives across the elements of national power in support of national security strategy."[10] Achieving national cybersecurity requires the development of human, technological and organizational resources and procedures that contribute to specific national objectives.[11]

States pursue different interests and objectives and follow different strategies to translate their resources into desirable outcomes. Proponents of strategic culture argue that states formulate national assumptions – based on their political, cultural, philosophical and cognitive characteristics – that limit the options they consider. Cultural legacies brought by different organizations can also play a role in framing issues and evaluating policy options.[12] These elements, as well as bureaucratic preferences and legal constraints, can be expected to produce national styles and preferences that shape the way nations user their cyber power.[13] However, analysts need to be careful not to make extreme generalizations that would seek to predict state behavior based solely on national circumstances and legacies.[14] While domestic factors are important in understanding national cybersecurity, a number of other influences – such as the structure of the international system and the particular characteristics of cyberspace – pose similar security challenges to decision-makers across the world. The following sections emphasize the national approaches to cyber power and security favored by the three most powerful nations in cyberspace: China, Russia and the United States. They emphasize a number of differences, but also some commonalities in the way these major powers guide and organize their actions in and through cyberspace.

China: controlling information

The development of the modern Chinese state and its emergence as a great power in cyberspace was not preordained. In the 1990s, China, while rapidly developing, lacked sufficient human and technical capacity in information communications technologies. This lack of endogenous capacity was confronted head-on in a 1998 book written by two Chinese PLA colonels, entitled *Unrestricted Warfare*.[15] In their book, Colonels Liang Qiao and Wang Xiansui proposed a new way of challenging potential adversaries without engaging in direct confrontation. To achieve this strategy, and exploit the rapidly evolving technological landscape, China began implementing an ambitious program of technological development. In 2000, then General Secretary of the Communist Party Jiang Zemin gave a series of seminal speeches in which he established the trajectory of China's information society and outlined a strategy to transform China into an advanced cyber power.[16]

These intentions were formally outlined in a 14-year plan that emphasized the priorities of a resurgent China in cyberspace. In tandem with developing the educational facilities and pushing for students to enter into information technology careers, the plan established the necessity of developing both internal controls on information and the capacity to exploit the information vulnerabilities of other states. Nearly 14 years later, China is technologically advanced and often dominates the quest for high-performance computing and Artificial Intelligence (AI). The nation currently benefits from a booming economy, and hosts close to a quarter of the global Internet population. Consequently, the Internet is an important enabler – and also a possible source of vulnerabilities – in the emergence of China as a great power.[17]

The authoritarian nature of the Chinese regime shapes its conception of cybersecurity and use of cyber power. At the domestic level, China has sought to control the flow of external information into the national sphere, to exert sovereignty over its society. For the Chinese government, Internet threats are not only technical but also informational. While various democratic nations, such as the United States and Sweden, monitor Internet traffic in and out of their country, China filters out unwanted content.[18] To control information Chinese authorities have developed a "golden shield," colloquially known as the Great Firewall of China. The Ministry of Public Security defines the boundaries of this wall, providing censorship guidelines that must be followed by ISPs and citizens alike. The Chinese Internet police relies on a combination of legislation, technologies and human workforce to enforce censorship and shut down websites, delete or redirect information and arrest dissident bloggers.[19]

This effort to censor the Internet aims to limit the influence of Western media and other news sources, which are seen as subversive tools that threaten the stability of the regime.[20] Chinese "netizens" do not have access to a number of foreign websites and applications, such as Facebook and Google Maps. Service providers are also forced to block access to websites presenting information on "subversive" movements and ideologies, such as the teachings of the Dalai Lama. In principle, Chinese censorship aims to limit separatism, terrorism and extremism. In practice, critics point out that information control also limits freedom of expression. In a detailed study of Chinese social media, Gary King and his colleagues found that Chinese censorship does not seek to systematically suppress government criticism on social media but attempts to "reduce the probability of collective action," such as protests.[21]

The Chinese government's ability to control Internet traffic on its territory provides a useful tool against external attacks. The government could shut off domestic access to the Internet in an effort to prevent major cyberattacks. However, experts have questioned the impermeability of the Great Firewall, noting that some activists have managed to bypass it.[22] Researchers have questioned the extent to which China is well equipped to confront technical and economic threats at home. The widespread use of pirate software in China creates vulnerabilities as their users do not automatically get access to security upgrades and patches.[23] Further concerns exist about the extent to which cyberspace has facilitated the development of a black-market economy, over which the government has limited control.[24]

At the international level, China is both a source and a target of cyber insecurity. The Chinese government knows that it cannot match the United States in conventional assets and has therefore sought to develop asymmetric means to wield informational power. This asymmetric approach seeks to turn the technical superiority of adversaries into a liability.

China has focused its efforts on cyber espionage and the theft of intellectual property in order to develop an informational advantage across the fields of economics, military affairs, politics and technology, and to weaken the operational efficiency of its adversaries.[25] This focus on information gathering is consistent with the Chinese strategy of pre-emption and "informationized war." The Chinese military wants to anticipate threats and act early to gain the initiative. This pre-emptive approach requires preparation and mobilization in peacetime, including the recruitment of a wide pool of talented personnel, as well as the continuous testing of adversaries' networks to uncover their strengths and vulnerabilities and signal intrusion capabilities. The information gathered through reconnaissance and espionage efforts can then be utilized to deceive or entice an opponent and adopt an appropriate strategy that will lead to the greatest gains.[26]

China is often decried in the West for its confrontational cyber posture and efforts to penetrate Western computer systems for military and economic gain. In the last two decades, a number of major cyber operations originating from China – from Titan Rain to APT1 – stole sensitive information from Western governments and industries. However, the extent to which Chinese-led APTs have translated into economic and military gains is unclear.

While these operations reflect an active stance, they might not be as aggressive as is commonly perceived. Some analysts argue that they reveal China's concerns about adversaries' efforts to penetrate its own government and private-sector systems.[27] Chinese authors writing about cyber warfare emphasize the role of the United States in driving cyber insecurity, and the need for China to develop cyber capabilities to maintain its sovereignty and protect itself from US destabilization.[28] For Valeriano, Jensen and Maness, Chinese cyber behavior reflects a desire to achieve balance with the United States and maintain power in Asia.[29] These concerns would explain why Beijing engages in cyber espionage and information manipulation rather than cyber degradation.

The organization of national cybersecurity in China is spread across multiple organizations. Jon Lindsay emphasizes the complex networks of overlapping committees and groups making decisions under the banner of the Chinese one-party government.[30] This institutional fragmentation has limited Chinese abilities to foster strong cybersecurity across the public–private divide, and weakened critical infrastructure protection. The PLA has invested significantly in its cyber warfare capabilities, both offensive and defensive. The responsibility for cyber operations in the Chinese military is generally attributed to the PLA General Staff's 3rd Department, which holds responsibilities for signals intelligence (SIGINT) and seems to play a primarily defensive role. The Chinese General Staff Department 418th Research Institute and its Unit 61539 are generally considered to be the Chinese Cyber Command. A number of other cyber units are co-located with civilian entities, specifically universities and schools.[31] Following a military reform launched in 2016, many of these units have been reorganized under a Strategic Support Force.

Chinese cyber operations also rely on entities and individuals that are not officially acting on behalf of the government and not directly tied to the PLA, allowing the government to formally deny any involvement and responsibility. Following Mao Tse Tung's notion of mobilizing popular support to wage a protracted struggle, Beijing has fostered the development of cyber militias and "patriotic hackers" organized in networks around the PLA and contributing to the development of Chinese cyber power.[32] According to some recent research, these militias bring together from 8 to 10 million individuals and primarily serve a defensive role.[33] The extent to which the PLA will effectively leverage and merge these disparate cyber capabilities remains to be seen.

Russia's holistic approach

Russia maintains a holistic approach to cybersecurity that considers strategic interactions across all the elements of power.[34] This approach is well suited to the all-encompassing nature of computer networks in modern societies. At the domestic level, Russian authorities have sought to control the flow of information and data in cyberspace to maintain national sovereignty. Following Tsarist and communist precedents, the government maintains a strong degree of state control on information to protect its regime and keep the loyalty of its people in check. Prior to the collapse of the Soviet Union, the KGB installed a System for Operative Investigative Activities at network junction points around the country. This system of devices has since evolved and now provides the FSB, Russia's Federal Security Service, with unprecedented surveillance capabilities on Russian networks.[35]

Russia has not built a Great Firewall, but the government supervises the media to make sure they promote patriotic values and traditions.[36]

Russian officials are particularly concerned with the influence of the Western information society and way of life. To limit Western influence and maintain its sovereignty, Russia has expressed a desire to develop an independent Internet and create its own domain name system that would limit external influences.[37] Russian law requires ISPs to host data belonging to Russian persons and entities on the Russian territory (to limit surveillance from other countries).[38] Beyond these technical measures, the Russian government has supported the development of a Russian ecosystem of Internet services, including the Russian social networking service VKontakte and the Russian search engine Yandex. The executive branch of government leverages this Russian segment of the Internet (also known as RUNET) as an instrument of power, both at home and abroad, to pursue Russian sovereignty.[39] RUNET provides Moscow with a tool to support a distinct digital subculture and influence former Soviet states like Georgia and Ukraine.

At the international level, Russia leverages cyberspace as an asymmetric means to engage with an adversary (the West) that is stronger in other elements (economy, military). Here, Russian use of cyber operations to project power and sow chaos contrasts with the more defensive outlook of Chinese cyber strategy. In Russia, cyber operations are construed as a form of information warfare that seeks to disrupt enemy civil–military facilities and systems, leadership, troops and populations.[40] Russian doctrine attributes great importance to the role of public perception and seeks to exploit psychological and cognitive factors as a part of a broader informational struggle. The aim is to manipulate the adversary's picture of reality, interfere with its decision-making process and influence its society to produce favorable conditions. The Russians use "reflexive control" to convey "to a partner or an opponent specially prepared information to incline him to voluntarily make the predetermined decision desired by the initiator of the action."[41]

In this context, cyber operations might seek to affect enemy information gathering and analysis, and manipulate the information disseminated in mass media and online. Such operations can be used to disorganize the structure of a society, distort public consciousness and affect elites and citizens alike. For example, Russian military movements in Eastern Ukraine were accompanied by Distributed Denial of Service (DDoS) attacks disrupting computer systems in Kyiv. Sowing such confusion can help to buy time in the initial stages of a conflict and thicken the fog of war.[42] Since 2016, Russian efforts to interfere in democratic elections across Western countries have become increasingly apparent. Russia has used cyber operations to gather protected information, alter some of its content and leak selected documents online to influence electorates. Russian trolls have used social media to foment societal tensions in the West, instill chaos and reinforce its position on the international scene. These actions have sent strong signals that Russia is a capable and dangerous cyber actor, but their overall utility as an instrument of power remains debatable.[43] Storybox 5.1 discusses Russian interference in the presidential elections in the United States (2016) and France (2017) to exemplify the Russian use and limits of cyber operations as an informational instrument of power.

Storybox 5.1 Russian interferences: Hit and miss

According to a declassified US intelligence community report, President Vladimir Putin ordered an influence campaign targeting the 2016 US presidential election.[44] This campaign sought to undermine public faith in the US democratic process and harm the electability of Secretary Clinton (initially a candidate for the Democratic Party presidential primaries). The Russian campaign relied on a messaging strategy that blended covert intelligence operations, mostly through cyber activity, with overt efforts by the government, state-funded media and social media users to delegitimize Clinton's candidacy. Russian military intelligence (General Staff Main Intelligence Directorate, or GRU) used online persona Guccifer 2.0 and the website DCLeaks.com to release data obtained through cyber operations to selected media outlets.

The crux of the operations relied on the GRU's ability to penetrate Democratic National Committee (DNC) networks from summer 2015 to 2016. Russian hackers compromised the personal email accounts of Democratic Party officials and stole large volumes of data. The US intelligence community assesses that the Russian services consider their cyber-enabled disclosure operation to be a "qualified success" because of its impact on public discussion in the United States.[45] Experts expect Russia to continue its propaganda and disinformation campaign to further exacerbate social and political fissures in the United States, and beyond.[46] This operation also served domestic purposes, drawing the Russian public's attention to flawed aspects of democratic institutions.[47]

* * *

In contrast to the success of its interferences in the 2016 US election, Russian efforts to influence the French presidential election of 2017

> failed to divide French society and affect outcomes. One key aspect of the Russian campaign in France was the leaking of information that had been captured from then-candidate Emmanuel Macron's presidential campaign. The Macron leaks were a combination of real emails and forgeries released a few hours before the final vote on the second tour of this election.
>
> Recent research on the failure of this operation to influence the French elections highlights a combination of structural factors and anticipatory measures. At the structural level, the two-round system of the French presidential elections makes it more difficult to identify potential candidates well ahead of the elections. The second round also provides an opportunity for the population to shift their support to a mainstream candidate. In this case, the mainstream candidate Emmanuel Macron faced a candidate for the extreme right party Rassemblement National. The quality of the French media environment, specifically the marginal role of tabloids and alternative websites, further limited the impact of the Macron leaks. In addition, the establishment of an independent administrative authority in charge of the integrity of the elections encouraged traditional media not to exploit the Macron leaks.[48]
>
> The French government and presidential candidates had the opportunity to learn from Russian influence operations in the United States, as well as similar efforts in the Netherlands and the United Kingdom. The French national cybersecurity agency (ANSSI) organized workshops to train political parties, and warned Macron about a potential attack. The Macron campaign team compartmentalized information and communicated only face-to-face on the most sensitive issues. They talked publicly about hacking attempts against them and even forged emails and fake documents to confuse the hackers with irrelevant information. These measures undermined the validity of the leaked documents and made the population doubt the authenticity of the material.[49]

Responsibility for Russian national cybersecurity falls on the FSB and its SIGINT unit, the Ministry of Internal Affairs (MVD) and the Foreign Intelligence Service (SVR). FSB and MVD are responsible for monitoring online information on extremist groups, for example. When doing so, they rely on national service providers and the companies at the basis of RUNET. Russian national cybersecurity relies on the synergy between the Russian security services and its business sector, both of which cooperate to purge RUNET of unwanted content.[50]

The Russian government has developed an ambivalent relationship with cyber criminals. The government tolerates, and sometimes encourages, hackers when they target adversaries. Reliance on hackers allowed Russia to maintain some distance from the well-coordinated cyberattacks that targeted Estonia in 2007 and Georgia in 2008, and to deny any responsibility. This reliance on hackers can be linked to the close ties between the Russian government and broader criminal networks.[51] Western analysts argue that the Russian government deliberately lets hacktivists and cyber criminals operate from its territory to "erode the boundaries of organized violence" and wage influence without resorting to open conflict.[52] The extent to which criminal organizations such as the Russian Business Network (RBN) are driven and coordinated by government entities is not clear, but they certainly seem to enjoy a degree of immunity.[53] Scholar Nikolas Gvodsev concludes that Russia's hackers might have struck a bargain with the government whereby they will be left alone – perhaps even politically protected – as long as they do not target the state and its key interests. This Russian strategy is not without risks, as criminals could, one day, turn against their political protectors.[54]

The United States: A pro-active cyber power

The United States is one of the most connected nations in the world – its economy, civilian infrastructure and government services are all highly dependent on cyberspace. Unlike China and Russia, the United States actively defends and promotes freedoms – specifically, freedom of speech – in cyberspace. The technological dependency and openness of the United States have created significant vulnerabilities that its adversaries have sought to exploit. The number of significant cyberattacks on the United States has required the government to adopt a very active stance on national cybersecurity and spawned the creation of a number of organizations and policies designed to enhance national cyber defense and resilience.

The US government has published dozens of strategic documents reflecting the growing importance of cyber power and national cybersecurity. Cyberspace emerged as a distinct national security policy area during the presidency of Bill Clinton when the White House established a structure to coordinate efforts across the public–private divide to "eliminate any significant vulnerability to both physical and cyber attacks on our critical infrastructure."[55] Since then, a variety of Defense, Military and National Security Strategies have identified cyber threats to critical infrastructure and services as a pressing national security threat.[56] The US approach emphasizes the importance of international alliances, specifically the North Atlantic Treaty Organization (NATO), in deterring shared threats and promoting stability in and through cyberspace.[57] The transatlantic alliance has been one of the main vectors supporting the development of strong and resilient cyber defense and cooperative cybersecurity in the West.

The US government has embraced cyberspace as an instrument of soft and hard power. The 2011 International Strategy for Cyberspace proposed to promote US values throughout cyberspace, including fundamental freedoms, privacy and respect for property. To achieve these objectives, the strategy sought to leverage defense, diplomacy and development. China and Russia consider US support for an open cyber environment, and specifically the spread of US-backed social media and Internet technologies like The Onion Router (TOR), as an effort to interfere in their domestic affairs. In a famous case of cyberattack discussed in the next chapter, the United States successfully deployed a computer worm to sabotage Iranian nuclear centrifuges.

In a government that traditionally divides responsibilities between multiple departments and across society, coordinating national cybersecurity policy and implementation presents a significant challenge. Critics note that the division of labor that characterizes American society limits the US ability to anticipate and respond to problems in a timely and coherent way.[58] To counter cyber threats, the US government has developed a number of platforms to promote common security standards, share information and coordinate threat assessments and responses across the public–private divide. However, these efforts remain limited by issues of privacy and trust between government and private-sector organizations.[59] Experts question the extent to which the private sector is ready to communicate with government entities about vulnerabilities. Equally, some government agencies remain reluctant to systematically share sensitive information with outsiders.[60] Such problems of public–private coordination are less apparent in China and Russia where the public authority of government is more sweeping and evident.

Responsibility for cybersecurity and related incidents is broadly divided into domestic and foreign responsibilities. The US Department of Homeland Security (DHS) is responsible for protecting critical infrastructure at home, from both physical and cyber threats. Its National Cybersecurity and Communications Integration Center (NCCIC) brings together public and private partners to coordinate cybersecurity efforts. The Department of Justice, acting through the Federal Bureau of Investigation, is the lead federal agency for threat response and law enforcement activities.[61] Both departments are expected to effectively coordinate their activities within their respective lines of effort, but the extent to which they do so in practice is not clear. Since 2009, the US has established a Cyber

Command, which brings together all components of the US military that work on cyber threats. USCYBERCOM was elevated to an independent unified command in 2018 under the direction of General Paul Nakasone, putting it on par with other warfighting commands and confirming the growing importance of digital combat. In May of 2018, USCYBERCOM reached full operational capability when the last of its 133 national mission teams became certified.

The latest Cyber Command "vision" points out that America faces competitors who are deliberately operating at a level below armed aggression. The document highlights a desire to defend forward – that is to say, to target adversaries' weaknesses, imposing costs on them so that they are forced to shift their resources to defense. Until August 2018, classified US Presidential Policy Directive 20 (PPD-20) imposed severe limitations on when, how and by whom offensive cyber operations could be authorized. In the summer of 2018, President Trump reportedly revised the standing direction and loosened the requirement that all offensive cyber operations required presidential approval.

In their analysis of US cyber strategy, Valeriano, Jensen and Maness present the United States as a sophisticated cyber power.[62] They argue that the notion of the precision strike has shaped the conduct of US cyber operations. Cyber capabilities are used to "infiltrate command networks, often through counterintelligence honeypots, and paralyze them at an opportune moment."[63] This approach utilizes cyber capabilities to gain information superiority, identify specific targets, and develop a sophisticated method to strike precisely at an opportune moment.

To stop or limit attacks by adversaries, the United States has sought to adopt a whole-of-government approach and liaise with partners across government, industry and academia.[64] US strategy recognizes the need for better alignment with the private sector, including ISPs and security companies. Other Western governments have faced similar coordination challenges and developed similar approaches. American allies such as South Korea and France have also established a Cyber Command (respectively in 2009 and 2016). The United Kingdom established a National Cyber Security Centre in 2016.[65] Governments increasingly coordinate their cybersecurity efforts through both bilateral and multilateral cooperation agreements.[66] As of October 2018, more than 83 countries had National Cybersecurity Strategy documents, each addressing the nuances and challenges, as well as interpretations, of the operating environment in and through cyberspace. A number of international organizations, including the African Union (AU), the Association of Southeast Asian

Nations (ASEAN), the EU and the UN, have set up working groups and developed strategies to coordinate national efforts to improve cybersecurity.[67]

Common lenses and challenges

The dynamics of national cybersecurity can be understood through the canon of international relations. In the realist tradition, cyberspace is an extension of the Hobbesian worldview in which states pursue their national interests by maximizing power. Chris Demchak and Peter Dombrowski argue that cyberspace, a man-made domain, cannot escape the "Westphalian world of virtual borders and national cyber commands."[68] In the digital realm, states strive to ensure their citizens' online safety, and the economic well-being of their nation. They also exert their power in cyberspace and push to assert national policies both at home and abroad. From this perspective, nation states are exerting their monopoly over the legitimate means of control of cyberspace. State control is apparent when governments require ISPs to share data with them and to filter out traffic. At the international level, Chinese Advanced Persistent Threats (APTs), the US cyber operation against Iranian centrifuges, and the Russian efforts to interfere with democratic elections in Western countries, all suggest that states are wielding power in cyberspace. As such, classic international relations debates about coercion, deterrence, escalation and alliance are increasingly central to the debates surrounding cybersecurity in social science.

Following a liberal internationalist tradition, some scholars have started to explore the emergence of international norms of behavior in cyberspace.[69] Nation states are growing increasingly interdependent and have much to lose from overt conflict in cyberspace. Evidence suggests that state-on-state cyberattacks and governments' efforts to control their domestic cyberspace have been tempered by the interdependencies of an increasingly globalized world.[70] Consequently, most governments want some degree of international cooperation. However, divergences over the governance of cyberspace highlighted in chapter 3 show that different models – some more supranational than others – continue to co-exist. These national differences can be explained by domestic factors such as regime type, and political and strategic culture.

Despite differences in national approaches to cybersecurity, most cyber powers confront common challenges in cyberspace. China, Russia and the United States all struggle to control and manage the various actors involved in cyberspace. These common challenges explain why nations that wield cyber power against each other cooperate on specific cybersecurity issues, such as the theft of banking information.[71] The rapid evolution of connected information technologies, from malicious codes to new applications to the Internet of Things (IoT), challenges governments' desire to control cyberspace domestically, and provides opportunities to wield power on a global stage. National cybersecurity is inherently transnational, and therefore requires the interaction of a plethora of different actors, only some of which have the resources and authority to coordinate effective responses.

Discussion questions

1. How can we study cyber power?
2. Contrast and compare the American, Chinese and Russian approaches to national cybersecurity.
3. How is the tension between centralization and decentralization visible in the organization of cybersecurity at the state level?

Further reading

Center for Strategic and International Studies, Cybersecurity and Cyberwarfare, Preliminary Assessment of National Doctrine and Organization, 2011, www.unidir.org/files/publications/pdfs/cybersecurity-and-cyberwarfare-preliminary-assessment-of-national-doctrine-and-organization-380.pdf.

Franklin D. Kramer, Stuart H. Starr and Larry K. Wentz (eds.), *Cyberpower and National Security* (Washington, DC: National Defense University, 2009).

NATO Cooperative Cyber Defence Centre of Excellence, "Cyber Security Strategy Documents," October 18, 2018, https://ccdcoe.org/cyber-security-strategy-documents.html.

Brandon Valeriano, Benjamin Jensen and Ryan C. Maness, *Cyber Strategy: The Evolving Character of Power and Coercion* (Oxford University Press, 2018).

6

Cyber war

Early International Relations scholarship on cybersecurity has been characterized by arguments about the forms, uses and effects of cyber warfare. Human history has seen the boundaries of the battlefield expand through technological transformations that continually redefine what it means to go to war, from land to sea, from air to outer space, and now to cyberspace. Since the early 1990s, security experts and media pundits have prophesied the dangers of cyber war, yet in the last decade a growing number of researchers have expressed skepticism. While the academic debate between the prophets and skeptics has remained contentious, militaries around the world have expanded their operations in and through cyberspace. People may not be directly killed by bits and bytes, but they can be harmed by those instruments of modern society that rely on cyberspace and its associated technologies. Understanding how states might leverage potential effects in and through cyberspace in times of war and conflict, and how cyber operations change the character of war, is important to policy-makers, military planners and students of cybersecurity.

War in the fifth domain

The long history of war and its near-continuous impact on human lives across the millennia have characterized the history of international relations, as scholars attempt to address ever-important questions on the causes of war and peace. From this perspective, it seems logical that, when confronted with a "new" domain, researchers should attempt to understand the occurrence of a new form of conflict and the conditions for peace. But what is cyber war? How different is it from war in other domains? Defining cyber war is crucial if we are to understand it, not least because of the economic, political and societal implications of waging war.

The spectrum of conflict in cyberspace encompasses everything from bullying and criminal activity to espionage and sabotage. At the violent end of the scale, cyberattacks can threaten critical infrastructure, economies, property and the well-being of citizens. There is no question that significant cyberattacks and incidents threaten national security, but this does not necessarily mean that they qualify as an act of war. Law scholar Michael Schmitt has argued that, thus far, cyberattacks have not been sufficiently organized, intense or destructive to constitute acts of war.[1] The US government holds that a cyberattack would have to "proximately result in death, injury or significant destruction" to qualify as an act of war.[2] However, the (proximate) effects of cyberattacks are not always clear. In practice, the current threshold set by international law is open to interpretation and is likely to evolve.

Since the beginning of the twenty-first century, thousands of NATO soldiers have fought in Afghanistan, Iraq and Syria without their countries being in a formal state of war. Many countries use force through military means without formally declaring war. Cyber war is no different.[3] A number of government officials and pundits have claimed that the United States is fighting a cyber war. However, legally speaking, this is not the case. Researchers have criticized the hysteria that surrounds the discourse on cyber war, with some even suggesting it to be impossible in practice.[4]

War is a political process through which groups of individuals threaten harm to influence an adversary. War – and, by extension, cyber war – will always be an instrument of politics. Although the political nature of war is constant, the conduct of war or warfare – typically through military operations – has evolved over time.[5] In the traditional understanding, two or more countries would go to war and their soldiers would confront each other on a battlefield using swords, bows, guns, gas, bombs, etc. With the advent of cyberspace, the belligerents and the type of engagements characterizing war have expanded across the three layers of cyberspace. Cyberspace has expanded the character and characteristics of war without affecting its inherently political and physical nature.

Cyber war is coming!

Most of the debate on cyber war is about its characteristics, and the extent to which cyberspace is transforming the conduct of war – or, more specifically, whether cyberspace is prompting fundamental changes in warfare. The notions of violence and force, which are often used to define war and warfare, are less apparent in cyberspace than in the physical world.[6] Thus, scholars have debated the form and effects of cyber war.

In the early 1990s, security researchers started considering the implications of the information technology revolution on the conduct of war. Experts debated the occurrence of a revolution in military affairs that would radically change the character of war.[7] In this context, two RAND Corporation scientists, John Arquilla and David Ronfeldt, published a scholarly article entitled "Cyberwar is Coming!" in 1993. In their article, Arquilla and Ronfeldt argued that the information revolution was altering not just the character of conflict – that is to say, the specific ways in which a conflict is waged (e.g. parties involved, terrain, technologies, etc.) – but also the nature of conflict, spurring a need for new military structures, doctrines and strategies. They introduced two original concepts to think about these new conditions: netwar and cyber war. The concept of netwar emphasized "societal-level ideational conflicts waged in part through internetted modes of communication."[8] They defined cyber war as military operations seeking to disrupt or destroy information and communication systems. Cyber war, the researchers noted, "is about organizations as much as technology. It implies new man–machine interfaces that amplify man's capabilities."[9] Reflecting on the implications of cyber war, Arquilla and Ronfeldt identified a number of puzzles that would capture the attention of researchers two decades later. What would cyber war look like? What would be the roles of and the relationship between offense and defense in cyber war? Could cyber victory be attained without destruction?

Increasingly complex communications and information infrastructures captivated the attention of American strategists and policy-makers for the next decade and beyond. But the key concept that drove the debate on the evolving character(istics) of war continued to be that of a revolution in military affairs, and not cyber war. For the proponents of the revolution in military affairs, new technology was enabling information to flow more freely from the battlefield to the headquarters and vice versa, leading to more network-centric forms of warfare.[10] While the advent of cyberspace certainly led to new efficiencies at the organizational level and evolving military structures and practices, few authors today would make the case that these changes qualify as a revolution in military affairs.[11]

In the mid-2000s, a number of cyberattacks drew extensive media coverage and prompted some experts to ask whether cyber war was (finally) emerging as a threat. In April 2007, a series of cyberattacks targeted Estonia following growing tension with Russia over the relocation of a World War II statue of a Soviet soldier to the outskirts of Tallinn. Waves of spam and automated online requests swamped Estonian servers, taking down dozens of websites and online services. The denial of service attack affected government services, newspapers and broadcasters, as well as banking services, causing millions of dollars of losses.[12] Though Estonia could not technically prove beyond a doubt who was behind the attacks, the government, leveraging substantial circumstantial data, pointed to its neighbor, Russia, and called on NATO for support. In an ensuing debate, international experts agreed that Russia was the most likely culprit, though direct responsibility could not be formally established. Were the attacks on Estonia an act of cyber war? For John Arquilla, these attacks qualify as a kind of "low-intensity war," in which the use of military force was applied selectively and with restraint to influence an enemy.[13] Yet, most experts find it difficult to conceive of a war in the absence of casualties and physical damage to property. In another notable case that took place a few months later, Israeli forces are suspected of using a cyberattack (Operation Orchard) to temporarily deactivate the Syrian air defense network. This attack allowed the Israeli air force to conduct a successful airstrike on a suspected nuclear reactor in Northern Syria.[14] For cybersecurity expert Gary McGraw, this attack is a case of cyber war "because the link to a kinetic effect is clear – a completely destroyed Syrian facility."[15] However, it could be argued that the Israeli airstrike caused this kinetic effect, and not the cyberattack.

The growing number of cyberattacks and intrusions worldwide, including against the United States, fueled the imagination of some American experts, keen to warn about the dangers of cyber war. In their book entitled *Cyber War*, Richard Clarke, a former special advisor on cybersecurity to the president, and Robert Knake, a former National Security Council staffer, imagined a scenario in which devastating cyberattacks would induce power blackouts, collapse air traffic control systems, and cause train and subway derailments and refinery and gas explosions causing several thousand deaths.[16] This vastly exaggerated scenario was reminiscent of the "electronic

Pearl Harbor," which experts had warned against as early as 1991.[17] This expression was then popularized by Secretary of Defense Leon Panetta in a 2012 speech:

> The most destructive scenarios involve cyber actors launching several attacks on our critical infrastructure at one time, in combination with a physical attack on our country. Attackers could also seek to disable or degrade critical military systems and communication networks. The collective result of these kinds of attacks could be a cyber Pearl Harbor; an attack that would cause physical destruction and the loss of life. In fact, it would paralyze and shock the nation and create a new, profound sense of vulnerability.[18]

Media and CEOs of cybersecurity companies also used the expression "cyber Pearl Harbor" – and others like "cybergeddon" – to attract readers and clients.[19] Skeptical observers have repeatedly pointed out that these scenarios have not materialized. But the hysteria around cyber war remained, and shaped the early scholarly debate on the topic.

Will cyber war take place?

In a widely read article, political scientist Thomas Rid argues that "Cyber War Will Not Take Place."[20] Rid examines examples of cyberattacks to raise a number of definitional questions, which framed the early debate on cyberspace and international security. He argues that all politically motivated cyberattacks are not war but sophisticated versions of sabotage, espionage and subversion. To support his argument, Rid carefully (some might say narrowly) defines cyber war. According to him, "any act of war has to have the potential to be lethal; it has to be instrumental; and it has to be political."[21] Following this definition, not a single cyber offense identified in the debate on cyber war would constitute an act of war on its own.

First, the lethality of cyberattacks is never direct; neither is it essential to the success of cyberattacks. It is conceivable that a cyberattack could cause a train to crash, or an electricity grid to stop working. Following these events, people could be killed or military units could be rendered defenseless. However, in practice, "no cyber offense has ever injured a person" and cyberattacks "need not be violent to be effective."[22] Second, Rid finds that most uses of cyber power are minimally – if at all – instrumental. The cyberspace component of an attack is rarely sufficient or central in forcing adversaries to change their behavior. Distributed Denial of Service (DDoS) attacks, for example, can limit a government's ability to communicate but won't force it to sue for peace. Third, Rid points out that political attribution of cyberattacks is rare. Though a cyberattack might be political, in the absence of attribution, the attack is depoliticized. Rid concludes that cyber war will not take place as long as cyberattacks continue to be characterized by the absence of violence, unclear goals and no political attribution.

Other types of activities seem to dominate the spectrum of conflict in cyberspace: crime, espionage, subversion and sabotage. None of these activities fulfills the three criteria Rid identifies. Cybercrime is apolitical, and criminals conceal their identity to protect themselves. Cyber espionage seeks to penetrate an adversary's system to extract sensitive information. Its purpose is not directly political – rather, it seeks to gather information to inform policies. Cyber subversion is political because it seeks to erode social bonds and trust in collective entities. However, cyberspace is a platform to reach out to an audience, but not the target of subversion. Finally, cyber sabotage – the deliberate attempt to weaken or destroy an economic or military system – is instrumental. However, its nature is predominantly technical and its targets are material things, not humans. Saboteurs can also avoid attribution and open violence.[23] Storybox 6.1 tells the story of the Stuxnet worm, a famous case of cyber sabotage – or cybotage – that dominated the early discussions on cyber war.

Storybox 6.1 Cybotage: From Stuxnet to Operation Olympic Games

In June 2010, computer security analysts working for Belarus company VirusBlokAda discovered a worm that intentionally targeted industrial equipment and software in a number of countries.[24] The malware used a previously unknown, or zero day, vulnerability to spread on computers via USB sticks. The malware, dubbed Stuxnet (a combination of the file names .stub and .MrxNext.sys) was designed to target a specific type of program used in industrial control systems that drive motors and switches. Further analysis revealed that the malicious code was highly sophisticated, using not one but four zero-day exploits as well as fraudulent certificates, and that Iran was the center of the infection. The malware had been specifically designed to covertly inject commands and sabotage industrial controllers used in the Natanz nuclear facility in Iran.[25]

Starting in 2008, Stuxnet generated small adjustments, manipulating the speed at which nuclear centrifuges in Natanz were spinning, to

> break them down. The attack reportedly took out nearly 1,000 of the 5,000 or so centrifuges Iran was using at the time to purify uranium. All the while, the computers controlling the centrifuges showed no sign of these physical changes and Iranian scientists thought they were confronting random breakdowns. Since the Iranian control system was air-gapped, nobody suspected a cyberattack. But the worm was transported via a thumb drive onto the air-gapped network and eventually spread beyond after an Iranian engineer connected his computer to the centrifuges and back to the Internet. Stuxnet was eventually discovered after infecting thousands of machines throughout the world.
>
> Reporters subsequently revealed that the attack was a joint operation between the US and Israeli intelligence services, codenamed "Olympic Games."[26] The two countries developed a new type of sabotage – some would even say a military-grade cyber weapon. Stuxnet was a tipping point in the debate on cyber war. This worm demonstrated that an offensive cyber capability could target and compromise a remote system to cause physical damage across international boundaries. Despite the damage Stuxnet inflicted on Iranian centrifuges, the Iranian nuclear program only experienced a temporary setback as a result of the covert operation.

While there is a broad consensus on the need to distinguish between war, crime, sabotage, espionage and subversion, Rid's claim that cyber war will not take place, and his focus on lethality as a criterion for war, have been more controversial.[27] In a response to Rid, John Stone argues that cyberattacks can be understood as acts of war. He reminds us that Clausewitz defined war as "an act of physical force" and argues that Rid conflates force, violence and lethality. Force is the capacity to cause physical damage to humans but also to objects. Force should not be conflated with lethality, or the ability to kill somebody. For Stone, "all wars involve force, but force does not necessarily imply violence – particularly if violence implies lethality".[28] From this perspective, acts of war do not need to kill humans – they can generate a large amount of violence by targeting the manufacturing capabilities of an enemy, for instance. Stone concludes that cyberattacks, particularly cyber sabotage, could constitute an act of war. However, the debate on cyber war remains unsettled. If Rid set the threshold for cyber war too high, Stone might have set it too low. Brandon Valeriano and Ryan Maness have criticized Stone's position, pointing out that "without violence, injury, and death, the term [war] loses much of its meaning and implication."[29]

When considering what exactly cyber war is, researchers have provided a significant contribution to the broader debate on the evolving character and nature of war. Overall, the debate on cyber war demonstrates how fuzzy and subjective a concept war can be. The use of the prefix "cyber" – denoting the use of computer network attacks to wage war – also has its limits. In the most extreme scenarios, where a cyberattack would end several thousand lives and disrupt the lives of millions of others, "cyber" becomes superfluous. A cyberattack of such a scale would lead to war, not cyber war.[30]

From cyber war to cyber conflict

Most International Relations scholars have moved beyond the hype. Myriam Dunn Cavelty was one of the first scholars to systematically criticize the hyperbole around cyber war. In her 2008 book on cybersecurity, she uses securitization theory to reveal the socially constructed nature of cyber threats in the US discourse.[31] Other approaches now appear to be more fruitful. John Sheldon, for example, focuses on cyber *power*, which he defines as "a form of influence in and from cyberspace."[32] Brandon Valeriano and Ryan Maness have emphasized the needs for systematic and theoretically informed empirical research to counter the cyber hype. They have used available data on cyber incidents and disputes to explore the significance of cyber *conflict*, which they define as "the use of computational technologies in cyberspace for malevolent and destructive purposes in order to impact, change, or modify diplomatic and military interactions among entities."[33] From this perspective, cyber war is only one possibility in the broader spectrum of cyber conflict. Their study of state rivalry in cyberspace, based on a database of incidents running from 2001 to 2011, shows that "the actual magnitude and pace of attacks do not match the popular perception."[34] So far, the fear of cyberattacks is greater than the damage they have caused. Their research supports the more moderate view that states have demonstrated restraint in their use of cyberattacks, mostly because of the potential for blowback, replication and collateral damage.[35] Yet new cases of cyberattacks challenge the moderate view. Storybox 6.2 examines attacks on the Ukrainian energy grid, in 2015 and 2016, which suggest that some of the cyber doom scenarios might not be as far-fetched as the most skeptic voices in the debate initially thought.

> **Storybox 6.2 Ukrainian blackouts**
>
> Since the Ukrainian revolution of 2014, which overthrew Kremlin-backed President Viktor Yanukovych, Russia has become increasingly aggressive toward its neighbor to the west. Following the revolution, Russia annexed the Crimean Peninsula, and launched a series of skirmishes in the eastern region of Donbas. Russian operations in Ukraine have also taken place in cyberspace, targeting multiple sectors of Ukrainian society – banking and finance, health, media, military, politics, transportation, etc. These attacks have allowed Russia to perfect its approach to cyber warfare and test Western resolve.[36]
>
> In December 2015, some 225,000 Ukrainians were left without electricity when hackers disabled 15 electricity substations and back-up power supplies. The attackers first conducted a phishing attack to lodge an all-purpose trojan known as BlackEnergy in the computer systems of specific Ukrainian power companies. They eventually gained access to industrial control software used to operate key equipment, and unloaded another code, named KillDisk, for destruction. The 2015 Ukrainian blackout lasted a few hours, until engineers manually switched the power on again. A year later, another attack took down a larger transmission station in Kiev for an hour. This second attack demonstrated more sophistication, using a piece of malware, "CrashOverride," that had been tailored specifically to sabotage the energy grid.
>
> Cybersecurity analysts believe that the same group of hackers – Sandworm – conducted the 2015 and 2016 attacks, and have expressed concern over this group's ability to refine its attacks and attempt to infiltrate US systems.[37] Most of the clues they have found, as well as the possible motives, for these attacks clearly point toward Russia.

Moderate voices recognize that the Internet will be a theatre of future conflict and that new cases may challenge their position. Yet they doubt that cyberattacks could decide the outcome of a conflict. First, cyberattacks remain limited because cyberspace is inherently linked to the physical world. Stuxnet, the most dramatic example of cyber sabotage that is publicly known, probably required a human using a flash drive to bypass the air gap protecting Iranian nuclear centrifuge systems. Second, cyberattacks are often limited in duration and have more readily reversible effects than conventional kinetic attacks. Stuxnet delayed but did not destroy capabilities, and the Ukrainian blackouts only lasted a few hours. Finally, cyberattacks do not destabilize international relations, because states exercise restraint in their use of cyber power. The risk, for Valeriano and

Maness, is that governments' excessive concern with cyber war will limit freedoms and innovation on and through the Internet.[38]

Another strand of research explores the potential motives behind cyber war to question its existence. For Erik Gartzke, the debate on cyber war has focused too much on means of cyberattacks (capabilities) and their outcomes (destruction and lethality), and not enough on the motives of those who are able to act.[39] Why would a state use cyberattacks to target an adversary? Force is traditionally used to punish, to conquer and to compel enemies to do things. Gartzke finds that most of the actors who are capable of harming their adversaries – online or elsewhere – do not do so, because they have insufficient reason to do so. Like Valeriano and Maness, he finds that cyberattacks on their own do not pose a threat that is significant enough to affect the political decisions of a sovereign nation. While cyberattacks might inflict costs on an adversary – for example by shutting down the electricity grid of a country – this damage can be fixed and there would be no long-lasting harm that could cause a shift in the balance of power.[40]

While researchers have pointed out that the anonymous nature of cyberattacks is a problem for defenders who might not be able to directly attribute them,[41] Gartzke adds that the absence of attribution is problematic for attackers. Why would an adversary attack and remain anonymous? Anonymity might protect an attacker from retribution but would also prevent him from getting credit for the attack. From the point of view of the victim, there can be no surrender if there is no attribution.[42] The attacker must then necessarily conclude that cyberattacks cannot achieve much without being associated with more conventional kinetic forms of military violence, where attribution is less problematic. In this context, cyberattacks are likely to remain a secondary tool, behind the use of conventional kinetic forces able to inflict unacceptable harm on an adversary.[43]

At a conceptual level, Gartzke's argument reinforces the point that what is distinctive about cyberspace, as a domain of operation, is that it is connected to all the other domains of military operation. This finding suggests that cyber power will most benefit well-established or strong military powers such as China, Russia and the United States, which can most effectively rely on their superior military power.[44] Indeed, most of the case studies of effective cyber operations discussed in the literature – including in this book – tend to focus on these countries. Cyber power should not be considered as an isolated instrument but in conjunction with other forms of warfare. Storybox 6.3 shows how Russia embraced a holistic use of cyberattacks during its 2008 conflict with neighboring Georgia.

Storybox 6.3 Leveraging cyberattacks: The Russo-Georgian war of 2008

In August 2008, Russia launched a series of large-scale overt cyberattacks to augment its on-the-ground military operation in Georgia. A number of patriotic citizen hackers launched DDoS attacks and defaced select websites belonging to dozens of government, news and financial institutions. As much as 35 percent of Georgia's Internet networks were affected. The networks used to launch the DDoS attacks, and the Georgian efforts to defend itself in cyberspace, spread far beyond the Russo-Georgian border, involving cyber infrastructure in over 60 countries.[45]

The cyber campaign against Georgia was carefully planned and closely coordinated with Russian military progress on the ground. The attacks diminished the Georgian government's ability to respond and communicate while Russian tanks were moving into South Ossetia in the early days of the campaign. This denial opened space for Russia to make gains at the strategic level and disseminate propaganda that pinned responsibility for the conflict on Georgia. These cyberattacks were not essential to the Russian intervention but they provided "marginal improvements to military effectiveness."[46]

The Russo-Georgian war was the first time in history that a cyberattack was so closely synchronized with a conventional military campaign.[47] Reflecting on how Russia leveraged cyberattacks to augment on-the-ground operations, John Arquilla concluded, in a nod to his 1993 article with David Ronfeldt, "Cyberwar Is Already Upon Us."[48] More measured voices have used this case to discuss the use of cyber power in war, rather than cyber war. Russia effectively mobilized the cyber power provided by patriotic citizens and hacker communities, limiting the ability of Georgia and the international community to attribute the cyberattacks to Russia, and to respond to them.[49] Though these attacks succeeded in limiting Georgia's ability to communicate, at the strategic level, Russian propaganda eventually failed to generate international consensus on their version of the events.

Cyberspace and military operations

In the last decades, advanced militaries across the world have developed institutions and doctrines to better integrate cyber power into military operations. The US government established a Cyber Command in 2009, and the United Kingdom a Joint Forces Cyber Group in 2013 to plan and coordinate cyber warfare operations. Since 2017, the "Commandement de cyberdéfense" leads French military operations in cyberspace. The Chinese People's Liberation Army's (PLA's) equivalent is the "Strategic Support Force."

Military operations in cyberspace can occur in various contexts, ranging from peacetime to high-intensity warfare. Peter Dombrowsky and Chris Demchak point out that cyberspace has "added layers of complexity to existing tactics and operations, and become increasingly influential in the strategic calculus of several major powers in the international system."[50] Cyber operations employ cyberspace capabilities to achieve objectives in and through cyberspace. Cyberspace is both a means and a target for militaries to exert power. Actions "in" cyberspace seek to deny or even manipulate an adversary's use of information systems and networks. The military also operates "through" cyberspace on a routine basis, using computers to support commanders' decisions. Core military functions such as Command and Control (C2) and logistical support rely on cyberspace to integrate, synchronize and direct operations at digital speeds. The network-centric character of modern militaries creates vulnerabilities that need to be defended.[51]

The US military distinguishes between offensive and defensive cyberspace operations. Offensive operations seek to disrupt the adversary's operations to deny them access to information systems, to deceive or manipulate adversaries, to degrade their capacity, or to destroy their computers or computer networks and applications. Defensive operations seek to detect, analyze and mitigate threats to computer networks, to preserve the ability to utilize cyberspace capabilities and to protect data, networks and systems.[52] Defensive operations can actively seek to jam or disrupt enemy offensive capabilities, or be more passive and block attacks. The distinction between offensive and defensive operations is useful, and provides a fruitful way to link military operations to strategic debates about the relationship and balance between offensive and defensive capabilities. However, this dichotomy has also been criticized for being too US-centric and overlooking alternative conceptions of cyberspace operations based on resilience, for instance.[53]

The use of the term "operations" should not obscure the fact that cyberspace capabilities affect all the levels of war, from tactics to operations and strategy. At the tactical level, cyberattacks are planned and code manipulations achieve specific military objectives. At the operational level, personnel are trained, resources are acquired and allocated to facilitate the implementation of the strategy at the tactical level. The strategic level establishes ideas and coordinates the elements of power – diplomacy, information, military, economy, etc. – to achieve national, and sometimes multinational, objectives.[54]

At all these levels, cyberspace capabilities are increasingly integrated with other domains. Since cyberspace underpins all other warfighting domains, it is best approached in a combined or integrated way. The American military talks about joint operations and multi-domain battle. Militaries across the world are learning to combine cyberspace capabilities with land, sea, air and space capabilities, and maneuver across all domains to maximize battlefield opportunities.[55] The Russo-Georgian war of 2008 is an example of cross-domain military operation, in which Russia leveraged cyberspace for a specific informational purpose along with more traditional maneuvers on land.

Conclusion

The debate on cyber war has been essential to helping establish cybersecurity in the field of IR. Early scholarship on the subject has sought to define the key terms that follow the prefix "cyber": war, warfare and operations, among others. The doomsday scenarios imagined by the first prophets of cyber war have not come to fruition, but they did have real-life consequences, triggering concern and responses from policy-makers. For the more moderate or skeptical voices in the debate, cyber hype has led to poor investments. The US government, particularly, has devoted vast resources to develop military cyber capabilities. Yet critics note that cybercrime, not cyber war, is the most prominent threat facing Western societies.

There is now a broad scholarly consensus that cyberspace has not revolutionized military affairs, but the debate on how cyberspace capabilities are transforming militaries remains open. There is no question that military institutions and doctrines have had to be adapted – if not created – to better take into account the emergence of a fifth domain of war. This domain presents some unique characteristics – for example, its man-made character – but has not fundamentally altered the nature of war. Cyberspace operations remain inherently linked and limited by humans, politics, culture and the fog of war. They should not be approached on a stand-alone basis, but in combination with other domains of warfare and human activity. The next chapter will explore how pre-existing concepts of deterrence, bargaining, the arms race and escalation, to name but a few, can help us understand national cybersecurity.

Discussion questions

1. What is the difference between cyber war and cyber warfare?

2. Do you agree with Rid's statement that "cyber war will not take place?"
3. To what extent is cyberspace transforming military affairs?

Further resources

Thomas Rid, *Cyber War Will Not Take Place* (London: Hurst, 2013).
Brandon Valeriano and Ryan C. Maness, *Cyber War versus Cyber Realities: Cyber Conflict in the International System* (New York: Oxford University Press, 2015), ch. 2.
Video: Ralph Langner, "Cracking Stuxnet, a 21st-century Cyber Weapon," TED Talk, March 2011, www.ted.com/talks/ralph_langner_cracking_stuxnet_a_21st_century_cyberweapon.

7

Non-state threats: From cybercrime to terrorism

Although states inspire the greatest fear in cyberspace, they are not the most prolific malfeasant actor category or the most pervasive threat to the average netizen. Three other categories of actors, each of which falls under the overarching designation of non-state actor, generate the majority of havoc that occurs in cyberspace. Criminals, hacktivists and terrorists in combination far exceed states in volume and variety of daily attacks and thefts that occur in and through cyberspace. Criminal actors constitute the largest and most substantial threat to cybersecurity, trailed at a substantial distance by hacktivists and terrorists.

The low barriers to entry and the wide reach and impact of cyberspace enable these non-state actors to pose security threats. For criminals, hacktivists and terrorists, the continued expansion of cyberspace and its associated technologies provides ample fertile ground for the development of capabilities within an environment that poses little risk to their physical safety. When asked why he robbed banks, the famous bank robber Willy Sutton responded: "because that's where the money is."[1] If criminals, hacktivists or terrorists were asked the same about their use of cyberspace, they would no doubt provide a similar response. For criminals, cyberspace is where the majority of the wealth and information of the world resides and transits each day. For hacktivists, it is the new public square, with moderate amounts of anonymity, allowing them to form robust groups able to work together with low costs for communications and organization. Lastly, for terrorists, cyberspace is where many potential recruits can be reached, and a medium through which they can elevate their power relative to states at a low cost and potentially high return on investment. This chapter examines each of these categories of actor and emphasizes their motivations and the threats they pose.

Cyberspace is ripe for exploitation by non-state actors in most, but not all, states. In states where cyberspace is open and accessible, non-state actors have substantial room to maneuver both legally and illegally. By contrast, in states where cyberspace is not friendly to non-state actors, such actors are often mobilized as quasi-deniable proxies to enhance the cyber power of a state. The threats posed by non-state actors in and through cyberspace are substantial and, while unlikely to result in catastrophic attacks rising to the scale and complexity of a state-sponsored act of cyber war, the volume of non-state attacks can substantially overwhelm and challenge a state's capacity to respond to specific incidents. Addressing non-state threats in cyberspace requires resources. The broad categories of non-state actors are examined independently below to highlight their unique utilization of cyberspace and the challenges they present to states, from criminological to national security threats.

Criminals

Cybercrime is by far the most prolific and arguably impactful threat in cyberspace. The proliferation of malware combined with its relative ease of use and online anonymity enable a panoply of criminal endeavors. The Federal Bureau of Investigation (FBI) Internet Crime Complaint Center, in its 2017 report on Internet crime, documented $1.4 billion in losses based on approximately 300,000 reports over the course of one year. Internet security firm McAfee estimates that total global cybercrime cost companies, individuals and governments between $445 and $608 billion dollars in 2017.[2] This equates to a global GDP loss of between 0.59 and 0.80 percent.[3] The impact of cybercrime varies widely by country, with North America, Europe and Central Asia, and East Asia and the Pacific, suffering the greatest financial losses.

Most conversations on cybercrime emphasize the financial losses incurred by victims. Cybercrime, however, encompasses multiple classes and categories of behavior. Early definitions of cybercrime focused on four categories of crime originating in, or occurring through, cyberspace or computers. These included cybertrespassing, deception and theft, cyber pornography and finally cyber violence.[4] For the purposes of this section, we examine cybertrespassing, deception/fraud/extortion, theft, violence, illicit commerce and a variety of sexual crimes. Cybercrimes involve criminal acts conducted on or with a computer, or within cyberspace. As this section illustrates, the expansion of cyberspace parallels a rise in criminal behavior online.

Cybertrespassing is the intentional unauthorized access to, or alteration, deletion, damage or destruction, or disruption of a computer, network, program or data. Trespassing in cyberspace is one of the most common criminal offenses and occurs across a variety of criminal contexts. One of the most famous examples of cybertrespassing was briefly examined in previous chapters when Mathew Broderick's character in the movie *WarGames* hacks into his school's computers to change grades, hacks into software vendors to steal games, and breaks into NORAD's computer systems. While *WarGames* was a work of fiction, there are regular attempts globally by students to hack into and alter grades, steal tests, or a variety of other acts that constitute cybertrespassing. For instance, in April 2018, hackers attempted to hack a Fairfax County, Virginia, high school to alter grades from Fs to As.[5] The perpetrators were caught and have been charged by local police.

Cyber deception/fraud/extortion is the deliberate obfuscation and manipulation of intent, characteristics (physical, logical or human persona) and behaviors in cyberspace for the purposes of gaining access to or altering the intended functioning of a computer, network, program or user. Deception is the primary means by which criminals manipulate human users. Deception in cyberspace is often referred to as social engineering and can enable cybertrespassing or other criminal activities. The most famous form of cyber deception is that of the Nigerian Prince email scam, which attempted to prey upon unsuspecting recipients who might willingly transfer money to an unverified third party. Cyber deception resulting in fraud or extortion can take the form of email system compromises, the theft of personal data for use in identify theft, denials of service to reorient users to other services or networks, malware or scareware that falsely present users with warnings of system compromise, phishing and spoofing – the use of fake documents, emails or text messages to enable access to computers or networks.

An increasingly prolific form of cyber extortion is the use of malware that, when installed on a target, encrypts all files on that system. Known as ransomware, these attacks require a system's owner to pay a fee in bitcoin or another cryptocurrency to unlock their files. Ransomware attacks have been targeted at a wide array of institutions, businesses and individuals. Targets unwilling to pay a ransom run the risk of total data loss. Such attacks are increasing in number and diverse in their targets. One widely publicized attack occurred in 2016 when a hacker encrypted portions of the San Francisco Municipal Transportation Agency including its ticket purchasing terminals and requested a $70,000 ransom. The transportation agency never considered paying the ransom and instead reinstalled the the software on impacted systems. The payment of a ransom is not a guarantee that files will be decrypted as some implementations of ransomware are poorly written and fail to decrypt data even when the ransom is paid, as was the case of WannaCry in 2017. As with most cyberattacks, ransomware nearly always begins with deception or fraud, often in the form of social engineering.

Deception for fraud and extortion is the most common method criminal actors use to violate computers and networks. Metadata spoofing, the alteration of sender information, and the replication of common visual identifiers within emails, text messages or other communications media are common tactics. Figure 7.1 is an example of a spoofed email using both metadata (the sender poses as Amazon) and visual replication (the Amazon logos) to deceive the recipient. Typosquatting is another common form of deception used by criminals to replicate the look of a known website and registers a similar domain name accessed through the accidental misspelling of an intended website (e.g. typing foogle.com instead of google.com).[6] Criminals often use broad deception techniques that work well against large numbers of individuals. This approach seeks to maximize return on investment for the criminal. In certain instances, criminals leverage specific techniques or information to "spear phish" or "whale" a single (individual) target who might prove to be a lucrative mark. However, more time and effort are required for tailored deception for fraud and extortion, with limited increases in the probability for success.

Cyber theft is the theft of data or resources from a computer or network. The most commonly considered form of cyber theft is that of data theft for use in fraud. Theft can be achieved through a variety of means but is most commonly instigated via the human persona layer. One of the largest incidents of cyber theft occurred in 2013 when hackers breached the point-of-sale systems of Target Corporation, the second-largest department store retailing in the United States, via the heating, ventilation and air conditioning units installed in stores. The hack resulted in the theft of 40 million debit and credit card numbers and 70 million records of personal information.[7] The theft of credit card information and personal data is a common occurrence. However, the Target hack led to a temporary multi-billion dollar decrease in Target's market capitalization, hundreds of millions of dollars in

Figure 7.1 Phishing email example

Source: Radius https://radius.ie/amazon-scam-alert/amazon-customers-tricked-with-ticket-verfication-number-phishing-email-473445-2/

lost sales during the 2013 holiday season, $200 million in credit and debit card reissuance costs for banks, and an $18.5 million settlement with 47 states. The incident itself was not isolated and was followed several months later by an equally large data breach of American home improvement supplies company Home Depot in 2014.[8]

The Target and Home Depot hacks are part of a larger trend in criminal activities online. These activities seek the centralized accumulation of data in repositories. Attacks against corporate databases, email servers, point-of-sale systems often emphasize the theft of personally identifiable information (PII) that results in financial damage well beyond the initial corporate victim of an attack. The loss of PII, which is subsequently sold online in dark markets, leads to identity theft and results in substantial harm to individuals least able to address such challenges.

Data theft by cyber criminals is rampant, and the intersection of theft and organized criminal activities is growing and rapidly becoming a multi-billion-dollar industry.[9] A relatively new form of cyber theft seeks to exploit the victim's computational power. The theft of resources for the creation of botnets, collections of enslaved computers, has been around for quite some time and was used in the 2007 Distributed Denial of Service (DDoS) attacks against Estonia and the 2008 attacks against the Republic of Georgia.[10] The purchase of enslaved machines in botnets is a readily available service on the dark web. Figure 7.2 is an image of the logo of the Tech service of the Islamic State, who provided information-technical solutions to avoid intelligence and law enforcement agencies. There are documented cases of members of the Islamic State purchasing DDoS capabilities via the dark web. The use of DDoS as a criminal tool to degrade or hold to ransom the websites of businesses, and the terrorist usage of the same tool to achieve political effects, highlight both the linkages between criminal and terror networks and the diffusion of tools and tactics across actor categories.

Figure 7.2 Logo of the Tech of the Islamic State

The utilization of botnets to create increasingly powerful DDoS attacks has begun to shift toward the creation of wealth through the theft of computational resources beyond extortion and political effects. Botnets stealing the computational resources of unsuspecting victims are available for sale in various time and scale increments.[11] While the theft of computer resources for botnets is not new, the rise of cryptocurrencies – virtual currencies representing monetary values equivalent to fiat currencies such as the US dollar – such as Bitcoin and Ethereum have resulted in the theft of computer resources for the purposes of mining for potential profits.[12] The theft of computer resources for cryptocurrency mining, a practice known as cryptojacking, steals the computer cycle resources, slowing down the functional operation of computers and increasing the energy consumption of those computers substantially.

Cyber theft for criminal ends is distinguishable from espionage in its profit-seeking motive. The breadth and depth of examples of cyber theft are far too numerous to list here. However, it is safe to say that, in line with the FBI statistics presented in the introduction to this chapter, the problem of cyber theft is growing.

Cyber violence is the utilization of cyberspace to achieve physical or psychological effects against target users or their systems. Unlike in the Bruce Willis action film *Live Free or Die Hard*, it is unlikely that hackers are going to cause remote computers to explode and kill their users anytime soon. This is not to say that hackers have not achieved physical violence against computers or their associated systems in recent years. One of the earliest incidents of physical criminal violence achieved through hacking occurred a decade ago, when a 14-year-old modified a TV remote and used it to maneuver and derail trams in the city of Lodz, Poland, injuring 12 people.[13] Hacks that induce physical violence have been rare, but hackers have demonstrated the possibility for criminals to achieve physical violence.

The more pernicious and common forms of criminal violence in cyberspace have been cyberbullying and cyberstalking. *Cyberbullying* is "the willful and repeated harm inflicted through the use of computers, cell phones, and other electronic devices."[14] Cyberbullying is a more modern take on conventional bullying that has resulted in suicides and murders, and has been indicated as a contributing factor in mass shootings.[15] Some studies indicate that up to 28 percent of all students experience cyberbullying during their secondary school education.[16] While often overlooked in discussions on cybercrime, cyberbullying is a criminal offense that has resulted in numerous criminal convictions.

Closely related to cyberbullying, *cyberstalking* is the "repeated use of the Internet, e-mail, or related digital electronic communication devices to annoy, alarm, or threaten a specific individual or group of individuals."[17] All 50 states in the United States and most nations have enacted laws pertaining to stalking. Cyberstalking extends criminal acts of stalking into cyberspace and creates a pervasive and damaging set of conditions that harms victims.[18] In 2013, three members of the Matusiewicz family were sentenced to life in prison for cyberstalking resulting in death, when the family members engaged in physical and online surveillance and abuse of their victims, the ex-wife of one of the defendants and one of her children, in the US state of Delaware.[19] Criminal cyberstalking can be both technical and nontechnical – however, the common linking factor is the use of computers and associated technologies to threaten and harass victims. Criminal violence in cyberspace is complex and often extends violent acts found in traditional criminal activities to the new domain. Although cyberstalking and cyberbullying are often beyond the scope of broad cybercriminal analyses, they are unfortunately very common and result in substantial harm to victims.

Illicit marketplaces are commerce sites commonly hosted in dark web services, such as I2P and Tor, which provide customers with access to drugs, guns, credit and debit cards, hacking tools, pornography or a range of other illegal wares. The most famous illicit market, also referred to as a dark market, was Silk Road. Silk Road was a one-stop shop for a variety of drugs and illegal goods, run by an American, Ross William Ulbricht, also known as the "Dread Pirate Roberts." On February 4, 2014, the FBI indicted Ulbricht for narcotics trafficking conspiracy.[20] Dread Pirate Roberts ran what was, at the time, one of the largest dark markets, with thousands of users engaged in illicit sales using cryptocurrencies.[21] Dark markets account for more than $100 million in yearly drug sales and leverage transnational shipping and postal services as couriers.[22] Despite repeated takedowns by government authorities around the world, these markets continue to redeploy and sell illicit items. Figure 7.3 is an image from a weapons site that has since been taken down, but which purported to sell everything from landmines to rockets. The use of hidden services within Tor to host dark markets is extremely controversial as the technical construction and operation of Tor is partially funded by the United States government and is the result of a naval research laboratory's project. The challenge of halting dark markets is ongoing and will probably expand as cryptocurrencies become more common and encryption technologies make anonymous commerce increasingly feasible.

Sexual crimes via cyberspace include the transmission of images of child pornography, rape, mutilation, bestiality, enslavement and a variety of other associated crimes facilitated by cyberspace. Among all forms of crime, US law enforcement considers child pornography to be the most serious and damaging form of criminal behavior in cyberspace.[23] The FBI estimated that its analysts reviewed more than 26 million images and videos of abuse in 2015 alone.[24] The National Center for Missing and Exploited Children (NCMEC) reported locating more than 10,500 victims of child pornography, with more than 4.4 million reports submitted.[25] One FBI investigation found a single website hosted within Tor had 200,000 registered users.[26] One man, Matthew Falder, leveraged cyberspace to blackmail 46 victims into sending increasingly explicit sexual images.[27] Three of his victims attempted to commit suicide.[28] The use of cyberspace for the facilitation of, transmission of images and video for, and blackmail

Figure 7.3 A dark net weapons market

of victims for the purposes of sexual crime, are unfortunately among the most common criminal activities within cyberspace. Very often, the investigation and subsequent prosecution of sex crimes facilitated in and through cyberspace require transnational cooperation among law-enforcement and intelligence agencies.

Although the impacts of economic cybercrime are often at the forefront of national and international discussions, the multitude of other criminal acts perpetrated in and through cyberspace is substantial and challenges all levels of jurisdictions from local communities to transnational bodies. Closely related, and often within the scope of cybercrime, is hacktivism. However, because the intentions of these individuals often – although not always – differ from "the purely criminal" intent, they are analyzed separately below.

Hacktivists

The term "hacktivist" combines "computer hacker" and "activist."[29] Hacktivism, while commonly associated with the collective known as Anonymous, has roots dating back to the early days of the Internet. Early hacktivists engaged in "digital sit-ins" by visiting sites or engaging in acts to consume the computer resources of an entity, to signal moral, ethical or political disfavor with the activities of an organization or entity.[30] Hacktivism commonly revolves around a variety of techniques meant to disrupt, or degrade, the operational status of servers or computers, through the use of Denial of Service (DoS) or DDoS attacks, social engineering, Cross-site scripting (XSS),[31] SQL injections[32] or other minimally to moderately technical attacks.

Although originally a means to engage in activism online for political, moral or ethical signaling, hacktivism expanded substantially when, in 2008, "anons" (anonymous users) of the popular site 4Chan formed an organic effort in response to a leaked video of actor Tom Cruise promoting the Church of Scientology.[33] Anons began coordinating efforts to attack the organization via various internet fora and chatrooms. Prior to the 2008 attacks on the Church of Scientology, many anons hacked or engineered targets for the lulz (a pluralization of the term "LOL": "Laugh Out Loud").[34] Much of the early lulz-inspired hacking targeted individuals engaged in child pornography, businesses or organizations that could be easily spoofed for "fun," and gave hackers a sense of power over their victims as well as amusement. Most of these hacks are criminal in nature, but distinguished from the profit-seeking, violent and sexually exploitative acts discussed in the previous section.

Individuals with a wide range of skills populate the ranks of hacktivist communities. The distribution of skills skews toward those with limited technical hacking abilities, but this does not limit their participation in the operations – or #Ops – that their community plans. Tools such as the Low Orbit Ion Cannon (LOIC) – a DoS application – enable any user to engage in coordinated operations established by Anonymous. However, the impact of LOIC is relatively small compared to that of botnets managed by some of the collective's more talented hackers.

Anonymous is famous for its creed:

We are Anonymous.
We are Legion.
We do not forgive.

We do not forget.
Expect us.

Anonymous is made up of members from nearly every country in the world. The collective functions as a decentralized and loosely coordinated group that plans and executes operations against various targets. Sometimes these operations are motivated politically, and sometimes they are for lulz. One of their most famous operations, Operation Avenge Assange, included attacking banking and credit card systems in response to the blocking of donations to file-sharing site Wikileaks, following the release of Chelsea Manning's documents. Operation Payback was a response to Bollywood companies attacking the popular peering site The Pirate Bay. Anonymous participants planned to attack Aiplex Software, the firm hired to DDoS The Pirate Bay, only to find it had already been DDoSed by an unknown hacktivist, and instead turned their attention to the Motion Picture Association of America (MPAA), the International Federation of the Phonographic Industry, the Recording Industry Association of America (RIAA) and the British Phonographic Industry.[35] In 2015, Anonymous famously declared "war" on the Islamic State in the aptly named "OPISIS."[36] #OPISIS arose following the attacks on Charlie Hebdo in Paris and sought to identify and take down ISIS-affiliated Twitter accounts and websites around the world. Experts have found the impact of #OPISIS on the operational capacity of the Islamic State was negligible.[37]

Although the most famous grouping of hacktivists is Anonymous, they are probably not the most impactful. "Patriotic" hackers generally fall under the same rubric of hacktivism. Members of Anonymous have been instrumental in signaling displeasure to states following a variety of diplomatic incidents. Alex Klimburg writes that states can motivate, and often work in tandem with, non-state hackers to signal intentions to other states.[38] There have been numerous incidents of "patriotic hackers" coming to the "aid" of states in times of perceived crisis. In 2001, following the mid-air collision of a US surveillance plane and a Chinese fighter aircraft, Chinese hackers defaced a number of prominent websites in the United States. In 2007 and 2008, Russian "patriotic hackers" closely timed DDoS, XSS, SQL injections and a variety of other attacks against both Estonia and the Republic of Georgia, when international relations between these states and Russia hit new lows.[39]

Criminal cyber activities – such as financial crimes, and violent, harassing and sexual acts online – are often motivated for a variety of nefarious reasons. Similarly, the motivations of hacktivists are equally diverse, and complex. Simply hacking for lulz would not constitute hacktivism, and instead is more akin to low-level criminal deviance. Hacktivism spans a gambit of motivations, from libertarian ideals of freedom of information and anarchic tendencies, on one side, to highly motivated patriotic or nationalistic tendencies on the other side of the spectrum. Despite the alignment of the state and hacktivists' motivations on the patriotic side of the spectrum in some instances, the position of hacktivists is not static. Today's patriotic hacker can be tomorrow's anarchist or libertarian, following changes in laws or government policies. Slightly outside of the spectrum of hacktivism, which ranges from libertarian–anarchistic to patriotic–nationalistic ideas, is yet another category, best described as nihilistic, which focuses on the absence of belief.

Hacktivism and hacktivists have found a prominent home within popular culture, yet the overarching difficulty in engaging in highly complex cyber capability development at the individual level, or even through decentralized collectives, remains one of the largest impediments to making this category of hackers a substantial threat. Over the last two decades, many organizations have learned to deal with the techniques employed by hacktivists, such as XSS, SQL injection and even DDoS, thus impairing their impact. Hacktivists often reuse tools and resources and attack 1-day or 1-day+ exploits – meaning that they leverage exploits that have previously been discovered and might have been patched. The resources available to hacktivists are substantial within deep and dark websites. By pooling their efforts, hacktivists are increasingly able to access capabilities and resources that exceed those of any one individual. Yet their ability to coordinate and undertake large-scale operations remains limited by a number of costs – for instance, those associated with surveillance and reconnaissance. While the threat hacktivists present to states is limited, they are still able to cause some damage and can embarrass or even harm individuals, corporations and governments through doxing (the search for and publishing of private or identifying information about an individual on the Internet for malicious intent) or social engineering, among a variety of other potential exploits.

Cyberterrorists

Since 9/11, an overwhelming amount of resources and research has been devoted to cyberterrorism. There have been many prognostications of forthcoming doom due to the terrorist use of cyberspace. Despite the multitude of articles written on the subject, both in the academic and the popular press, and the large number of successful cyberattacks conducted by "cyberterrorists," relatively few have resulted in meaningful consequences. Most terrorist-perpetrated cyberattacks have come in the form of XSS, SQL injection or the release of documents already publicly available. While the impact of terrorist cyberattacks has centered mainly on website defacement and document dumps of quasi-private information, terrorist use of cyberspace has changed the way in which terrorists organize, recruit and plan operations in the physical world. Early debates put a great deal of emphasis on understanding and preventing potential terrorist attacks in and through cyberspace. In the last few years, experts have increasingly emphasized the use of cyberspace for the organization and planning of terrorist incidents.

Cyberterrorists differ from both cyber criminals and hacktivists primarily in their motives. Differentiating between the motives of some cyberterrorists and some hacktivists requires walking a very thin line. At its most basic, cyberterrorism is the use of cyberspace to commit terrorism.[40] This definition begs the question of what constitutes terrorism. Terrorism, according to Bruce Hoffman, "is violence – or, equally important, the threat of violence – used and directed in pursuit of, or in service of, a political aim."[41] This definition, though it is debatable, reveals the greatest impediment to terrorism in cyberspace: the ability to commit or credibly threaten violence. Few violent cyber incidents have occurred in the young history of cyber conflict, other than accidental hacking and the use of a reprogrammed remote control in Poland by a teenager to crash streetcars. These incidents do not fit with common definitions of terrorism because they were apolitical. Achieving political violence through cyberspace is extremely difficult and requires a complex set of skills that can often only be provided by multiple individuals working together within a stable environment. Creating politically violent effects in cyberspace often requires advanced persistent presence within a remote system, which necessitates intelligence, surveillance and reconnaissance, and often command and control (C2) capabilities. The costs associated with developing a violent cyberattack are comparatively low for state actors, relative to other weapon systems, yet they are high for non-state actors such as terrorists, absent third-party funding. Storybox 7.1 discusses some of the hackers and hacks of the Islamic State in Iraq and Syria (ISIS).

> **Storybox 7.1 The ISIS hackers**
>
> Throughout late 2014 and into 2015, a group of ISIS-affiliated hackers known as teaMp0ison claimed credit for a variety of hacks, including the hacking of the Twitter and YouTube accounts of US Central Command (CENTCOM) on the same day that US President Barack Obama gave a speech on cybersecurity.[42] Hackers posted a variety of Tweets with missives against the United States and the coalition battling ISIS. One post said "In the name of Allah, the Most Gracious, the Most Merciful, the CyberCaliphate continues its CyberJihad," while another said: "American soldiers, we are coming, watch your back."[43] While briefly in control of CENTCOM's accounts, the hackers also posted what they claimed were classified documents stolen from CENTCOM and other US military and intelligence agencies. These claims were subsequently debunked.[44]
>
> Analysis from the University of Toronto's Citizen Lab found evidence that ISIS-affiliated groups also probably engaged in targeting of human rights activists and others in Syria through social engineering and spyware.[45] Analyses from multiple sources indicate that the level of hacking skill within the various hacking teams in ISIS was relatively low. The cyber jihadis used a variety of readily available social engineering techniques and malware.
>
> The most prominent ISIS hacker on teaMp0ison was a British Pakistani man named Junaid Hussain. Hussain had a previous criminal record, including an arrest for hacking into the email account of former British Prime Minister Tony Blair in 2012.[46] Junaid, other hackers from teaMp0ison, and other groups including Lizard Squad attempted to form what they referred to as the "Cyber Caliphate."[47] The Cyber Caliphate engaged in low- to moderate-level hacking and extensive social engineering. In addition to their hacking prowess, members including Hussain became well-known ISIS propagandists.
>
> Junaid Hussain is thought to have been added to the Disposition Matrix, a US government "kill list" for high-level targets, primarily because of his propaganda efforts and ability to inspire "lone-wolf" terrorism, rather than his hacking skills. Hussain was killed in a drone strike on August 24, 2015, according to US government sources.[48] He is the only known hacker to have been deliberately targeted by a drone strike.

Although cyberterrorists have attracted much attention, their skill levels tend to be low to moderate. Those few terrorists who do possess substantial hacking skills have so far been unable to regroup and achieve a level of coordination comparable to large criminal enterprises, hacker collectives such as Anonymous, or states. Yet, despite a lack of numbers, members of Al-Qaeda and ISIS, among other terrorist groups, have made substantial headway into cyberspace in a variety of contexts. Most notably, hacker groups such as the "Cyber Caliphate" and others are responsible for a variety of website defacements and doxing.[49]

Cyberterrorists to date have almost exclusively gone after low-level targets, generally websites with known vulnerabilities. However, with state assistance from sponsoring regimes such as Iran, cyberterrorists might be able to substantially increase their capabilities. Although cyberterrorists are not presently a major threat to states, their attacks do impose costs and challenge a variety of smaller actors. Cyberterrorist doxing efforts have proven particularly disturbing and have led to the release of personal information on public officials around the world – most notably on members of the US military. Often the release of documents is accompanied by calls within terrorist propaganda channels to target the individuals named in the documents. To date, there are no known instances in which individuals named within such documents were subsequently killed by terrorists.

Terrorists most commonly use cyberspace to organize and coordinate their activities, communicate propaganda and recruit new members.[50] In November 2008, terrorists from Lashkar-e-Taiba (LeT) killed more than 172 people in an attack on hotels and streets in Mumbai, India. Subsequent investigations found that the terrorists had leveraged mobile communications, online groups and Google Earth mapping to plan and organize the resources for the attack. Since then, dozens of physical attacks have similarly relied on cyberspace to plan and coordinate terror in the physical world. One of the most notable attacks occurred in 2015 when ISIS-inspired attacks on Paris led to the deaths of 137.

The reach and messaging of terrorist organizations are both extended and amplified within cyberspace. Services such as Twitter and Facebook provide a readily available and accessible platform for group organization and mobilization.[51] While the use of these platforms by terrorists is widespread, it is not without challenges. Intelligence and law-enforcement agencies have long sought to use the open distribution of information on these platforms to identify, interdict, or capture terrorists in advance of, or following, attacks. Their efforts have forced terrorists to adopt new tactics to avoid being caught, using encryption and software or protocols that enable or facilitate anonymity.[52] Terrorists have also shown a moderate level of interest in the utilization of cryptocurrencies such as bitcoin, to evade restrictions on money laundering and financial transfers for criminal or illicit purposes.[53]

Starting in 2015, the US Army Cyber Command (ARCYBER) began directly targeting ISIS and Al-Qaeda networks in what has become known as Joint Task Force (JTF) Ares. This effort has sought to identify and neutralize the online presence of various terrorist organizations.[54] Some US policy-makers have criticized this initiative, feeling that JTF Ares did not accomplish enough.[55] US military efforts to engage and counter online terrorist organization and coordination has been frustrated by the speed with which terrorists have been able to quickly and effectively reconstitute their online networks. Attempts to remove terrorists from cyberspace have been frequently referred to as a "whack-a-mole" concept, after the famous carnival game where a player attempts to bonk one mole on the head, only to have others quickly rise to take its place in nearby locations. For the foreseeable future, the challenge of combatting terrorists online is likely to remain. New reports indicate an increased effort by transnational terrorist organizations to leverage the dark net to recruit and organize out of sight of intelligence and law-enforcement agencies.[56] Given the trend towards more online coordination, it is likely that future terrorists will organize and generate effects that challenge states, leading to attacks or exploits that are comparable to those orchestrated by larger hacker collectives and criminal organizations.

The non-state actor(s)

Although the biggest threats to national security in cyberspace originate at the state level, non-state actors pose substantial challenges across a variety of interest areas central to the functioning of stable societies. Malicious non-state actors cost individuals, businesses and states vast sums of money on an annual basis, and their use of the Internet for criminal or terrorist activities harms the reputations, and degrades the digital and physical safety, of the average netizen. Curtailing malicious activities in cyberspace is time-consuming and costly.

To date, state efforts to do so have been unsuccessful, even in repressive countries such as China and Russia. China, through its use of the Great Firewall and domestic surveillance mechanisms, has one of the most censored and controlled domestic cyberspaces in the world. Yet, despite all these controls, China remains home to a substantial number of bots, cyber criminals and hacktivists who actively seek to avoid censorship and surveillance.[57] Since the 1980s, Russia has used a variety of means to control its growing domestic cyberspace. Most notably, Russia has employed intercept devices that monitor all traffic on domestic networks and can engage in deep-packet inspection of that traffic.[58] Russia, too, remains one of the most prolific points of origin for cybercrime.

The use of control, censorship and surveillance in domestic cyberspaces tends to affect the civil liberties of citizens, in direct contravention of many of the goals originally promoted by early users and developers of the Internet. And while these controls often limit domestic cyber criminals targeting domestic actors – for instance, Russian cyber criminals are less likely to hack other Russians or the Russian government, and Chinese cyber criminals are less likely to hack other Chinese – these measures are unlikely to apply beyond the state's borders. Hacktivists from repressive countries are also more likely to target their ire outside of their domestic cyberspaces.

The proliferation of cybercrime is likely to continue and intensify as more and more users and their computers come online. Cyberspace is a target-rich environment. The saying goes that there are two types of people or companies in cyberspace: those who have been hacked and know it, and those who have been hacked and don't know it. Statistically, the probability of being hacked in cyberspace in a given year is greater than 100 percent. These hacks are almost always the result of criminals attempting to steal information or data to generate a profit.

At the international level, states banded together as early as November 23, 2001 to sign the Budapest Convention on Cybercrime. More than 56 countries are signatories of the convention, which seeks to harmonize laws relating to cybercrime and facilitate multilateral legal assistance (MLAT) to investigate and prosecute cyber criminals. Although the Budapest Convention has a broad base of adoption, it does not cover a number of important countries, including Russia and China.

Since the signing of the Budapest Convention, the volume of cybercrime has increased substantially and shows no signs of abatement. There is rarely a week that passes in which there is not a news story detailing a large cyber breach of a major company, hospital or organization. What these articles often overlook is the heavy toll that the cybercrime can have on individuals, in the form of identity theft or stolen financial resources. Non-state actors who actively seek to violate the laws of states – whether for profit, lulz or terrorist objectives – challenge law-enforcement and intelligence agencies at all levels. At the lowest levels of criminal jurisdiction, most police departments simply do not have qualified staff to assess or investigate cybercrime. In higher jurisdictions, the volume of cases is overwhelming. In the near term, the challenges faced by states in addressing non-state cyber threat actors are likely to grow.

Discussion questions

1. Who are non-state actors in cyberspace and why do they create so many problems for states?
2. Why is cyberterrorism so difficult to accomplish?
3. What is the impact of cybercrime on individuals within different societies?

Further reading

Marc Goodman, *Future Crimes: Everything Is Connected, Everyone Is Vulnerable and What We Can Do About It* (New York: Doubleday, 2015).

Parmy Olson, *We Are Anonymous: Inside the Hacker World of LulzSec, Anonymous, and the Global Cyber Insurgency* (New York: Back Bay Books, 2013).

Gabriel Weimann, *Terrorism in Cyberspace: The Next Generation* (New York: Columbia University Press, 2015).

8
Organizing deterrence and defense in cyberspace

Cyberspace presents substantial security challenges requiring state and non-state actors, public and private entities, to engage in defensive actions to ensure the Confidentiality, Integrity and Availability (CIA triad) of data and the systems that use and depend upon data for their intended functioning. While much of the defensive nature of cyberspace revolves around the development of ever more sophisticated technical devices and software programs, there remains a robust need for states to implement a "mosaic" of deterrence strategies, ranging from deterrence by denial to deterrence by punishment, to organize their cyber defense.[1] Technical solutions combined with policies intended to deter adversaries from engaging in undesired behaviors and actions form the bulwark behind which actors organize to protect cyberspace.

Fundamental cybersecurity begins with an understanding of how to maintain and defend a network or system (computer) against error and malicious actors who either directly or indirectly target the pillars of the CIA triad. Beyond the maintenance and defense of systems and networks, cyber actors across all levels of jurisdiction find it increasingly necessary to identify ways to impose costs on malicious actors. Imposing costs can occur in a variety of ways, through acts of punishment or denial, and can occur within or across domains of interaction (meaning they can occur in cyberspace and in the physical world).

Defense and deterrence in cyberspace are about weighing costs and benefits, risks and rewards in an attempt to find a balance where the defender state, company, organization, school, individual or any actor in between is able to achieve their goals and objectives. Defense in cyberspace is unique and tailored. Although certain practices span actors and levels, there is no single solution to the challenges present within cyberspace.

This chapter examines the concepts of cyber defense and deterrence, first by examining micro-level policies and technologies to defend networks, computer systems and users in cyberspace, and second by evaluating the applicability and current status of deterrence strategies and policies being used by different levels of government. Cyber defense and deterrence both center on the goal of preventing the unintended use of cyberspace and its components. Understanding the challenges confronting cyber defense and deterrence, and the many ways different actors attempt to address them, provides perspective and illustrates why organizing for defense in cyberspace is and will remain difficult.

Technical cyber defense and deterrence by denial

Cyber defense and deterrence by denial form two sides of the same coin. Together, they technically, financially and psychologically impose costs on potential adversaries by increasing the level of difficulty associated with penetrating computers and networks. The three layers of cyberspace – physical, logical and persona – provide a useful roadmap for thinking about cyber defense and deterrence. When focusing on cyber defense using technical solutions, the emphasis is on designing or reinforcing systems, networks and their users against errors, both intentional and unintentional, as well as deliberate acts of malfeasance, at every step along the way from an individual computer system to a complex network. Defense is the balancing of costs and benefits over time. There is no such thing as perfect defense in cyberspace. All defense is based on the choices and needs of the users or organizations who own a system or network. Every choice has costs, both financially and functionally.

Cyber defense starts early. Even before the component parts of a computer system are developed, its designers are forced to make choices that impact its future security. The more complicated the design of hardware, in particular the Central Processing Unit (CPU) or Graphical Processing Unit (GPU), the fewer the number of potential manufacturers, the more difficult an eventual CPU will be to validate and assess for errors. Complexity can be the enemy of security because it can hide accidental and deliberate errors. At the physical level of cyberspace, each processor, hard-drive, memory component and so on, throughout the computer, adds complexity.

After the initial design of these components, firms must decide where to source their component parts. In a process known as supply chain management, firms make decisions about where and how to manufacture the component pieces – that is to say, both the hardware and software – of a computer system. Supply chain security is so important in the manufacture and distribution of products that in 2012 the United States released a "National Strategy on Global Supply Chain Management," which encourages firms to assess and mitigate related risks.[2] Many countries now impose requirements on manufacturers related to where and how various computer systems are developed, as well as the chain of custody that tracks components within computer systems between their initial manufacture and their eventual delivery to government clients. Detailed sourcing requirements for computer system components are time consuming and expensive. Such requirements are imposed to prevent the injection of deliberate vulnerabilities into products prior to their delivery.

The physical components of the systems being delivered are only part of the production process for an end user. A computer system comprised only of its physical parts is little more than a box of plastic, silicon and metals. To operate a computer system requires software that directs the functioning of the physical components. There are multiple layers of software that operate on each computer system. Most consumers interact with their computers via a Graphical User Interface (GUI) operating system, such as Mac OS, Windows 10, Linux, iOS or Android. These operating systems are immensely complicated computer programs comprised of millions of lines of code developed in dozens of countries around the world. To mitigate errors – both deliberate and accidental – within code, the firms and collectives (in the case of Linux) who develop software are encouraged to use what is called a "security development lifecycle" (SDL). SDL is a process used to reduce maintenance costs and increase the reliability of software. This process encourages developers to systematically plan, design, code, test and maintain the software they produce. Software products that fail to use a security development lifecycle are much more susceptible to vulnerabilities and therefore have weaker defenses.

For most users, from individuals to small and medium-sized firms, the process of security development for their devices ends prior to their delivery. Computer systems are delivered with hardware and software components ready for end-user configuration and further optional security measures such as anti-virus software, firewalls or similar end-user strategies based on their specific needs and requirements. However, for militaries and governments, the delivery of products starts a second defensive process of hardware and software verification. The more sensitive the use of a product, the more this product is scrutinized before deployment. Government organizations like the US Army take the verification of their systems, even non-sensitive systems like the Non-Classified Internet Protocol Router Network (NIPRnet) very seriously, and request the source code for the operating systems of computers they allow on their network. The Army then heavily modifies and reduces the functionality of many attributes of these operating systems in an effort to further alleviate potential vulnerabilities. Moreover, many governments, firms and even universities limit how, and what, devices are allowed to connect to their computer networks, in what is referred to as network access control. Some organizations even limit which software programs are permitted on end-user systems.

Each of the actions above attempts to minimize potential vulnerabilities prior to the initial use of a computer system or network. Despite all these efforts, all computers remain vulnerable to a variety of exploitations at every level. In the case of Spectre and Meltdown, hardware vulnerabilities identified in Intel chips (CPUs) enabled hackers to access data and information on computer systems.[3] Software vulnerabilities known as zero-days (vulnerabilities not previously identified) reside within every software program on every computer. The more complex the computer hardware and the more complex the computer software, the higher the risk of vulnerability. Developing such complex systems without robust security development lifecycles results in an overwhelming mix of defensive challenges prior to a computer's initial use.

After initial product delivery and configuration by an end user, defensive cyberspace actions shift to the protection of individual computer systems (host-based defense), groupings of computer systems within a computer network (networked-based defense) and efforts to prevent human users from deliberately or inadvertently introducing weaknesses into either a computer system or network (human user defense). For each of these types of action, both technical and policy measures seek to minimize potential vulnerabilities and enhance defense. No single policy or technical solution provides sufficient defense to prevent all attacks. Rather, a combination of defensive technical and policy measures are typically implemented to reduce the likelihood and subsequent impact of an attack. Moreover, all defensive solutions are specific to the peculiarities of the computer systems, networks and users being protected. However, some policy and technical solutions, such as password protection of computers, are generally applicable across use cases.

There are multiple approaches to cyber defense. The most widely used globally are outlined in a series of publications by the US National Institute of Standards and Technology (NIST) known as the NIST-800 series. The NIST-800 series of publications provides templates for the development of cyber defense that can be tailored across organization types. Many organizations and governments across the world use these publications as a guide. These publications document best practices and outline how and why organizations should establish certain policy mechanisms to bolster cyber defenses and reduce vulnerabilities. For example, the NIST-800 series presents best practices on password security and network access controls, encryption standards and configurations of networks. Altogether, there are more than 177 unique publications in the NIST-800 series, and further specific documentation relevant to critical infrastructures, e-commerce and cloud computing in the NIST-500 and the NIST-1800 series. These policy and technical recommendations are intended to reduce the risks users and operators of computer systems and networks face.

Beyond policy mechanisms highlighted in the NIST publications, hundreds of firms specialize in cyber defense. Many of these firms offer technical solutions that reside on computer systems (host-based defense) or on networks (network-based defense). Host-based defensive measures on computer systems include everything from anti-virus software and firewalls, such as Windows Defender, to access controls such as passwords and biometric identification. Each new defensive measure on a computer system can make it more resistant to cyberattacks – however, host-based defensive measures are not without trade-offs. Anti-virus scanners can consume the processing power of computers making them run slower. Passwords and biometrics can limit the number of people who can use a computer, making it more difficult to share expensive devices within families or organizations. Firewalls can inadvertently block traffic or programs that a user wants to use. Implemented properly, host-based defensive measures can enhance the security of a computer system without imposing too many costs on the functionality of the system itself.

Patch management is one of the most important host-based defensive measures. Many software vendors release "patches" – updates to software that fix bugs (vulnerabilities) or improve the functionality of software. Microsoft historically released patches regularly on what it referred to as "Patch Tuesday." As new vulnerabilities are discovered, the vendor attempts to quickly find solutions to these vulnerabilities. Once a solution is developed, it pushes these to the end user. In most instances, end users are required to install these patches. Users often ignore these updates and, as a result, their computer system remains vulnerable over time. A failure to install released patches substantially increases the risk of compromise because, once a patch is released, malicious actors can learn about the vulnerability the patch seeks to mitigate. Thus, while installing a patch increases defenses in cyberspace, a failure to do so does not merely maintain the previous level of risk, but actually results in an increased risk and therefore a weakened defense.

Not all actors are able to immediately install released patches on their computer systems or networks. Some actors, particularly those who use specialized computer systems – such as electronic medical records systems in hospitals or critical infrastructure providers – utilize custom versions of common software. Therefore, a power company such as Duke Energy might not have Windows 10 installed, but instead have Duke Energy Windows 10. A patch installed on customized software platforms, particularly those involved in critical infrastructure, can result in incompatibilities of existing software and hardware components and result in substantial damage. The release of a new patch results in a rapid race to implement the patch in such a way that it is compatible within each unique operating environment. The process of patch customization can take days, weeks and even months. During this period, the unpatched systems remain vulnerable to a publicly known vulnerability.

The goal of network defense is to protect not just a single computer system but many systems all within a network. There are two broad types of network defense: internal and perimeter. Internal network defense seeks to manage and prevent the spread of malware or malicious activity between computer systems within a network. Perimeter defense seeks to prevent the introduction of malware or stop malicious activities from entering a network. Network defenses commonly rely on a series of technologies known as intrusion detection systems (IDSs), intrusion prevention systems (IPS) or a hybrid intrusion detection and prevention system (IDPS). Most IDSs use one of three common detection methods to identify malicious traffic attempting to enter or transit within a network. First, signature-based detection compares traffic attempting to enter or already in a network to known or preconfigured attack patterns. This defense only works against known vulnerabilities (pre-existing malware) and therefore is less adaptable to rapid changes in the threat environment. The second type of IDS uses a statistical anomaly-based detect schema. Statistical anomaly-based detection uses snapshots of normal network behavior to create a "baseline." If a network exceeds this baseline, an anomaly-based detect schema identifies that there is anomalous activity that needs to be stopped. This type of defense is prone to false positives (identifications of problems where none exists) as traffic patterns change over time within and between networks. The third type of IDS is stateful-protocol analysis detection. This type of analysis focuses on predetermined profiles of normal activity. When non-normal activity occurs, it alerts human network defenders. Detecting malicious traffic is only the first step; a new class of products referred to as intrusion prevention systems attempts to stop an intrusion in progress. An IPS that detects a malicious remote connection to its network will halt the transfer of network traffic between the malicious connection and its network. IPS systems commonly work in tandem with IDS systems to ensure the defenses of a network.

Network and host-based security systems have substantially improved technical cyber defenses. Yet they remain vulnerable to advances such as polymorphic malware, which attempts to identify the defensive measures of a network or computer system and overcome them by changing their form. Human users pose another type of vulnerability that is difficult to mitigate – for example, when they inadvertently or knowingly introduce malicious software into a network. Technical defense is in many ways a game of whack-a-mole, in which defenders are constantly trying to plug holes all the while new holes keep arising. The future of technical defense is likely going to include the use of Artificial Intelligence (AI) to assist in the surveillance, monitoring and maintenance of computer systems and networks. One project developed by the Defense Advanced Research Projects Agency (DARPA) and named Mayhem has shown substantial progress against the world's top hackers at two recent hackers' events.[4]

Organizations across all levels are also developing agreements and institutions to facilitate the exchange of threat indicators. In the United States, a series of high-level public–private organizations called Information Sharing and Analysis Centers (ISACs) have formed around various critical industries. Organizations such as E-ISAC (electricity sector), FS-ISAC (financial services), Auto-ISAC (automotive), Aviation-ISAC, DIB-ISAC (defense industrial base) and more than a dozen other formal organizations share threat indicators between corporate and governmental partners in an attempt to get ahead of threats. These organizations are fee-based and the level of requisite defensive capabilities necessary to utilize the information they share remains above most small to medium firms. In the United States, a second, lower tier of organizations was proposed to address the challenges facing small to medium-sized organizations. These information-sharing organizations are called Information Sharing and Analysis Organizations (ISAOs). Both ISAOs and ISACs are designed to streamline the sharing of information horizontally within sectors, and vertically between sectors and the government. For example, these organizations can help with sharing indicators of compromise quickly, to minimize the time from indicator discovery to remediation. While some sectors' ISACs and ISAOs have become very robust and enable better defense, others remain relatively weak. In sum, cyber defense cooperation varies from one sector to another.

The ISAC and ISAO model is being explored around the world. In 2017, the European Agency for Network and Information Security released a study on cooperative models for information sharing and analysis centers and collated best practices for implementation within Europe. The same year, the Financial Services ISAC (FS-ISAC) started building partnerships in Asia and began the process of developing centers headquartered in Singapore. Defense sharing and coordination are also growing within military alliances. In November 2017, the North Atlantic Treaty Organization (NATO) began the process of developing a Cyberspace Operations Center to foster cyber defense cooperation amongst partner nations.

Despite increases in information sharing across all levels, there remain strong incentives for many firms to be less than forthright regarding their breaches. Legal and reputation issues related to their products or services often constrain or slow organizations from sharing timely information that might prevent breaches within other organizations. While the trend is toward sharing, too much sharing might reveal weaknesses or cause clients to seek new firms. Incentivizing firms to share often requires negotiating policies that reduce the risks – including the legal liability – involved in sharing information about a compromise.

Beyond sharing threat information within organized networks, Internet and digital services providers have been pushed to address a variety of security challenges more directly. In 2012, US Internet Service Providers (ISPs) voluntarily began to work on addressing issues such as botnets, domain name fraud and Internet route hijacking. Many ISPs and telecommunications providers are currently seeking to address security challenges associated with data that reside both within their service areas and amongst their clients. However, there is no uniform international organizing principle and the ability of ISPs, Internet Exchange Points (IXPs) and content delivery firms to provide improved security has been met by legal challenges that have limited their success in liberal democracies and facilitated repression and censorship in more authoritarian states. The securitization of network traffic by the providers of the Internet remains a substantial challenge.

Combined, the technical and policy solutions examined in this section foster what International Relations scholars call deterrence by denial. Each of the steps undertaken above to build the defenses of computer systems and the networks they are a part of, as well as their users, increases the relative costs associated with attack. Denying vectors of attack across the three layers of cyberspace minimizes risks and requires potential adversaries to incur increased costs when attacking. Yet, despite all the available technology and policy, defense in cyberspace is and will probably remain for the foreseeable future inherently vulnerable. Each step undertaken to increase defense reduces risks, but no one solution – nor all in combination – eliminates risk. The inherent weaknesses of cyber defense via technical and policy solutions at the organizational level have pushed states and other sub-national jurisdictions to seek new means to deter malicious actors from engaging in cyberattacks. The next section focuses on the macro-policy options available to states and jurisdictions in their continuing efforts to create effective cyber defenses.

Defense through deterrence by punishment

Since defense in cyberspace is intrinsically imperfect, governments need to use various mechanisms to deter cyber threat actors. At its most basic, deterrence seeks to dissuade a potential adversary by signaling that the costs and or risks of a given course of action they might take outweigh the benefits.[5] The most commonly examined form of deterrence emphasizes punishment. Deterrence by punishment operates at the international, national and sub-national levels. Deterrence that occurs at, or below, the national level most commonly falls into criminological frameworks that emphasize the individual level of analysis. Research in this area might seek to answer questions such as: how to deter a hacker from attacking a local company for profit? Deterrence at the international level most commonly occurs through inter-state interactions, but also includes state-to-non-state interactions such as states interacting with transnational terrorist organizations.

In all cases, deterrence requires specific, credible signals backed up by sufficient resolve to exact punishment.[6] Deterrence requires specificity. Specificity at the state level is the identification of which acts perpetrated by another state constitute a violation that would cross a pre-identified "red line" or core interest of a state. Specificity within states is codified as acts that violate law. A violation by a state or non-state actor can both cross a "red line" and violate the national laws of the state it is attacking. Often a victim state will identify the types of violation and engage in deterrence through both domestic legal proceedings to punish the perpetrator and international actions for the same purpose. Credibility is the ability to exact punishment on a violator of a legal or political "red line." Establishing credible punishments for cyberattacks is extremely challenging. Generally, the credibility of the state is not in doubt within states. The notion of *de facto* sovereignty holds that a state has the power to enforce the law within its territorial boundaries. Most states consistently demonstrate their resolve to enforce the law, thanks to policing and judicial systems. By contrast, when states interact amongst themselves, it is often difficult to signal both credibility – the ability to respond – and resolve – the will to respond.

Whether in the physical world or in cyberspace, exacting punishment requires accurate and timely attribution. Attribution in cyberspace is a substantial challenge to effective cyber deterrence.[7] Whether attempting criminological deterrence or interstate deterrence, accurately identifying the perpetrator of a digital attack requires substantial digital forensic and contextual information.[8] Attribution must also occur in a timely manner. If a perpetrator of a digital crime is not identified within the statute of limitations, he or she cannot be charged with a crime. While in interstate deterrence there is no formal statute of limitations, responding in an untimely manner to an attack is likely to be misinterpreted as a new attack.

Signals are the mechanism by which a state alerts potential violators of red lines or laws. The repeated prosecution of those who violate the law generally provides robust and unambiguous signals at the state and sub-state levels. Very often, these signals are ignored because criminal actors believe they are "able to get away with a crime." A perpetrator's belief that he or she can get away with a crime is rooted in an evaluation of the likelihood of being caught relative to the costs of being caught. While some crimes are driven by impulses, most cybercrimes require careful planning and foresight. At the domestic level, the process of establishing deterrence through criminological approaches – in particular, the prosecution of individuals or groups who violate the law – is hampered not by specificity or credibility, but rather by a lack of resolve to provide sufficient capabilities for law enforcement to attribute cyberattacks to a perpetrator at a level sufficient for criminal prosecution. When the deterrence of criminal actors is imperfect, violations of the law are more likely to occur than if it caught the perpetrator of every crime. Even if all crimes were prosecuted, it is likely that individuals would still, for a variety of reasons, attempt criminal acts in and through cyberspace.

Despite substantial resources, specific legal frameworks and a credible source of power, states are unable to achieve perfect criminological deterrence. All of the legal specificity present within a state and the credibility found within a criminological framework for the prosecution of crime is largely absent at the international level. The consensus among scholars and practitioners is that deterrence in cyberspace is plagued by a number of issues.[9] Cyberspace presents at least three core challenges to deterrence. First, victims of cyberattacks are often unaware that an attack has occurred. The average discovery time for data breaches in 2017 was 191 days.[10] Distinguishing between random or expected malfunctions in networks and systems and deliberately induced malfunctions is difficult and requires substantial resources, both human and financial. Moreover, after initial detection, data breaches in 2017 averaged 66 days between identification and containment.[11]

Second, beyond knowing that a cyberattack is occurring and preventing the damage from spreading, attributing the attack to a specific actor is often imprecise or dependent on substantial forensic analysis and contextual geopolitical factors that allow reasonable attribution to a given actor. In the case of Russian hacks of the Democratic National Committee (DNC) in 2015–16, the perpetrators' techniques, tactics and procedures provided both the forensic and geopolitical context necessary for reasonable attribution. Jon Lindsay points out that "attribution requires great technical expertise, analytical skill, and organizational coordination."[12] He goes on to write that, despite the attribution problem being hard to solve, it is more difficult in less vital instances of attack than it is in comparably important instances in which the amount of available information drawn from both forensic and non-forensic (geopolitical) means increases. More simply, the more geopolitically significant an attack, the more information about that attack is likely to be available, consequently making attribution easier. For deterrence to be credible, attribution is important.[13] The absence of accurate and substantiated attribution can lead to unnecessary escalation and retaliation against a third party that did not perpetrate a cyberattack. A response predicated on faulty attribution, or based on attribution with insufficient evidence, could even be in violation of international law.[14]

Third, international law requires that retaliation (the punishment side of deterrence) be proportionate. The calibration of a proportionate response to a cyberattack is difficult. Several factors must be taken into account, such as time, perceptions of proportionality, and existing technical capacity to respond. The average time it takes to recognize that an attack is under way or has taken place is almost 200 days. Moreover, the time to contain such an attack is approximately 60 days. Lengthy delays in actuating deterrence weaken the credibility associated with threats of punishment. If a state waited six months to respond to a conventional kinetic or nuclear attack, the credibility of a threatened punishment would be almost entirely lost. Following 9/11, it only took the United States a few weeks to have the first Central Intelligence Agency (CIA) operators and Special Forces responding to Taliban and Al-Qaeda in the remote reaches of Afghanistan. Time is important for deterrence at any level, from punishing a criminal within a "statute of limitations" to punishing states for violating a red line. Calibrating the timing of the (counter-) attack and the subsequent perception of this attack by an adversary is difficult. If retaliation through cyberspace occurs but the state being punished does not recognize it has been attacked for more than 200 days, it is uncertain whether the punishment is in response to a violation of a stated red line, or is itself a new attack.

The proportionality of a retaliatory response is further challenged by the complexities of cyberspace itself. A successful cyberattack against a power station might warrant a successful return cyberattack against the attacking nation's electric grid. But, unlike in the physical world where bombs, missiles and the planes that carry them are reliable and work across a wide range of relevant cases, in cyberspace developing a retaliatory attack against an adversary takes time to plan, engineers to scope the consequences of various effects, and lawyers to assess whether the retaliation meets international legal standards. Such a process also assumes there is a proportionate target to attack. This might not always be the case. For instance, the United States presents a target-rich environment for would-be state hackers. But a state such as the Democratic People's Republic of Korea (DPRK – North Korea) has relatively few connections to cyberspace, and even fewer that constitute proportionate targets for a retaliatory cyberattack. Since readily available proportionate retaliatory cyberattacks are not a certainty, states are forced to consider options that extend beyond cyberspace. These cross-domain options – for instance, retaliating to a cyberattack through economic sanctions – cause decision-makers to worry about potential conflict escalation and have been used sparingly.

Although many nations state their intention to retaliate to cyberattacks, the evidence that states actually do retaliate is far from conclusive.[15] There are few definitive cases in which there was a clear retaliatory response to a cyberattack. This situation can be explained by the fact that no single attack rises to the level of an "armed attack" or "a use of force" necessary under international law for a state to retaliate. Instead, the vast majority of cyberattacks occur just below the threshold of "armed attack" or "use of force." Cyber adversaries can essentially bleed their targets dry of information without doing any physical harm.[16] Storybox 8.1 explores the claim that Chinese cyber theft and espionage operations have caused the greatest transfer of wealth in human history.

Storybox 8.1 The greatest transfer of wealth in human history

In 2005, *Time* magazine ran an article about Shawn Carpenter, an employee at Sandia National Laboratories who had discovered a security breach within the Sandia computers.[17] Carpenter alerted US Army Counterintelligence, who later turned the investigation over to the Federal Bureau of Investigation (FBI). What Carpenter encountered at Sandia was the beginning of one of the most pervasive intelligence penetrations of the US Department of Defense (DoD) and national laboratories up to that point – an operation codenamed "Titan Rain." But Titan Rain was only the beginning and was followed by more than 38 substantial breaches involving hundreds of government agencies and departments in dozens of countries around the world, as well as hundreds more private companies and human rights activists, including the Dalai Lama, over the next ten years.[18]

The story of Titan Rain and the subsequent mass theft, espionage and surveillance programs undertaken by the Chinese began when two People's Liberation Army (PLA) Colonels, Liang Qiao and Wang Xiansui, published a book entitled *Unrestricted Warfare*.[19] In their volume, the colonels emphasized a new series of military strategies to undermine the strategic and tactical position of an adversary without triggering a military conflict. Within the next five years, China began a rapid trajectory of informatization across the whole of its society, and developed a strategy focused on China's need to develop its technological prowess. Titan Rain and the broader Chinese cyber theft and espionage campaign have now become one of the most visible aspects of this strategy.

Throughout the more than 38 uniquely named operations, Chinese-affiliated actors stole terabytes-worth of data. Yet no single attack constituted an armed attack or a use of force. China's sustained theft and espionage are considered by many to be the single largest transfer of wealth (via intellectual property theft) in human history.[20]

In 2013, cybersecurity firm Mandiant released a detailed report on one Chinese actor: Unit 61398.[21] Less than a year later, the US Department of Justice indicted five members of this unit on 31 charges. Little more than a year after the indictment, rumors began circulating through official corridors in Washington, DC, that the United States was developing severe sanctions in response to repeated Chinese hacking.[22] The sanctions were being timed with an upcoming 2015 summit between Chinese President Xi Jinping and US President Barack Obama. Upon receiving word of the impending sanctions, China dispatched a high-level delegation to forestall their implementation.[23] Negotiations appeared to work out when both leaders reiterated a strong commitment to cybersecurity during a joint press conference at the close of the summit. The following year, cybersecurity firm FireEye (which bought Mandiant) released a follow-up report that indicated that Chinese economic espionage had significantly declined following the 2015 summit.[24]

This example illustrates the use of multiple levels of deterrence, ranging from a criminological approach to a formal and credible signal of impending retaliation in the form of sanctions. The initial indicators of success in response to this approach appear to have been a decline in economic espionage, but the long-term results of this deterrent approach remain uncertain. However, the process of deterring China from engaging in economic espionage in cyberspace took more than ten years, and in the end resulted not from retaliatory response in cyberspace, but through a cross-domain threat of sanctions and the use of indictments.

Conclusion: The painful reality

The painful reality for defense and deterrence in cyberspace is that there remains, for the foreseeable future, no fool-proof means of protecting computers, networks or their users in cyberspace. Since the challenges facing cyber defenders are so great, cyberspace is often referred to as an offense-dominant domain.[25] A preponderance of data currently indicates that defense in cyberspace is difficult, but primarily against the threats of espionage and theft. Some scholars contend that the balance between offense and defense is of little consequence, and that investments in cyber capabilities achieve goals, rather than espionage, such as the attack on Iran's nuclear facilities at Natanz demonstrate defense dominance.[26] They claim that the development costs of the exploits used to damage these nuclear facilities exceeded the defensive costs undertaken by Iran to protect their networks and facilities, and the costs of repair to those facilities once damaged. These direct costs–benefit analyses are helpful for conceptualizing raw inputs, but fail to consider the psychological impact that cyberattacks have. In the case of Iran, the Stuxnet worm caused significant distress and concern for engineers and within the military. In the absence of information on the source of their system failures, it was assumed they were experiencing technical difficulties due to poorly sourced goods or engineering.

There are very few examples of cyberattacks that have achieved violent effects resulting in the physical destruction of property. Cases such as the Stuxnet attack on Iran's nuclear facilities at Natanz, the Iranian hacking of a spillway dam,[27] cyberattacks on a German steel mill in 2014,[28] and several others are relatively rare but stand out in the public consciousness. When attacks occur that rise to the level of an armed attack or use of force, they often make the problem of deterrence substantially easier. The more pervasive forms of theft and espionage require states to consistently develop and implement both technical and policy mechanisms to address increasingly sophisticated threats that do not readily fit within international legal frameworks related to acceptable retaliation. The costs of organizing for cyber defense are expected to grow. In 2004, the global cybersecurity market was worth $3.5 billion; by 2017, that number exceeded $120 billion.[29] Estimates are that, over the next five years, total global expenditures will exceed $1 trillion.[30]

Countries and companies are in a technical and financial race that seems unsustainable and appears to be making little dent in the overall trends of crime and espionage. Hardly a day goes by without a news story discussing yet another breach of a company or government agency somewhere in the world. To address the unsustainable nature of defense in cyberspace, states are trying to deter adversaries from engaging in further cyberattacks through multilateral institutions and bilateral signals. Yet, with a few exceptions, deterrence in cyberspace has largely failed to dissuade adversaries from attacking networks and the computers within them.

Discussion questions

1. Why are deterrence and defense so difficult in cyberspace?
2. What makes attribution so important to deterrence?
3. What should states prioritize – defense or deterrence?

Further resources

The Cyber Defense Review, at https://cyberdefensereview.army.mil.

Martin C. Libicki, *Cyberdeterrence and Cyberwar* (Santa Monica, CA: RAND, 2009), www.rand.org/content/dam/rand/pubs/monographs/2009/RAND_MG877.pdf.

National Institute of Standards Computer Security Resource Center, https://csrc.nist.gov/publications/sp800.

9

Cybersecurity and democracy

Cyberspace has provided a platform for the expansion of democracy. At national and local levels, e-government offers new forms of accessibility to public services. The Internet is sometimes described as a "liberation technology," fostering democratization throughout the world. However, as our daily lives increasingly rely on the Internet and its connectivity, governments have also used cyberspace to expand their surveillance efforts, fostering important debates and concern about civil liberties in the digital era. While social media played a key role in the Arab Spring and the EuroMaidan movement, their effect cannot be separated from broader political and societal implications. Authoritarian governments, fearing the power of social media, have not hesitated in restricting or banning access to certain parts of their domestic Internets, using broad surveillance powers to curtail free speech. Cyberspace is a powerful medium for mobilizing citizens and organizing democracy, yet it can also be used by states to control and manipulate their societies and limit human freedom.

Democracy and security in cyberspace

Early Internet enthusiasts championed notions of freedom and independence. They envisioned that cyberspace would liberate humans due to its decentralized nature. The Internet did not need a constitution, or a political process, it was an emancipatory space controlled by users and established to share ideas and experiments: World Wide Web users were free to express themselves and interact however they wanted. This openness, and the liberties provided by the Internet, were essential to its early success. However, as researchers Ronald Deibert and Rafal Rohozinski note, "just because a technology has been invented for one purpose does not mean that it will not find other uses unforeseen by its creators."[1]

Governments have always been and remain dominant actors in cyberspace, and have used the Internet to further both democracy and national security. From this perspective, cyberspace has simply provided new ground for pre-existing processes and tensions, between democracy and security, to express themselves. At the end of the twentieth century, governments embraced the Internet to develop new instruments of governance. The Internet offered a new means to provide citizens with information about public services, political processes and choices, a practice known as e-government. Increasingly, digital devices became tools to facilitate online citizens' participation in political processes – for example, through online voting.[2] Together, these new modes of action were expected to promote greater efficiency and effectiveness, and a more citizen-centric government.[3] However, as state actors expanded their digital footprint, the percentage of the population with access to computers remained relatively low, and the development of e-democracy stalled.[4]

At the dawn of the twenty-first century, a growing number of countries invested in national cybersecurity, re-affirming the pre-existing tension between security and democracy. This tension is particularly clear when focusing on the national level of analysis. National security can be defined as the possibility for inhabitants of a state to live in the absence of internal and external threat to the quality of their life and values. To protect our way of life, including the democratic system of government and liberal democratic values such as freedom of speech and privacy, intelligence and security agencies use special powers that threaten, and sometimes infringe upon, these values. In democracies, security agencies seek to defend an open society by secret means. Beyond strategic-level declarations, governments keep most of their cybersecurity practices secret, to protect the methods through which they wield cyberpower. Throughout the world, cyber commands, signals intelligence agencies and domestic law-enforcement agencies operate secretly to protect the comparative advantages they develop over their adversaries. Their reliance on secrecy limits governmental transparency and, by extension, democratic accountability. Without sufficient information on government cyber operations, citizens cannot assess the decisions public authorities make on their behalf. Instead, they have to rely on representatives – the head of government and select members of parliament – who have access to sensitive government information and make cyber policy decisions.

Cybersecurity policy decisions are particularly important because government security agencies benefit from surveillance powers that encroach upon individual privacy. Privacy, defined as the condition of being free from observation or disruption by other people, is an international human right guaranteed by the Universal Declaration of Human Rights of 1948 and the International Covenant on Civil and Political Rights of 1966. International law holds that individuals have the right to consent to or refuse the use of their personal data by secondary or third parties. Interference with this right must be justified by government authorities. Government officials generally invoke national security to deploy special surveillance powers. In this context, surveillance, in and beyond cyberspace, is supposed to constitute a temporary restriction to the rights of a few suspect individuals, accepted in the pursuit of the greater societal interest of national security.

The extent to which governments do indeed use cyber surveillance in exceptional circumstances is a point of debate. Domestic security services collect information in cyberspace to identify and monitor suspected criminals, spies and terrorists. They sometimes monitor political dissenters and opposition groups – subversive elements – who have the potential to turn to violent action or (in autocratic countries) threaten the legitimacy of the regime. Government security services have struggled historically to differentiate legitimate political dissenters from subversive elements that truly threaten society.[5] What constitutes legitimate government surveillance is contentious and constantly evolving. Government overreach in this domain can stymie public debate and freedom of expression. Public expectations regarding surveillance can sometimes also have a "chilling effect" on society, in the sense that the simple awareness of the existence of surveillance can restrain social activism and free expression. At the extreme end of the spectrum, excessive government surveillance threatens democracy, instead of protecting it.

There are many ways privacy can be threatened online. Internet users all leave a digital footprint when they visit websites, send emails and submit information online. Some elements are left intentionally – a birth date or a picture shared on Facebook, for instance. Other data are left unintentionally by visiting websites and clicking on links. Each computer has an IP address that is used to surf on the web, which reveals the location and type of device used to access specific parts of the Internet.[6] Data on Internet browsing habits can help governments, private companies and malicious actors identify individuals online. Storybox 9.1 discusses growing public concern about online privacy in the aftermath of the global surveillance disclosures of 2013.

> **Storybox 9.1 The global surveillance disclosures of 2013**
>
> In Spring 2013, international media revealed details of a global surveillance network set up by the US National Security Agency (NSA) and partner agencies across the world. The revelation emanated from a cache of highly classified documents stolen by then NSA contractor Edward Snowden. Snowden leaked these documents to a group of journalists who subsequently published them in newspapers such as the *Guardian*, the *Washington Post* and *Der Spiegel*. The Snowden leaks contained thousands of top secret documents shedding light on the surveillance efforts of the "Five Eyes" network – comprised of intelligence agencies in Australia, Canada, New Zealand, the United Kingdom and the United States – and partner countries (including Denmark, France, Germany, Israel, Italy, the Netherlands, Norway, Singapore, Spain and Switzerland).
>
> The most widely discussed revelations focused on a series of programs with mysterious codenames, such as PRISM and XKeyscore. Through the implementation of PRISM, the NSA uses selectors – an email address, for instance – to collect stored Internet communications from major companies including Apple, Google and Skype. According to a PowerPoint presentation leaked by Edward Snowden, PRISM is the main source of raw intelligence used for NSA analytic reports.[7] Another program, XKeyscore, allowed the NSA and a number of partner agencies in other countries to search and analyze global Internet data.
>
> These revelations caused outrage around the world because they suggested that the US government and its partners were collecting Internet data in bulk. For many critics and concerned citizens around the globe, these revelations raised the specter of omnipresent government surveillance described in George Orwell's dystopian novel *Nineteen Eighty-Four*, or practiced by the East German Ministry for State Security, the Stasi.[8]
>
> Critics question whether government agencies should be allowed to collect data on large populations of presumably innocent people. While modern intelligence agencies do collect tremendous amounts of data, they do not actively monitor and analyze all the individuals whose data have been collected. From the perspective of the US government, PRISM and XKeyscore were originally authorized by Congress, and legal. Beyond legalities, the global surveillance disclosures raised public awareness and triggered a broad public debate on Internet surveillance.

The debate on Internet privacy expands well beyond the reach of government intelligence agencies. Both government and private-sector organizations are data hungry and seek to obtain personal information online to inform and orient their decisions.[9] The amount of data they gather is particularly worrying because no organization seems to be immune to data breaches that can leave sensitive personal information in the hands of criminals.[10] In response to growing concerns about online privacy, the European Union passed the General Data Protection Regulation (GDPR) to harmonize data protection across Europe. GDPR allows European users to have easier access to the data that website owners hold about them, and establishes a clear responsibility for organizations to obtain the consent of people they collect information about, among other measures.[11] One hope is that creating more accountability for organizations that handle people's personal information will force them to develop more comprehensive data protection policies and assessments.

A liberation technology

Optimists argue that cyber technologies can help foster social change that encourages liberal democratic values. Scholar Larry Diamond defines liberation technology as "any form of information and communication technology that can expand political, social, and economic freedom," from computers to mobile phones to the Internet and social media.[12] Social media platforms like YouTube and Twitter can be used to report news, express opinions and expose wrongdoing. From this perspective, online media provide powerful tools for transparency and monitoring government activities. The practice of cyberactivism, a form of political mobilization in and through cyberspace, relies on the Internet to organize political activities such as demonstrations and street protests.[13]

There is no question that, in some circumstances, the Internet does empower individuals and strengthen civil society. Larry Diamond details how China's blogosphere has provided room to open a domestic public sphere, in spite of strong government censorship.[14] In one case, online indignation forced the Chinese government to investigate the death of a rural migrant, Sun Zhigang, after he was incarcerated and beaten to death by local police in the city of Guangzhou. The government eventually decided to change its national regulation and closed the detention centers that were used to hold rural migrants in custody prior to repatriation.[15] In 2011, social media facilitated the Arab Spring, a series of demonstrations, protests and riots that spread from Tunisia to the rest of the Arab world. In a region where freedom of speech and freedom of press are limited, youth used the Internet to exchange political ideas, spread information and organize protests against repressive governments.[16] Storybox 9.2 examines the role digital media played in the EuroMaidan movement, which has affected Ukrainian politics since 2013.

> **Storybox 9.2 The EuroMaidan movement**
>
> In 2013, a wave of demonstrations and protests followed the Ukrainian government's decision to suspend the signature of an association agreement with the European Union. The movement, which began on November 21, 2013 in Maidan Nezalezhnosti (Independence Square) was nicknamed "EuroMaidan," and supported through a number of social media accounts such as @euromaidan on Twitter and the евромайдан–euromaydan page on Facebook. With the help of digital media, fueled by growing public concern with government corruption and human rights violations, among other issues, the movement grew significantly. Protests eventually led to the 2014 Ukrainian revolution, ousting Ukrainian President Viktor Yanukovych and resulting in the overthrow of his government.
>
> Activists, news media and political scientists have all pointed out the importance of social media in the EuroMaidan movement. Social media helped mobilize the population rapidly, sometimes leading to near-spontaneous actions. Digital tools helped protesters connect to one another – thanks, for example, to the use of hashtags.[17] Following Yanukovych's decision not to sign the EU agreement, activists promptly assembled online to criticize the administration. Social media helped activists communicate about the protest, and the broader situation in Ukraine, to domestic and international audiences. They also helped activists organize protests, sharing information about flyers and slogans, setting up a legal assistance service for victims of government repression, and field hospitals for protesters.[18]
>
> The use of social media also provides a uniquely detailed source of data for researchers to study social movements and a number of other phenomena relevant to national and international politics. However, the digital world cannot provide a window into everything. Social media were an important part of the success of the EuroMaidan movement, but not the sole facilitator. Pre-existing social networks and other types of media – digital, in print, and television – interacted with social media to amplify the protest and bring about social and political change in Ukraine.[19] Scholars continue to debate the extent to which digital platforms can foster durable change and sustained civic engagement. In addition to technology, a number of other variables affect political change, including political culture, leadership and the level of organization within a movement.[20]

The US government famously embraced the potential of the Internet as a tool for democracy promotion in its 2011 International Strategy for Cyberspace. This strategy expressed US support for fundamental freedoms and privacy in cyberspace and offered to support civil-society actors in achieving these freedoms throughout the world.[21] Then-Secretary of State Hillary Clinton famously defended Internet freedom, noting that "governments should not prevent people from connecting to the Internet and websites or each other."[22] This notion builds on pre-existing civil and political rights and is often attached to online free expression and the right to access the Internet to connect to others.[23] In practice, the US government has supported the development of software, including The Onion Router (Tor), that provide online protection by disguising the source and endpoint of online interactions. Tor allows individuals to surf the web without anyone knowing who and where they are. Egyptian dissidents relied on Tor to protect their identity during the Arab Spring.

However, cyberspace is not a one-dimensional domain dominated by its potential for liberation. Two-thirds of all Internet users live in countries where criticism of the government is subject to censorship.[24] China and Russia, among other nations, perceive Internet freedom as a way for Western culture and values to infiltrate their societies and foment dissent. The contrast could hardly be starker between these different perspectives on what constitutes a security risk or a right.[25]

While the Internet may have been invented with the ideals of freedom of expression and access to information in mind, other purposes have emerged throughout its development. Pessimistic voices in the debate on cybersecurity and democracy highlight governments' capabilities to control and filter the Internet to identify and punish dissenters. Critics point out that governments can leverage their concerns about cyber warfare to securitize cyberspace and justify extraordinary surveillance measures to the population. The same social media used to organize popular protest and widen the public sphere in the Arab world and beyond can be used by governments to identify dissenters and put them in jail.

Reductions in Internet freedom can take many forms. Filtering technologies, such as the Great Firewall of China, limit citizens' access to specific sites and resources in cyberspace. Governments can monitor and track online activities, to support arrests and prosecutions based on behaviors or actions in cyberspace.[26] The Chinese government has tried to eliminate anonymous communications and networking by requiring the registration of real names to blog or comment, and monitoring cyber cafes. However, there is simply too much information online for governments to monitor everything.

A multiplicity of national approaches to what is allowed on the Internet continues to dictate its use. Even in the most advanced liberal democracies, complete freedom of expression on the Internet does not exist. Among other limitations, liberal democracies have been keen to protect intellectual property, legislating on music rights and cracking down on illegal download platforms, such as Napster and The Pirate Bay. Citizens are also protected from online slander and hate speech in various countries. Other countries chose to more directly restrain access to Internet websites and services based on national values. In Pakistan, laws concerning blasphemy have been used to ban access to Facebook, which hosted cartoons of the Prophet Muhammad.[27]

In the last decade, the emergence of alternative news websites and fake news raised important questions on the impact of Internet on the public debate. Larry Diamond emphasizes "the fine line between pluralism and cacophony, between advocacy and intolerance, and between the expansion of the public sphere and its hopeless fragmentation."[28] While the Internet can help establish a public debate and support civil society, it can also divide people and foment dissent.[29] Cyberspace, in turn, is what people make of it.

Whose cybersecurity?

While a significant part of the International Relations literature on cyberspace focuses on nation states, understanding the effect of cybersecurity on individuals is equally important. Aaron Brantly argues that the main losers in the current cyber arms race are not states but the activists who are struggling to keep up with the tremendous resources of state actors and corporations that invest in cybersecurity, cyberespionage and cyber operations. As states develop more powerful cyber capabilities, they can use them not only against their adversaries but also on civilian populations.[30] For instance, a company based in the United Kingdom developed a complex spyware named FinFisher. This software was sold and used by repressive regimes in Egypt, Bahrain and Uganda to spy on political opponents.[31] In other cases, innovations developed for cybercrime are re-used by governments to spy on foreign agents, or even on their own citizens.[32] Brantly shows that the development of new cyber capabilities is often followed by decreases in civil liberties, and argues that major democracies should invest more significantly in facilitating freedom of connection and expression online.

The recognition of the imbalance between the power of governments and companies and of civil society has fostered the emergence of public interest groups supporting Internet freedom. Organizations such as the Citizen Lab – an interdisciplinary laboratory based at the University of Toronto – the Electronic Frontier Foundation (EFF) and others actively support less capable cyber actors. The weak position of civil-society actors is reinforced by what one author calls their careless practices. In one stunning example, advocacy group Reporters Without Borders unknowingly propagated a link to a malicious website posing as a Facebook petition to release the Tibetan activist Dhondup Wangchen.[33] To combat these kinds of mistakes, organizations like the Citizen Lab provide free support to human rights groups and teach them best practices in cybersecurity. Storybox 9.3 presents the findings of an investigation co-led by the Citizen Lab, and shows some of the difficulties confronted by public interest groups in this context.

Storybox 9.3 GhostNet

In a seminal report entitled "Tracking GhostNet," an international team of researchers led by the Citizen Lab at the University of Toronto uncovered a vast electronic spying operation infecting 1,295 computers in 103 countries. Their investigation started when researchers at the University of Toronto were asked by the office of the Dalai Lama to examine its computers for signs of malware. Their initial analysis found that the computers had indeed been infected, and the team decided to pursue their investigation through technical scouting and laboratory analysis. The researchers set up a honey-pot computer that helped them identify malicious servers and observe the tactics, techniques and procedures used by the attacker(s) to infect computers and to access and retrieve data from them.[34]

Their analysis opened a window into a broad cyber operation that had infiltrated hundreds of computers throughout the world, stealing troves of potentially sensitive documents, mostly in Asian countries.[35] The main tool used by the hackers behind GhostNet – an open-source and widely available trojan known as gh0st RAT – allowed attackers to gain complete control of a computer.[36] This malware was used to retrieve data from high-value targets located in ministries of foreign affairs, embassies, international organizations and NGOs.

Though the researchers could not directly attribute the computer network exploitation, they found that four control servers were based

> in China, and one in Southern California. However, they remained reluctant to pin responsibility on the Chinese government. Another state actor could have compromised proxy computers in China to achieve deniability. Non-state actors, working for profit or out of patriotism, could also have conducted the operation.[37]

Protecting information stored on digital devices and communicated through cyberspace has become easier in the last decade, not least thanks to the effort of organizations such as the Citizen Lab, the EFF and the Guardian Project.[38] These organizations recommend a number of free tools that are available online to support digital privacy. This includes software that provide disk encryption, email encryption, secure text messages and video services, secure browsing services and virtual private networks, to name a few. These tools are particularly important for activists living in undemocratic countries, where failing to secure online activities can become the difference between freedom and incarceration.[39] They can also be important in democracies, to help users protect their online activities from cyber criminals and other online threats. Most online freeware provides sufficient cyber defense against neighbors, colleagues and common cyber criminals. However, the capabilities of specialized companies and many governments are much more difficult to protect against. In those more extreme cases, effective cybersecurity might require users to adapt and limit the ways they use computers. While highly secure browsing and communication is possible, there is no perfect cybersecurity.

Encryption and cyber (in)security

The debate on encryption gained prominence in the 1990s, when the administration of President Bill Clinton proposed for federal law-enforcement agencies to hold a decryption key that would facilitate wiretaps. Opponents were disturbed that this would give undue power to government officials, and the government proposal was eventually terminated.[40] Advocates of strong public encryption – such as the EFF – point out that the "power of ciphers" protects citizens when they communicate, bank and shop online. For them, more cryptography is inherently beneficial. On the other side, critics – mostly government intelligence and security agencies – point out that encryption protects "foreign spies, terrorists and criminals when they pry, plot and steal."[41] For Daniel Moore and Thomas Rid, these antithetical positions are overstated and flawed. The problem is less with encryption itself than how it is used. They argue that encryption should be used as often as possible, but not all the time, especially not as it relates to cryptographically enabled services.[42] They recommend encrypting personal communications and data to enable better privacy and freedom of speech. However, they condemn the use of encryption for online exchange platforms and marketplaces, specifically on the dark web – a distinct cyberspace network supporting cryptographically hidden sites and accessible through specific software like Tor. These services provide anonymous browsing and hosting of exchanges through a browser. While anonymous browsing should be welcomed, anonymous exchanges are more problematic. Research shows that encryption helps develop marketplaces that mostly benefit criminals who want to sell or buy fake passports, drugs, weapons and other illegal goods and services. For Rid and Moore, the individuals creating these websites should have to give their names to service providers. Outside of these specific circumstances, user anonymity should be protected to support free speech.[43] The solution Rid and Moore provide is helpful, but it does not resolve the dilemma over encryption. Storybox 9.4 examines the case of the San Bernardino shooters in the United States and presents the dispute that ensued over the decryption of a mobile phone, between the US Federal Bureau of Investigation (FBI) and Apple.

Storybox 9.4 The Apple–FBI debate over digital privacy

The rise of encryption limits government agencies' ability to access data on digital devices. Technology companies such as Apple have used encryption as a marketing tool. Developing encryption locks that are difficult, sometimes even impossible, to break is a selling point to attract customers who want to protect their digital data. Strong encryption has frustrated law-enforcement agencies, which have repeatedly asked companies such as Apple to provide them with a key to access encrypted data on their customers' digital devices and support their investigations. But IT companies have been reluctant to do so. They are concerned that any means of bypassing encryption would create a weakness that hackers and foreign spies might be able to exploit against their customers.

The dispute between Apple and the FBI concerns the extent to which a US court can compel manufacturers to assist government in unlocking mobile phones whose data is encrypted. In 2015 and 2016, Apple

> received and objected to a dozen court orders seeking to compel the company to use its capabilities to extract data from iPhones to assist criminal investigations. In the most well-known case, the FBI tried to force Apple to create new software that would enable it to unlock an iPhone used by Syed Rizwan Farook, one of the shooters involved in a terrorist attack in San Bernardino, California, that killed 14 and injured 22. FBI officials said that the data in Farook's phone might hold vital clues for their investigation. The company refused to cooperate on the grounds that it would violate its right to due process, claiming that forcing it to write new software would be a violation of free speech (writing code can be considered as a form of free speech in the United States). From Apple's perspective, helping law enforcement to bypass the phone password protection would create unwanted vulnerabilities in its products. Privacy advocates, Apple and other technology companies were also worried that cooperating with the government would create a precedent. If Apple complied with the US government, it might then be forced to cooperate again in the future, and not only with US agencies but perhaps also with China, Russia and other less democratic countries.[44]
>
> Eventually the US government withdrew its request to Apple after it reached out to an Israeli cybersecurity company that was able to unlock the device.[45] Since then, Apple has developed stronger encryption on its newer devices, making it technically impossible to unlock passwords or extract data from the devices it produces. The *Apple* v. *FBI* story raises broader questions about trust in the digital era. Who should we trust our digital data with? The government? Technology companies? Or only ourselves?

Conclusion

The advent of cyberspace has expanded traditional debates about security and democracy in the digital world. Early Internet users were very attached to the free flow of information and conceived of cyberspace as a haven of freedom. However, the expansion of cyberspace has also been marked by the development of new security tools and threats. These tools have been used by governments to monitor populations for good and bad reasons. But they have also been available beyond government, to activists seeking to advance democracy and to criminals seeking to protect their identity.

Long-existing tensions between liberal democratic values and security practices have not disappeared in cyberspace. States are still trying to regulate this difficult area to fight the use of cybersecurity by malicious actors, and limit their own encroachments on fundamental freedoms. New information and communication technologies do not guarantee freedom or control. Why and how cyberspace is used largely depends on political and societal factors that vary across the globe. The Internet does not create fundamentally new choices between security and democracy, but provides an evolving platform for reaffirming these choices.[46] In this sense, the Internet is what people make of it. Cyberspace is a cause for both optimism and pessimism, and, as such, illustrates the complexity of modern societies.

Discussion questions

1. How far should governments be able to encroach on liberties to provide for cyber security?
2. Has cybersecurity become essential to democracy?
3. Was Apple right to resist the FBI demand to crack an iPhone linked to the San Bernardino attacks?

Further reading

Ronald J. Deibert, *Black Code: Surveillance, Privacy, and the Dark Side of the Internet* (Toronto: McClelland & Stewart, 2013). An eponymous documentary directed by Nicholas de Pencier was released in 2016.

Timothy Edgar, *Beyond Snowden: Privacy, Mass Surveillance, and the Struggle to Reform the NSA* (Washington, DC: Brookings Institution, 2017).

10

The futures of cybersecurity

The future of cybersecurity will be complex. As humans invest more time and resources in cyberspace, the digital realm will become increasingly multifaceted, and so will cybersecurity. In the coming decades, cyberspace will continue to grow in influence at all levels of society. The number of Internet-enabled devices is expected to expand substantially from 20 billion in 2020 to more than 100 billion by 2050. These devices will pervade every aspect of modern life, from the rise of smart cities to new biotechnologies, and collect zettabytes-worth of data daily, requiring increasingly robust capabilities to process, interpret and secure big data. Quantum computing and other novel technologies are poised to expand processing power at unfathomable rates, redefining human–machine interactions. The confluence of greater numbers of devices, increasing automation and faster computing offers both challenges and opportunities for the future of cybersecurity. Yet, despite all the technological advances over the horizon, the inherently human – and therefore complex and imperfect – nature of cybersecurity will remain.

The best experts in any field frequently get it wrong when they write about *the future*. Futurists prefer to discuss an array of alternative *futures* to reflect the infinite number of possible permutations originating in the present. Using scenarios to plot possible futures can help strategic planning and identify research priorities, but they should not be treated as predictions. In the best cases, they are informed hypotheses whose implications can orient cybersecurity planning and practices.[1] For example, Jason Healey, the Director of the Cyber Statecraft Initiative at the Atlantic Council in Washington

DC, imagines five possible futures of cyber conflict and cooperation based on three key factors: offense–defense balance, the intensity and kinds of cyber conflict, and the intensity and kinds of cyber cooperation. His "most likely" scenario is one that imagines cyberspace as a "conflict domain" where cyber terror and cyber war co-exist with normal use of the Internet for communication and commerce. Another plausible scenario plots a balkanized Internet divided by national interests and intranets. Healey's preferred future is a "paradise cyberspace" that is secure, and where espionage, warfare and crime are all extremely difficult.[2]

Thinking about a multitude of different possible futures for cybersecurity keeps the door open for different understandings of cyberspace to co-exist. This concluding chapter focuses on possible developments and highlights some of the puzzles confronting scholars and practitioners as they ponder over the shape that a desirable cyber future might take. A common method for thinking about futures is to extrapolate from current trends to anticipate changes. The sections below highlight three interconnected trends that are frequently discussed in the contemporary debate on cybersecurity: the Internet of Things (IoT), the rise of big data and Artificial Intelligence (AI), and the deepening of human–machine interactions. These trends offer a small window into the future that allows us to examine some – but not all – of the key developments in the field, related threats and opportunities, and their policy implications. Given the growing complexity of cyberspace as a socio-technical domain, greater engagement from the humanities and social sciences will improve our understanding of cybersecurity. To tackle emerging challenges, researchers need to study how humans and societies interact in and through the digital realm.

Toward an ever more interconnected world: The Internet of Things

The IoT will significantly expand the physical and digital frontiers of cyberspace in the next decades. The concept of IoT is best understood as an ecosystem of connected sensors attached to everyday devices and appliances, from vehicles to door locks, thermostats, fridges, security cameras and so on.[3] Together, these sensors "collect and transmit data (sensing)," feed it to "systems that interpret and make use of the aggregated information (processing), and actuators that, on the basis of this information, take action without direct human intervention (actuation)."[4] According to one estimate, the number of objects connected to the IoT will reach 50 billion in 2020, and 100 billion by 2025.[5] The growing physical presence of connected devices will significantly increase the flow of data in cyberspace, and will require the development of new standards to maintain interoperability between billions of connected digital tools.

With applications in every sector of society, from agriculture to finance and health, the IoT will significantly expand the scope and scale of cybersecurity needs. Each new Internet-enabled device provides an entry point into cyberspace, as well as new opportunities to shape human lives in and through cyberspace in both positive and negative ways. Presently, IoT devices are a major point of weakness in the cybersecurity landscape. Many devices lack basic security features and rely upon default passwords, giving attackers easy access to them.

Experts warn that the emergence of the IoT will boost cyberattack capabilities. The growing ecosystem of devices already provides fertile ground for hackers to develop large botnets. The convergence of billions of devices across multiple sectors is likely to increase the potential scale of these disruptions. A single attack will be able to affect more devices and users, and is likely to result in amplified socio-economic effects.[6] The IoT will also open new vectors for holding individual data or access to ransom. For example, hackers might one day lock users out of their personal vehicle, home or appliances until a ransom is paid.

The more we interact with the Internet in our everyday life, the larger the data footprint we leave behind. Interconnected devices increasingly transfer large amounts of personal data in cyberspace, generating deeper concerns about privacy, and raising the political stakes of cybersecurity. The IoT will increase surveillance capacities to an unprecedented level, allowing resourceful cyber actors to collect new types of data in greater quantities. In 2018, media revealed how popular fitness trackers allowed companies to monitor the movement of national security professionals working in military bases around the world.[7] An interconnected system of billions of sensors provides a tremendous source of information, not only for governments to conduct domestic and foreign surveillance, but also for data-hungry companies and non-state threat actors.[8]

While none of the risks highlighted in this section is fundamentally new, their scale and scope are likely to significantly affect the way users approach cybersecurity. When cyberspace is everywhere, traditional boundaries between the home and workplace, public and private sphere, and related security practices will become harder to distinguish.[9] In a future in which the IoT dominates our daily lives, cybersecurity will become just security.[10] Who or what will guarantee the confidentiality, integrity and availability of our data in this future?[11] Key security actors, in governments and beyond, will need to develop new concepts and technologies to protect and process the massive amounts of data generated by the IoT.[12]

Big data and artificial intelligence

According to IBM, humans create 2.5 trillion megabytes of data every day.[13] With the advent of the IoT, increasingly large amounts of data will be captured from humans, machines and their environment. By the year 2020, worldwide data production is expected to reach 3,500,000,000,000 trillion gigabytes.[14] The ability to process such large volumes of data is one of the defining challenges of big data, but volume alone is not sufficient to define this new norm. The velocity at which data are produced or changed, and the variety of data types, also contribute to the complexity of big data. Scholars and practitioners generally define big data as "the information assets characterized by such a high volume, velocity and variety [as] to require specific technology and analytical methods for its transformation into value."[15]

Individuals and organizations confronted with an ever-increasing volume, velocity and variety of data will need assistive technology to extract information and meaning out of them.[16] Emerging practices such as machine learning, a form of AI, will support this process and redefine cybersecurity. According to an industry report, 87 percent of US cybersecurity professionals and 60 percent of those in Japan report their organizations are already using AI as part of their cybersecurity strategy.[17] A computer using machine learning can learn and adapt its code (operating instructions) and underlying algorithms (predictive mathematical frameworks) to new inputs without assistance from human programmers. This learning process leverages AI to perform tasks faster and more accurately than a human user attempting to keep up with a deluge of data such as malware samples.[18] In the years ahead, machine-learning models will help identify, anticipate and respond more swiftly to cyber threats, including malware, malicious Internet Protocols (IPs) and websites. Quantum computing, a branch of computer science poised to revolutionize the processing of data, is likely to offer the first major revolution in fundamental computer architectures and logic since their invention prior to World War II. Quantum computers will allow for more complicated computational structures beyond binary 1s and 0s. Such advances, paired with new forms of code and algorithms, are expected to undermine most current forms of encryption and offer potentially revolutionary advances in computational power that could make the most computationally intensive tasks solvable in far shorter periods of time. Advances such as quantum computing and AI are expected to open up new areas of research for fields as diverse as medicine and physics.

In this data-intensive context, cybersecurity will increasingly be about controlling data and the tools to process them. The convergence of big data, cloud computing and the IoT will generate huge amounts of personal data, increasing public concern about the availability of personal data in cyberspace.[19] Many experts expect a deterioration of privacy in the future, which will be mirrored by an increasing level of societal acceptance of infringement on privacy.[20]

Powerful big data tools will allow those that wield them to better target their interactions with individual users. Similarly, hackers could exploit big data and machine learning to better identify potential targets and develop more sophisticated attacks, by such techniques as narrowing down the probable passwords used by a target. The growing role played by AI will force security professionals to adapt their practices to focus increasingly on overseeing machines. AI is unlikely to work perfectly and the potential for error will remain, not least because bias limits computers and the humans who develop and use them. In one notable case, a crime prediction tool, which combined criminal data to tell officers where to focus their prevention efforts, was found to significantly amplify racially biased policing.[21] While machine learning and AI offer many promises, humans will remain essential to develop, use, make sense of and secure cyberspace.

Human–machine interactions

A third trend suggests that the boundaries between humans and machines will become increasingly blurred. Contemporary research on the brain–machine interface already allows humans to interact with computers by thought. The merging of biological data and digital devices presents tremendous opportunities to improve standards of living. In one famous medical experiment, a tetraplegic patient was able to directly control robotic prosthetic limbs thanks to electrodes placed in his brain.[22]

But some commentators worry about the risks of bio-surveillance and, specifically, their impact on privacy. A scenario developed by the Center for Long-Term Cybersecurity at the University of

Berkeley hypothesizes an "Internet of Emotion" in which computer devices – directly able to track our hormone levels, heart rate, facial expressions and voice – will be able to read our emotions and touch "the most sensitive aspects of human psychology." In this future, the report concludes, "managing and protecting an emotional public image and outward mindset appearance become basic social maintenance."[23] In the worst case, this is a future in which Internet users' privacy will increasingly fall prey to psychological manipulations and blackmail.

The possibility of a future in which AI directly augments human intelligence has encouraged researchers to examine the need for appropriate human-centered safeguards and ethical considerations in the development of AI technologies.[24] In recent years, a number of prominent TV shows – from *Black Mirror* to *Westworld* – have used fiction to explore the ethical implications of a future dominated by new forms of AI. As AI becomes more prominent, the role of humans will evolve increasingly toward oversight and management of computer systems. Automation requires guardians to ensure the continuity of the values, ethics and policies that define human societies. Prominent thinkers are currently debating whether humans should always have the ultimate say in this context, or whether machines might be able to act as their own masters.[25]

Either way, both humans and machines will continue to generate cybersecurity vulnerabilities. Humans will continue to forget to install the latest security patch, fall for phishing attacks, and leave flash drives containing personal information on public transport. Computers will continue to bug, and display system flaws or coding vulnerabilities. Cybersecurity will remain necessary to maintain acceptable – though not perfect – levels of trust between humans and machines.

Conclusion: Adapting to the evolving cybersecurity environment

Understanding current trends and alternative futures provides a good foundation for considering the need for new cybersecurity policies and regulations. As computer systems and their interactions with humans become more diverse and complex, experts worry about the extent to which governments, businesses and broader society will be able to maintain security and privacy online.[26] Many of the cybersecurity trends discussed in this conclusion suggest a future in which privacy will decrease. If this is the case, policies and regulations will need to adapt to maintain acceptable levels of privacy. Commentators worry that the fast pace of technological change is outstripping laws and policies.[27] For instance, researchers have expressed concern that current cybersecurity policies do not adequately address human vulnerabilities, such as the insider threat, and the risk posed by individuals bringing their own devices to work.[28]

In a highly complex and decentralized environment, multiple divides – between countries, industries and organizations – will require more coordinated efforts to develop coherent cybersecurity regulations and practices. Cybersecurity scholar Benoit Dupont warns that "the escalation and acceleration of data flows may lead to a dilution of security responsibilities if adequate regulatory obligations are not developed and implemented."[29] The concept of multistakeholderism, introduced in chapter 3, might not be enough to overcome these divisions. New concepts and theories will be necessary to better understand and explain the governance of cybersecurity, and to help decision-makers develop and implement common regulations.

The growing complexity of cyberspace and cybersecurity threats will widen the gap between those that can achieve some degree of security and those that cannot. An ISOC report on *Paths to Our Digital Future* identifies a growing divide, not between those who have and do not have access to the Internet, but between those who have the skills and capabilities to protect their data and those who do not.[30] In a highly complex and divided environment, powerful states, companies and collectives will continue to dominate, while individual users struggle to understand the implications of their online activities.

Cybersecurity is a booming sector that will require not only new technologies but also a steady influx of human talent.[31] The dearth of cybersecurity skills is already a major problem for many organizations. The tremendous growth of cybersecurity occupations poses pressing challenges in the fields of talent acquisition and education. The search for cyber talent will continue to create opportunities for non-state actors and companies, but also groups of hackers, to sell their services to the highest bidders. Education and training will remain essential to foster tomorrow's cybersecurity workforce.

A seminal report by the Internet Society on the future of the Internet notes that "new thinking, new approaches and new models are needed across the board, from Internet policy to addressing digital divides, from security approaches to economic regulations."[32] This book has provided a starting point for understanding some of the defining concepts and issues confronting contemporary cybersecurity. While cybersecurity has long been considered a topic for engineers and computer scientists, the last two decades have witnessed growing engagement from scholars and students in the social sciences and humanities. These disciplines are uniquely placed to make sense of the rapid changes and multiple dimensions of cybersecurity. From the individual to the organizational, national and international, the social sciences have a unique capacity to contribute to the analysis of cybersecurity.

Throughout the book, we have shown how the study of human and social relationships – specifically of politics and international relations – provides insights into cybersecurity. Despite the pessimism and technological determinism that mark some of the debate on the futures of cyberspace, the human and political nature of cyberspace also provides ground for optimism. Whatever the future of cybersecurity will be, understanding its core challenges and the role humans continue to play in shaping this domain is essential.

Notes

Introduction

1 Norbert Wiener, *Cybernetics: Or, Control and Communication in the Animal and the Machine* (New York: MIT Press, 1961).
2 John Arquilla and David Ronfeldt, "Cyberwar Is Coming!" *Comparative Strategy* 12/2 (1993): 141–65.
3 US Joint Chiefs of Staff, Joint Publication 3-12 (R), "Cyberspace Operations," Washington, DC, 2013.
4 Chris Demchak and Peter Dombrowski, "Cyber Westphalia: Asserting State Prerogatives in Cyberspace," *Georgetown Journal of International Affairs* (2013): 29–38.
5 William Gibson, *Neuromancer* (New York: Ace Books, 1984).
6 Craig Timberg, "The Real Story of How the Internet Became So Vulnerable," *Washington Post*, May 30, 2015, www.washingtonpost.com/sf/business/2015/05/30/net-of-insecurity-part-1.
7 AV-Test Institute, "Malware," www.av-test.org/en/statistics/malware.
8 Symantec, "Norton Cyber Security Insights Report Global Results 2017," www.symantec.com/content/dam/symantec/docs/about/2017-ncsir-global-results-en.pdf.
9 Jonathan Vanian, "Here's How Much Businesses Worldwide Will Spend on Cybersecurity by 2020," *Fortune*, October 12, 2016, fortune.com/2016/10/12/cybersecurity-global-spending.
10 Alina Sylyukh, "A Year After San Bernardino and Apple–FBI, Where Are We on Encryption?" National Pubic Radio, December 3, 2016, www.npr.org/sections/alltechconsidered/2016/12/03/504130977/a-year-after-san-bernardino-and-apple-fbi-where-are-we-on-encryption.
11 Aaron F. Brantly, "Innovation and Adaptation in Jihadist Digital Security," *Survival* 59/1 (2017): 79–102.

12 David E. Sanger and William J. Broad, "Pentagon Suggests Countering Devastating Cyberattacks with Nuclear Arms," *New York Times*, January 16, 2018, www.nytimes.com/2018/01/16/us/politics/pentagon-nuclear-review-cyberattack-trump.html.

1 The expanding scope of cybersecurity

1 Paul E. Ceruzzi, *Computing: A Concise History* (Cambridge, MA: MIT Press, 2012), 27; Graeme Philipson, "A Short History of Software," in *Management, Labour Process and Software Development: Reality Bites*, ed. Rowena Barrett (New York: Routledge, 2005), 14–15.
2 Ceruzzi, *Computing*, 6–7.
3 Loyd Searle, "The Bombsight War: Nordern vs. Sperry," *IEEE Spectrum* (1989): 60–4.
4 Ceruzzi, *Computing*, 33–7, 41.
5 Ceruzzi, *Computing*, 46–7.
6 Philipson, "A Short History of Software," 15–17.
7 Beverley Steitz, "A Brief Computer History," 2006, http://people.bu.edu/baws/brief%20computer%20history.html.
8 Philipson, "A Short History of Software," 18.
9 Ceruzzi, *Computing*, 58–63.
10 Brad A. Myers, "A Brief History of Human–Computer Interaction Technology," *ACM Interactions* (1998): 47–8.
11 Martin Campbell-Kelly, William Aspray, Nathan Ensmenger and Jeffrey R. Yost, *Computer: A History of the Information Machine* (New York: HarperCollins, 2017), 186–8.
12 Camille Ryan and Jamie M. Lewis, *Computer and Internet Use in the United States: 2015* (Washington, DC: US Census Bureau, 2017), 3.
13 Pew Research Center, "Global Computer Ownership," March 18, 2015, www.pewglobal.org/2015/03/19/internet-seen-as-positive-influence-on-education-but-negative-influence-on-morality-in-emerging-and-developing-nations/technology-report-15.
14 Derek S. Reveron, "An Introduction to National Security and Cyberspace," in *Cyberspace and National Security: Threats, Opportunities, and Power in a Virtual World*, ed. Derek S. Reveron (Washington, DC: Georgetown University Press, 2012), 7.
15 David C. Mowery and Timothy Simcoe, "Is the Internet a US Invention? An Economic and Technological History of Computer Networking," *Research Policy* 31 (2002): 1369–70.
16 Reveron, "An Introduction to National Security and Cyberspace," 7; Michael Warner, "Intelligence in Cyber – and Cyber in Intelligence," in *Understanding Cyber Conflict*, ed. George Perkovich and Ariel E. Levite (Washington, DC: Georgetown University Press, 2018), 24.
17 Peter W. Singer and Allan Friedman, *Cybersecurity and Cyberwar: What Everyone Needs to Know* (Oxford University Press, 2014), 16.
18 Mowery and Simcoe, "Is the Internet a US Invention?" 1373.

19 Mowery and Simcoe, "Is the Internet a US Invention?" 1373.
20 Barry M. Leiner, Vincton G. Cerf, David D. Clark, et al., "The Past and Future History of the Internet," *Communications of the ACM* 40/2 (1997): 104.
21 Mowery and Simcoe, "Is the Internet a US Invention?" 1372.
22 Ceruzzi, *Computing*, 123; Thomas Rid, *Rise of the Machines: A Cybernetic History* (London: Scribe, 2016), 181–94.
23 Gibson, *Neuromancer*, 69.
24 Mowery and Simcoe, "Is the Internet a US Invention?" 1375.
25 A supercomputer has a high level of performance compared to general-purpose computers in use at the time.
26 Mowery and Simcoe, "Is the Internet a US Invention?" 1371; Ceruzzi, *Computing*, 131.
27 Mowery and Simcoe, "Is the Internet a US Invention?" 1376–7.
28 Singer and Friedman, *Cybersecurity and Cyberwar*, 20.
29 Mowery and Simcoe, "Is the Internet a US Invention?" 1378; Edward Skoudis, "Evolutionary Trends in Cyberspace," in *Cyberpower and National Security*, ed. Kramer, Starr and Wentz, 149.
30 "A Brief History of Wi-Fi," *The Economist*, June 10, 2004, 26; Ceruzzi, *Computing*, 139–40.
31 Darcy DiNucci, "Fragmented Future," *Print* 53/4 (1999): 32.
32 Milton L. Mueller, *Networks and States: The Global Politics of Internet Governance* (Cambridge, MA: MIT Press, 2010), 1; Mary McEvoy Manjikian, "From Global Village to Virtual Battlespace: The Colonizing of the Internet and the Extension of Realpolitik," *International Studies Quarterly* 54/2 (2010): 381–401.
33 Skoudis, "Evolutionary Trends in Cyberspace," 156–7.
34 White House, National Security Decision Directive 145, "National Policy on Telecommunications and Automated Information Systems Security (U)," September 17, 1984, 1.
35 Clifford Stoll, *The Cuckoo's Egg: Tracking a Spy Through the Maze of Computer Espionage* (New York: Doubleday, 1989); Wayne Madsen, "Intelligence Agency Threats to Computer Security," *International Journal of Intelligence and CounterIntelligence* 6/4 (1993), 413–88; Clifford Stoll, "Stalking the Wily Hacker," *Communications of the ACM* 31/5 (1988): 484–97.
36 John Arquilla and David F. Ronfeldt, *Cyberwar is Coming!* (Santa Monica, CA: RAND, 1992); Eric Harnett, "Welcome to Hyperwar," *Bulletin of the Atomic Scientists* 48/7 (1992): 14–21.
37 Michael Warner, "Cybersecurity: A Pre-history," *Intelligence and National Security* 27/5 (2012): 781–99.
38 Fred Kaplan, *Dark Territory: The Secret History of Cyber War* (New York: Simon & Schuster, 2017), 57–79.
39 Vin McLellan, "Case of the Purloined Password," *New York Times*, July 26, 1981, F4.
40 British Broadcasting Corporation, "Bill Gates's Desert Island Playlist," January 31, 2016, www.bbc.co.uk/news/magazine-35442969.

41 For a short timeline of cybercrimes, see Symantec, "Cybercrime Time-Line," www.symantec.com/region/sg/homecomputing/library/cybercrime.html.
42 Andrew Murray, *Information Technology Law: The Law and Society* (Oxford University Press, 2016), 357–8.
43 Jessica Johnston, *Technological Turf Wars: A Case Study of the Computer Antivirus Industry* (Philadelphia: Temple University Press, 2009).
44 This test was first revealed by CNN, which has also made a video of the test available on its website. See Jeanne Meserve, "Mouse Click Could Plunge City into Darkness, Experts Say," *CNN*, September 27, 2007, http://edition.cnn.com/2007/US/09/27/power.at.risk/index.html.
45 White House, "The National Strategy to Secure Cyberspace," February 2003, ix.
46 For an overview of cybersecurity organizations and strategies in a number of developed countries, see: NATO Cooperative Cyber Defence Centre of Excellence, "National Cyber Security Organisation," https://ccdcoe.org/national-cyber-security-organisation.html.
47 Lev Grossman, "Attack of the Love Bug," *Time*, May 15, 2000, 37.
48 "Turk, Moroccan Nabbed in Huge Worm Case," *CNN*, August 26, 2005, http://money.cnn.com/2005/08/26/technology/worm_arrest; Skoudis, "Evolutionary Trends in Cyberspace," 167.
49 Mandiant Threat Intelligence Center, "APT1: Exposing One of China's Cyber Espionage Units," 2011, 20, www.fireeye.com/content/dam/fireeye-www/services/pdfs/mandiant-apt1-report.pdf.

2 What is cyberspace?

1 Kaplan, *Dark Territory*.
2 Tibi Puiu, "Your Smartphone Is Millions of Times More Powerful Than All of NASA's Combined Computing in 1969," October 12, 2015, www.zmescience.com/research/technology/smartphone-power-compared-to-apollo-432.
3 Rid, *Rise of the Machines*.
4 Gibson, *Neuromancer*.
5 Greg Conti and David Raymond, *On Cyber: Towards an Operational Art for Cyber Conflict* (n.p.: Kopidion Press, 2017).
6 Thomas C. Folsom, "Defining Cyberspace (Finding Real Virtue in the Place of Virtual Reality)," *Tulane Journal of Technology and Intellectual Property* 9/1 (2007): 75.
7 Kuehl cited in Franklin D. Kramer, "Cyberpower and National Security: Policy Recommendations for a Strategic Framework," in *Cyberpower and National Security*, ed. Franklin D. Kramer, Stuart H. Starr and Larry K. Wentz (Washington, DC: National Defense University Press, 2009), 4.
8 *Oxford Dictionaries*, s.v. "Electronic," https://en.oxforddictionaries.com/definition/electronic.

9 *Oxford Dictionaries*, s.v. "Electromagnetic Spectrum," https://en.oxforddictionaries.com/definition/electromagnetic_spectrum.
10 US Joint Chiefs of Staff, Joint Publication 3-12 (R), "Cyberspace Operations."
11 Brandon Valeriano and Ryan C. Maness, *Cyber War Versus Cyber Realities: Cyber Conflict in the International System* (New York: Oxford University Press, 2015); Lucas Kello, *The Virtual Weapon and International Order* (New Haven, CT: Yale University Press, 2017); Alexander Klimburg, *The Darkening: The War for Cyberspace* (New York: Penguin Books, 2017).
12 Amy Nordrum, "Popular Internet of Things Forecast of 50 Billion Devices by 2020 Is Outdated," *IEEE Spectrum*, August 18, 2016, https://spectrum.ieee.org/tech-talk/telecom/internet/popular-internet-of-things-forecast-of-50-billion-devices-by-2020-is-outdated.
13 Om Malik, "Gigaom | 100G, 200G, 400G: Internet's Core Is Getting Fatter to Meet Our Tech Planet's Bandwidth Demand," August 16, 2013, https://gigaom.com/2013/08/16/100g-200g-400g-internets-core-is-getting-fatter-to-meet-our-tech-planets-bandwidth-demand.
14 Ramakrishnan Durairajan, Paul Barford, Joel Sommers and Walter Willinger, *InterTubes* (New York: ACM Press, 2015), 565–78.
15 Tom Parfitt, "Georgian Woman Cuts Off Web Access to Whole of Armenia," *Guardian*, April 6, 2011, www.theguardian.com/world/2011/apr/06/georgian-woman-cuts-web-access.
16 Maddie Stone, "What Would Happen if a Massive Solar Storm Hit the Earth?" August 20, 2015, https://gizmodo.com/what-would-happen-if-a-massive-solar-storm-hit-the-eart-1724650105.
17 David Kravets, "It's Official: Sharks No Longer a Threat to Subsea Internet Cables," *ArsTechnica*, July 10, 2015, https://arstechnica.com/tech-policy/2015/07/its-official-sharks-no-longer-a-threat-to-subsea-internet-cables.
18 Louis Matsakis, "What Would Really Happen if Russia Attacked Undersea Internet Cables," *Wired*, January 15, 2018, www.wired.com/story/russia-undersea-internet-cables.
19 Asma Ali Zain, "Cable Damage Hits One Million Internet Users in UAE," *Khaleej Times*, February 4, 2008, www.khaleejtimes.com/nation/general/cable-damage-hits-one-million-internet-users-in-uae.
20 "Packet Switching History," www.livinginternet.com/i/iw_packet_inv.htm.
21 Lawrence G. Roberts, "The Evolution of Packet Switching," *Proceedings of the IEEE* 66/11 (1978): 1307–13.
22 Katie Hafner and Matthew Lyon, *Where Wizards Stay Up Late: The Origins of the Internet* (New York: Simon & Schuster, 1996).
23 Vinton G. Cerf and Robert E. Kahn, "A Protocol for Packet Network Intercommunication," *Data Communications of the IEEE Communications Society* 22/5 (1974): 1–13.
24 Matthew G. Naugle, *Network Protocols* (New York: McGraw-Hill Professional, 1999).

25 "Exploiting Heartbleed," Infosec Institute, April 18, 2014, http://resources.infosecinstitute.com/exploiting-heartbleed.
26 Brian Krebs, "AshleyMadison Hack – Krebs on Security," September 23, 2015, https://krebsonsecurity.com/tag/ashleymadison-hack.
27 Adrian Bridgewater, "20% of Cyber-Attacks Attributed to Conficker Worm," *SCMagazine*, December 7, 2015, www.scmagazineuk.com/news/20-of-cyber-attacks-attributed-to-conficker-worm/article/535571.
28 Brett Hawkins, "Case Study: The Home Depot Data Breach," SANS Institute InfoSec Reading Room, January 2015, www.sans.org/reading-room/whitepapers/breaches/case-study-home-depot-data-breach-36367; Xiaokui Shu, Ke Tian, Andrew Ciambrone and Danfeng Yao, "Breaking the Target: An Analysis of Target Data Breach and Lessons Learned," *arXiv* (January 2017): 1–10.
29 Ron Ross, Michael McEvilley and Janey Carrier Oren, *Systems Security Engineering* (Gaithersburg, MD: National Institute of Standards and Technology, 2016).
30 Dan Mayer, "Ratio of Bugs Per Line of Code," November 10, 2012, www.mayerdan.com/ruby/2012/11/11/bugs-per-line-of-code-ratio.
31 Lance Ulanoff, "Ford Ready to Innovate, but Not at the Expense of Customer Needs," *Mashable*, May 21, 2015, https://mashable.com/2016/05/31/mark-fields-ford-codecon; David Flynn, "New Mercedes-Benz E-Class Has More Lines of Computer Code Than an Airbus A380," *Australian Business Traveller*, August 30, 2016, www.ausbt.com.au/new-mercedes-benz-e-class-has-more-lines-of-computer-code-than-an-airbus-a380.
32 Ben Collins and Joseph Cox, "Jenna Abrams, Russia's Clown Troll Princess, Duped the Mainstream Media and the World," *Daily Beast*, November 2, 2017, www.thedailybeast.com/jenna-abrams-russias-clown-troll-princess-duped-the-mainstream-media-and-the-world.
33 Ned Kock, "E-Collaboration and E-Commerce in Virtual Worlds," *International Journal of E-Collaboration* 4/3 (2008): 1–13.
34 Aaron F. Brantly, "The Cyber Losers," *Democracy and Security* 10/2 (2014): 132–55.
35 Paul Syverson, "A Peel of Onion," *Proceedings of the 27th Annual Computer Security Applications Conference ACM* (2011): 123–37.
36 Aaron F. Brantly, *The Decision to Attack: Military and Intelligence Cyber Decision-Making* (Athens: University of Georgia Press, 2016).
37 A plausibly deniable operation that pretends to originate from a third party.
38 Marc Goodman, *Future Crimes: Everything Is Connected, Everyone Is Vulnerable and What We Can Do About It* (New York: Doubleday, 2015); Brantly, "Innovation and Adaptation in Jihadist Digital Security."
39 Steve Durbin, "Insiders Are Today's Biggest Security Threat," *Recode*, May 24, 2016, www.recode.net/2016/5/24/11756584/cyber-attack-data-breach-insider-threat-steve-durbin.
40 Fran Howarth, "The Role of Human Error in Successful Security Attacks,"

SecurityIntelligence, September 2, 2014, https://securityintelligence.com/the-role-of-human-error-in-successful-security-attacks.

3 Governing cyberspace

1. Château de Bossey, "Report on the Working Group on Internet Governance," June 2005, www.wgig.org/docs/WGIGREPORT.pdf.
2. Laura DeNardis, *Protocol Politics: The Globalization of Internet Governance* (Cambridge, MA: MIT Press, 2009).
3. Steven Levy, *Hackers: Heroes of the Computer Revolution* (Sebastopol, CA: O'Reilly Media, 2010), 7–10.
4. Janet Abbate, *Inventing the Internet* (Cambridge, MA: MIT Press 2000); Hafner and Lyon, *Where Wizards Stay Up Late*.
5. Network Working Group, "Request for Comments: 2, [unknown title]," n.d., https://tools.ietf.org/html/rfc2, and "Request for Comments: 3, Documentation Conventions," April 1969, https://tools.ietf.org/html/rfc3.
6. Sandra Braman, "The Interpenetration of Technical and Legal Decision-Making for the Internet," *Information, Communication & Society* 13/3 (2010): 309–24.
7. Network Working Group, "Request for Comments: 322, Well Known Socket Numbers," March 26, 1972, https://tools.ietf.org/html/rfc322.
8. Network Working Group, "Request for Comments: 1083, IAB Official Protocol Standards," December 1998, https://tools.ietf.org/html/rfc1083.
9. Jovan Kurbalija, *An Introduction to Internet Governance*, 7th edn. (Geneva: DiploFoundation, 2016).
10. US Government, "Improvement of Technical Management of Internet Names and Addresses; Proposed Rule," in *Federal Register*, vol. LXIII (Washington, DC: Office of the Federal Rgister, 1998).
11. Laura DeNardis, *The Global War for Internet Governance* (New Haven, CT: Yale University Press, 2014).
12. Ryan Singel, "Pakistan's Accidental YouTube Re-Routing Exposes Trust Flaw in Net," *Wired*, February 25, 2008, www.wired.com/2008/02/pakistans-accid.
13. Arielle Pardes, "What Is GDPR and Why Should You Care?" *Wired*, May 24, 2018, www.wired.com/story/how-gdpr-affects-you.
14. Bill Marczak and John Scott-Railton, "Keep Calm and (Don't) Enable Macros: A New Threat Actor Targets UAE Dissidents – the Citizen Lab," Citizen Lab, May 29, 2016, https://citizenlab.ca/2016/05/stealth-falcon.
15. Fergus Hanson, *Revolution @State: The Spread of EDiplomacy* (Sydney: Lowy Institute for International Affairs, 2012).
16. Sue Pleming, "U.S. State Department Speaks to Twitter Over Iran," Reuters, June 16, 2009.
17. Netmundial, "NetMundial Multistakeholder Statement," Sao Paulo, Brazil, 2014.

18 Jeremy Malcolm, "Internet Governance and the NETmundial Initiative: A Flawed Attempt at Turning Words into Action," Electronic Frontier Foundation, August 28, 2014, www.eff.org/deeplinks/2014/08/internet-governance-and-netmundial-initiative-flawed-attempt-turning-words-action.
19 Robert O. Keohane and Joseph S. Nye, *Power and Interdependence: World Politics in Transition* (Boston: Little, Brown, 1977).
20 Alexander Wendt, "Anarchy Is What States Make of It," *International Organization* 46/2 (1992): 391–425.
21 Mark Raymond and Laura DeNardis, "Multistakeholderism: Anatomy of an Inchoate Global Institution," *International Theory* 7/3 (2015): 572–616.
22 Adam Segal, "Holding the Multistakeholder Line at the ITU," Council on Foreign Relations, October 21, 2014, www.cfr.org/report/holding-multistakeholder-line-itu.
23 Milton Mueller, *Will the Internet Fragment? Sovereignty, Globalization and Cyberspace* (Malden, MA: Polity, 2017).
24 Bob Price, "Portugal Hints at What the American Internet Could Eventually Look Like Without Net Neutrality," *Business Insider*, December 14, 2017, www.businessinsider.com/net-neutrality-portugal-how-american-internet-could-look-fcc-2017-11.
25 Melissa Locker, "John Oliver Is Calling on You to Save Net Neutrality, Again," *Time*, May 8, 2017, http://time.com/4770205/john-oliver-fcc-net-neutrality.
26 Video: Burger King, "Whopper Neutrality," January 24, 2018, www.youtube.com/watch?v=ltzy5vRmN8Q.
27 Council of Europe, Convention on Cybercrime, Budapest, November 23, 2001, www.coe.int/en/web/conventions/full-list/-/conventions/rms/0900001680081561.
28 Alex Grigsby, "The UN GGE on Cybersecurity: What Is the UN's Role?" Council on Foreign Relations, April 15, 2015, www.cfr.org/blog/un-gge-cybersecurity-what-uns-role.
29 Michael N. Schmitt, *Tallinn Manual on the International Law Applicable to Cyber Warfare: Prepared by the International Group of Experts at the Invitation of the NATO Cooperative Cyber Defence Centre of Excellence* (Cambridge University Press, 2013); Michael N. Schmitt and Liis Vihul, *Tallinn Manual 2.0 on the International Law Applicable to Cyber Operations* (Cambridge University Press, 2017).
30 Heather Harrison Dinniss, *Cyber Warfare and the Laws of War* (New York: Cambridge University Press, 2012).
31 Aaron F. Brantly, "The Most Governed Ungoverned Space: Legal and Policy Constraints on Military Operations in Cyberspace," *SAIS Review of International Affairs* 36/2 (2016): 29–39.
32 Catherine Lotrionte, "A Better Defense: Examining the United States' New Norms-Based Approach to Cyber Deterrence," *Georgetown Journal of International Affairs* (2016): 75–88.

4 Cyber capabilities and insecurity

1. US Joint Chiefs of Staff, Joint Publication 3-12 (R), "Cyberspace Operations."
2. Stanley Sandler, *World War II in the Pacific: An Encyclopedia* (New York: Routledge, 2015).
3. Michael Dobbs, *One Minute to Midnight: Kennedy, Khrushchev, and Castro on the Brink of Nuclear War* (New York: Vintage Books, 2009).
4. Homer, *The Iliad & the Odyssey* (New York: Barnes & Noble Books, 2008).
5. Peiter Mudge Zatko, "If You Don't Like the Game, Hack the Playbook," presentation at DARPA Cyber Colloquium, November 7, 2011, Arlington, VA.
6. Aaron F. Brantly, "Public Health and Epidemiological Approaches to National Cybersecurity: A Baseline Comparison," in *US National Cybersecurity: International Politics, Concepts and Organization*, ed. Damien Van Puyvelde and Aaron F. Brantly (New York: Routledge, 2017), 91–109.
7. IBM Global Technology Services, "IBM Security Services 2014 Cyber Security Intelligence Index," https://media.scmagazine.com/documents/82/ibm_cyber_security_intelligenc_20450.pdf.
8. Author conversation with Vice Admiral Nancy A. Norton, March 2018.
9. Dan Mayer, "Ratio of Bugs Per Line of Code," Mayerdan, November 10, 2012, www.mayerdan.com/ruby/2012/11/11/bugs-per-line-of-code-ratio.
10. Dick O'Brien, "ISTR Ransomware 2017," *Internet Security Threat Report*, July 2017, www.symantec.com/content/dam/symantec/docs/security-center/white-papers/istr-ransomware-2017-en.pdf.
11. O'Brien, "ISTR Ransomware 2017."
12. National Audit Office, "Investigation: WannaCry Cyber Attack and the NHS," October 27, 2017, www.nao.org.uk/report/investigation-wannacry-cyber-attack-and-the-nhs.
13. Alejandro Calleja and Juan Caballero, *A Look Into 30 Years of Malware Development from a Software Metrics Perspective* (Cham: Springer, 2016), 325–45.
14. Brett Stone-Gross, Ryan Abman, Richard A. Kemmerer, Christopher Kruegel, Douglas G. Steigerwald and Giovanni Vigna, "The Underground Economy of Fake Antivirus Software," in *Economics of Information Security and Privacy III*, ed. Bruce Schneier (New York: Springer, 2013), 55–78.
15. Brian Krebs, "Shadowy Russian Firm Seen as Conduit for Cybercrime," *Washington Post*, October 13, 2007, A15.
16. Rhys Blakely, Jonathan Richards and Tony Halpin, "Cybergang Raises Fear of New Crime Wave," *The Times*, November 10, 2007, p. 13.
17. David Bizeul, "Russian Business Network Study," 2007, www.bizeul.org/files/RBN_study.pdf.

18 John Markoff, "Before the Gunfire, Cyberattacks," *New York Times*, August 13, 2008, A1.
19 Bizeul, "Russian Business Network Study."
20 Shadow Server Foundation, "AS40989 RBN as RBusiness Network," www.shadowserver.org/wiki/uploads/Information/RBN-AS40989.pdf.
21 John Leyden, "Bulletproof Hosts Stay Online by Operating Out of Disputed Backwaters," *Register*, October 5, 2017, www.theregister.co.uk/2017/10/05/bulletproof_hosting.
22 David E. Sanger, David Barboza and Nicole Perlroth, "China's Army Is Seen as Tied to Hacking Against U.S.," *New York Times*, February 19, 2013, A1.
23 Mandiant Threat Intelligence Center, "APT1."
24 Mandiant Threat Intelligence Center, "APT1."
25 Mandiant Threat Intelligence Center, "APT1," 8.
26 Mandiant Threat Intelligence Center, "APT1," 3.
27 Mandiant Threat Intelligence Center, "APT1," 2.
28 Giora Engel, "Deconstructing the Cyber Kill Chain," *DarkReading*, November 18, 2014, www.darkreading.com/attacks-breaches/deconstructing-the-cyber-kill-chain/a/d-id/1317542; Lockheed Martin, "The Cyber Kill Chain," www.lockheedmartin.com/en-us/capabilities/cyber/cyber-kill-chain.html.
29 Sydney J. Freedberg Jr., "Cyber Command Lawyer Praises Stuxnet, Disses Chinese Cyber Stance," *Breaking Defense*, March 12, 2012, https://breakingdefense.com/2012/03/cyber-command-lawyer-praises-stuxnet-disses-chinese-cyber-stanc.
30 Kim Zetter, *Countdown to Zero Day: Stuxnet and the Launch of the World's First Digital Weapon* (New York: Broadway Books, 2014).
31 Jason Healey, *A Fierce Domain: Conflict in Cyberspace, 1986 to 2012* (Arlington, VA: Cyber Conflict Studies Association, 2013).
32 Aaron F. Brantly, Nerea M. Cal and Devlin P. Winkelstein, *Defending the Borderland: Ukrainian Military Experiences with IO, Cyber, and EW* (West Point, NY: US Army Cyber Institute, 2017), www.dtic.mil/dtic/tr/fulltext/u2/1046052.pdf.
33 US Department of Justice, "Fugitive Computer Hacker Arrested in North Carolina," February 15, 1995, www.justice.gov/opa/pr/Pre_96/February95/89.txt.html.
34 Chris Williams, "Today the Web Was Broken by Countless Hacked Devices – Your 60-Second Summary," *Register*, October 21, 2016, www.theregister.co.uk/2016/10/21/dyn_dns_ddos_explained.
35 Mandiant Threat Intelligence Center, "APT1."
36 Stoll, *The Cuckoo's Egg*.
37 Herbert Lin, "Operational Considerations in Cyber Attack and Cyber Exploitation," in *Cyberspace and National Security*, ed. Reveron, 37–56.
38 David E. Sanger, *The Perfect Weapon: War, Sabotage, and Fear in the Cyber Age* (New York: Crown Publishers, 2018).

39 Aaron F. Brantly, "The Violence of Hacking: State Violence and Cyberspace," *Cyber Defense Review* 2/1 (2017): 1–19.
40 Richard A. Clarke and Robert K. Knake, *Cyber War: The Next Threat to National Security and What to Do About It* (New York: Ecco, 2010).
41 Kello, *The Virtual Weapon and International Order*; Thomas Rid, "Cyber War Will Not Take Place," *Journal of Strategic Studies* 35/1 (2012): 5–32; Erik Gartzke and Jon R. Lindsay, "Weaving Tangled Webs: Offense, Defense, and Deception in Cyberspace," *Security Studies* 24/2 (2015): 316–48.
42 Richard Forno and Anupam Joshi, "How U.S. 'Cyber Bombs' Against Terrorists Really Work," *Scientific American*, May 13, 2016, www.scientificamerican.com/article/how-u-s-cyber-bombs-against-terroristsreally-work.

5 National cybersecurity and strategy

1 Damien Van Puyvelde and Aaron F. Brantly (eds.), *US National Cybersecurity: International Politics, Concepts and Organization* (Abingdon: Routledge, 2017), 2–3.
2 See Brandon Valeriano, Benjamin Jensen and Ryan C. Maness, *Cyber Strategy: The Evolving Character of Power and Coercion* (Oxford University Press, 2018).
3 For a classic definition, see Arnold Wolfers, "National Security as an Ambiguous Symbol," *Political Science Quarterly* 67/4 (1952): 483–4.
4 Alan G. Stolberg, "Crafting National Interests in the 21st Century," in *U.S. Army War College Guide to National Security Issues*, vol. II: *National Security Policy and Strategy*, ed. J. Boone Bartholomees Jr. (Carlisle, PA: Strategic Studies Institute, 2012), 13–14.
5 Joseph S. Nye, "Get Smart: Combining Hard and Soft Power," *Foreign Affairs* 88/4 (2009): 160–3.
6 John Sheldon, "The Rise of Cyberpower," in *Strategy in the Contemporary World*, ed. John Baylis, James J. Wirtz and Colin S. Gray (Oxford University Press, 2013), 306.
7 Daniel T. Kuehl, "From Cyberspace to Cyberpower: Defining the Problem," in *Cyberpower and National Security*, ed. Kramer, Starr and Wentz, 39.
8 National Telecommunications and Information Administration, "Initial Estimates Show Digital Economy Accounted for 6.5 Percent of GDP in 2016," March 15, 2018, www.ntia.doc.gov/blog/2018/initial-estimates-show-digital-economy-accounted-65-percent-gdp-2016; Xinhua, "China's Digital Economy Surges 18.9%, Drives Growth," *China Daily*, July 20, 2017, www.chinadaily.com.cn/business/2017-07/20/content_30179729.htm.
9 Joseph S. Nye, "Hard, Soft, and Smart Power," in *The Oxford Handbook of Modern Diplomacy*, ed. Andrew F. Cooper, Jorge Heine and Ramesh Thakur (Oxford University Press, 2013).

10 Kramer, Starr and Wentz (eds.), *Cyberpower and National Security*, xvi.
11 Kuehl, "From Cyberspace to Cyberpower: Defining the Problem," 41–2.
12 W. Alexander Vacca, "Military Culture and Cyber Security," *Survival* 53/6 (2011): 159.
13 James J. Wirtz, "Cyber War and Strategic Culture: The Russian Integration of Cyber Power into Grand Strategy," in *Cyber War in Perspective: Russian Aggression against Ukraine*, ed. Kenneth Geers (Tallinn: NATO Cooperative Cyber Defence Centre of Excellence, 2015), 30.
14 Alastair Iain Johnston, "Thinking about Strategic Culture," *International Security* 19/4 (1995): 32–64; R. Uz Zaman, "Strategic Culture: A 'Cultural' Understanding of War," *Comparative Strategy* 28/1 (2009): 82–3.
15 Nigel Inkster, *China's Cyber Power* (Abingdon: Routledge, 2016).
16 Greg Austin, *Cyber Policy in China* (New York: Polity, 2014).
17 Jon R. Lindsay, "Introduction. China and Cybersecurity: Controversy and Context," in *China and Cybersecurity: Espionage, Strategy, and Politics in the Digital Domain*, ed. Jon R. Lindsay, Tai Ming Cheung and Derek S. Reveron (Oxford University Press, 2015), 1–2.
18 Kathrin Hikle, "How China Polices the Internet," *Financial Times*, July 25, 2009, 2.
19 Lindsay, "Introduction. China and Cybersecurity," 10–11.
20 Chris Demchak and Peter Dombrowski, "Rise of a Cybered Westphalian Age," *Strategic Studies Quarterly* 5/1 (2011): 45.
21 Gary King, Jennifer Pan and Margaret E. Roberts, "How Censorship in China Allows Government Criticism but Silences Collective Expression," *American Political Science Review* 107/2 (2013): 326–43.
22 Valeriano, Jensen and Maness, *Cyber Strategy*, 146.
23 Singer and Friedman, *Cybersecurity and Cyberwar*, 139.
24 Zhuge Jianwei, Gu Lion, Duan Haixin and Taylor Roberts, "Investigating the Chinese Online Underground Economy," in *China and Cybersecurity*, ed. Lindsay, Cheung and Reveron, 87–120.
25 Singer and Friedman, *Cybersecurity and Cyberwar*, 142; Valeriano, Jensen and Maness, *Cyber Strategy*, 144–5.
26 Timothy L. Thomas, "Nation-State Cyber Strategies: Examples from China and Russia," in *Cyberpower and National Security*, ed. Kramer, Starr and Wentz, 468–75.
27 David E. Sanger and Nicole Perlroth, "N.S.A. Breached Chinese Servers Seen as Security Threat," *New York Times*, March 22, 2014.
28 Lindsay, "Introduction. China and Cybersecurity," 17.
29 Valeriano, Jensen and Maness, *Cyber Strategy*, 146.
30 Lindsay, "Introduction. China and Cybersecurity," 7.
31 Ronald J. Deibert, *Black Code: Surveillance, Privacy, and the Dark Side of the Internet* (Toronto: McClelland & Stewart, 2013), 21–6.
32 Valeriano, Jensen and Maness, *Cyber Strategy*, 150.

33 Robert Sheldon and Joe McReynolds, "Civil–Military Integration and Cybersecurity: A Study of Chinese Information Warfare Militias," in *China and Cybersecurity*, ed. Lindsay, Cheung and Reveron, 190; Nigel Inkster, "The Chinese Intelligence Agencies: Evolution and Empowerment," in *China and Cybersecurity*, ed. Lindsay, Cheung and Reveron, 35–7.
34 Dmitry (Dima) Adamsky, "From Moscow with Coercion: Russian Deterrence Theory and Strategic Culture," *Journal of Strategic Studies* 41/1–2 (2018): 41–2.
35 Andrei Soldatov and Irina Borogan, *The Red Web: The Struggle Between Russia's Digital Dictators and the New Online Revolutionaries* (New York: Public Affairs, 2015).
36 Thomas, "Nation-State Cyber Strategies: Examples from China and Russia," 483–4.
37 Tracy Staeder, "Why Russia is Building Its Own Internet," *IEEE Spectrum*, January 17, 2018, https://spectrum.ieee.org/tech-talk/telecom/internet/could-russia-really-build-its-own-alternate-internet.
38 Sergey Medvedev, "Data Protection in the Russian Federation: Overview," *Thomson Reuters Practical Law*, December 1, 2017.
39 Nicholas Gvodsev, "The Bear Goes Digital: Russia and its Cyber Capabilities," in *Cyberspace and National Security*, ed. Reveron, 175.
40 Thomas, "Nation-State Cyber Strategies: Examples from China and Russia," 476; Gvodsev, "The Bear Goes Digital," 175.
41 Timothy L. Thomas, "Russian Reflexive Control, Theory and the Military," *Journal of Slavic Military Studies* 17/2 (2004): 237.
42 Wirtz, "Cyber War and Strategic Culture," 35.
43 Valeriano, Jensen and Maness, *Cyber Strategy*, 110.
44 Office of the Director of National Intelligence, "Background to 'Assessing Russian Activities and Intentions in Recent US Elections': The Analytic Process and Cyber Incident Attribution," January 6, 2017.
45 Office of the Director of National Intelligence, Background to "Assessing Russian Activities and Intentions in Recent US Elections," 5.
46 Matthew Rosenberg, Charlie Savage and Michael Wines, "Russia at Work on U.S. Midterms, Spy Chiefs Warn," *New York Times*, February 14, 2018, A1.
47 Valeriano, Jensen and Maness, *Cyber Strategy*, 131.
48 Jean-Baptiste Jeangène Vilmer, "Successfully Countering Russian Electoral Interference: 15 Lessons Learned from the Macron Leaks," CSIS Brief, 2018, 2–4.
49 Jeangène Vilmer, "Successfully Countering Russian Electoral Interference."
50 Gvodsev, "The Bear Goes Digital," 179.
51 Julie Anderson, "The Chekist Takeover of the Russian State," *International Journal of Intelligence and CounterIntelligence* 19/2 (2006): 247–50.
52 Sergei Modsetov cited in Gvodsev, "The Bear Goes Digital," 176.

53. Jack Jarmon and Pano Yannakogeorgos, *The Cyber Threat and Globalization: The Impact on U.S. National and International Security* (New York: Rowman and Littlefield, 2018), 133–7.
54. Gvodsev, "The Bear Goes Digital," 180–1.
55. White House, Presidential Decision Directive/NSC-63, "Critical Infrastructure Protection," May 22, 1998.
56. See, for example, White House, "National Strategy to Secure Cyberspace," 2003; "National Defense Strategy of the United States of America," March 2005, 16; "National Military Strategy for Cyberspace Operations," December 2006; "National Defense Strategy of the United States of America," June 2008, 1; "National Defense Strategy of the United States of America," 2011; "National Security Strategy of the United States of America," December 2017, 12–13; "National Defense Strategy of the United States of America: Sharpening the American Military's Competitive Edge," 2018, 6.
57. US Department of Defense, "The Department of Defense Cyber Strategy," April 2015, 15, 27.
58. Richard J. Harknett, "United States Cyber Command's New Vision: Why It Matters," *Lawfare*, March 23, 2018, www.lawfareblog.com/united-states-cyber-commands-new-vision-what-it-entails-and-why-it-matters.
59. Scott Jasper, "U.S. Cyber Threat Intelligence Sharing Frameworks," *International Journal of Intelligence and CounterIntelligence* 30/1 (2016): 53–65.
60. Damien Van Puyvelde, "From Information to Cybersecurity: Bridging the Public–Private Divide," in *US National Cybersecurity*, ed. Van Puyvelde and Brantly, 177–94.
61. White House, "Presidential Policy Directive 41 – United States Cyber Incident Coordination," July 26, 2016.
62. Valeriano, Jensen and Maness, *Cyber Strategy*, 195.
63. Valeriano, Jensen and Maness, *Cyber Strategy*, 179.
64. US Cyber Command, "Achieve and Maintain Cyberspace Superiority: Command Vision for US Cyber Command," 2018.
65. UK Government, "National Cyber Security Strategy 2016 to 2021"; Ministère de la Défense, "Pacte Défense Cyber," February 7, 2014; Saïd Haddad, "Le Cyberespace ou la construction d'un 'champ de confrontation à part entière'," in *La Cyberdéfense. Politique de l'espace numérique*, ed. Amaël Cattaruzza, Didier Danet and Stéphane Taillat (Paris: Armand Collin, 2018), 44–51.
66. See, for example: White House, Remarks by President Obama and President Park of the Republic of Korea in Joint Press Conference, October 16, 2015, https://obamawhitehouse.archives.gov/the-press-office/2015/10/16/remarks-president-obama-and-president-park-republic-korea-joint-press.
67. NATO Cooperative Cyber Defence Centre of Excellence, "Cyber Security Strategy Documents," October 18, 2018, https://ccdcoe.org/cyber-security-strategy-documents.html and "Incyder: International Cyber Developments Review," https://ccdcoe.org/incyder.html.

68 Demchak and Dombrowski, "Rise of a Cybered Westphalian Age," 35.
69 Brian Mazanec, "The Outlook for Constraining International Norms for Offensive Cyber Operations," in *US National Cybersecurity*, ed. Van Puyvelde and Brantly, 40–54.
70 Jon R. Lindsay and Derek S. Reveron, "Conclusion: The Rise of China and the Future of Cybersecurity," in *China and Cybersecurity*, ed. Lindsay, Cheung and Reveron, 346–7; Jarmon and Yannakogeorgos, *The Cyber Threat and Globalization*, 98.
71 John Rollins, "U.S.–China Cyber Agreement," *CRS Insight*, October 16, 2016, https://fas.org/sgp/crs/row/IN10376.pdf. For an analysis, see Gary Brown and Christopher D. Yung, "Evaluating the US–China Cybersecurity Agreement, Part 1: The US Approach to Cyberspace," *Diplomat*, January 19, 2017, https://thediplomat.com/2017/01/evaluating-the-us-china-cybersecurity-agreement-part-1-the-us-approach-to-cyberspace.

6 Cyber war

1 Michael Schmitt, "Classification of Cyber Conflict," *Journal of Conflict & Security Law* 17/2 (2012): 245.
2 Harold Hongju Koh, "International Law in Cyberspace," Keynote Address at the US Cyber Command Inter-Agency Legal Conference, September 18, 2002.
3 Singer and Friedman, *Cybersecurity and Cyberwar*, 120.
4 See, for example: Mike McConnell, "To Win the Cyber-war, Look to the Cold War," *Washington Post*, February 28, 2010.
5 Colin Gray, *Another Bloody Century: Future Warfare* (London: Orion Books, 2006), 37.
6 Karl von Clausewitz, *On War* (New York: Random House, 1943), 3.
7 Gray, *Another Bloody Century*, 105.
8 Arquilla and Ronfeldt, "Cyber War is Coming!" 144.
9 Arquilla and Ronfeldt, "Cyber War is Coming!" 147.
10 See for example, Donald Rumsfeld, "Transforming the Military," *Foreign Affairs* 81/3 (2002): 20–32; John Ferris, "A New American Way of War? C4ISR, Intelligence and Information Operations in Operation 'Iraqi Freedom': A Provisional Assessment," *Intelligence and National Security* 81/3 (2003): 155–74; Eliot Cohen, "Changes and Transformation in Military Affairs," *Journal of Strategic Studies* 27/3 (2004): 395–407.
11 See, for example, David Betz, "The Mystique of 'Cyberwar' and the Strategic Latency of Networked Social Movements," *Strategic Insights* 10 (2011): 61–76; Martin C. Libicki, "Why Cyber War Will Not and Should Not Have its Grand Strategist," *Strategic Studies Quarterly* 8/1 (2014): 30.
12 Damien McGuinness, "How a Cyber Attack Transformed Estonia," BBC, April 27, 2017, www.bbc.co.uk/news/39655415.

13 John Arquilla, "Cyberwar Is Already Upon Us: But Can it Be Controlled?" *Foreign Policy* 192 (2012), 84.
14 David A. Fulghum and Robert Wall, "Israel Shows Electronic Prowess," *Aviation Week & Space Technology*, November 25, 2007.
15 Gary McGraw, "Cyber War Is Inevitable (Unless We Build Security In)," *Journal of Strategic Studies* 36/1 (2013): 112.
16 Clarke and Knake, *Cyber War*, 64–8.
17 US House of Representatives, Committee on Science, Space, and Technology Subcommittee on Technology and Competitiveness, Hearing: Computer Security, Statement of Winn Schwartau, 102nd Congress, 1st sess., June 27, 1991, 10; Neil Munro, "The Pentagon's New Nightmare: An Electronic Pearl Harbor," *Washington Post*, July 16, 1995, C3.
18 US Department of Defense, Remarks by Secretary Panetta on Cybersecurity to the Business Executives for National Security, New York City, October 11, 2012, http://archive.defense.gov/transcripts/transcript.aspx?transcriptid=5136.
19 See, for example: Gordon Corera, "If 2017 Could Be Described as 'Cyber-geddon', What Will 2018 Bring?" BBC, 30 December 2017, www.bbc.co.uk/news/technology-42338716; video: Kevin Mandia, "FireEye CEO Says Midterm Elections Are Vulnerable to a Russian Hack," *Bloomberg*, February 20, 2018, www.bloomberg.com/news/videos/2018-02-20/fireeye-ceo-says-midterm-elections-vulnerable-to-russia-hack-video. For a media critique, see: Ryan Singel, "Richard Clarke's *Cyber War*: File Under Fiction," *Wired*, April 22, 2010, www.wired.com/2010/04/cyberwar-richard-clarke.
20 Rid, "Cyber War Will Not Take Place"; Rid, *Cyber War Will Not Take Place* (London: Hurst, 2013).
21 Rid, "Cyber War Will Not Take Place," 6.
22 Rid, "Cyber War Will Not Take Place," 10.
23 Rid, "Cyber War Will Not Take Place," 15–27.
24 Kim Zetter, "How Digital Detectives Deciphered Stuxnet, The Most Menacing Malware in History," *Wired*, July 11, 2011.
25 Ralph Langner, "To Kill a Centrifuge: A Technical Analysis of What Stuxnet's Creators Tried to Achieve," November 2013, www.langner.com/wp-content/uploads/2017/03/to-kill-a-centrifuge.pdf.
26 Ellen Nakashima and Joby Warrick, "Stuxnet Was Work of U.S. and Israel Experts, Officials Say," *Washington Post*, June 2, 2012.
27 McGraw, "Cyber War is Inevitable (Unless We Build Security In)," 109–19; Timothy J. Junio, "How Probable is Cyber War? Bringing IR Theory Back in to the Cyber Conflict Debate," *Journal of Strategic Studies* 36/1 (2013): 125–6.
28 John Stone, "Cyber War *Will* Take Place!" *Journal of Strategic Studies* 36/1 (2013): 103.
29 Valeriano and Maness, *Cyber War Versus Cyber Realities*, 29.
30 Betz, "The Mystique of 'Cyberwar,'" 65.

31 Myriam Dunn Cavelty, *Cyber-Security and Threat Politics: US Efforts to Secure the Information Age* (London: Routledge, 2008), 1–7.
32 Sheldon, "The Rise of Cyberpower," 306.
33 Valeriano and Maness, *Cyber War versus Cyber Realities*, 5. See also Chris C. Demchak, *Wars of Disruption and Resilience: Cybered Conflict, Power, and National Security* (Athens: University of Georgia Press, 2011).
34 Brandon Valeriano and Ryan Maness, "The Fog of CyberWar," *Foreign Affairs*, November 21, 2012, www.foreignaffairs.com/articles/2012-11-21/fog-cyberwar.
35 Valeriano and Maness, *Cyber War versus Cyber Realities*, 16; Jon R. Lindsay, "Stuxnet and the Limits of Cyber Warfare," *Security Studies* 22/3 (2013): 401–4.
36 Curt Merlo, "How an Entire Nation Became Russia's Test Lab for Cyberwar," *Wired*, June 20, 2017, www.wired.com/story/russian-hackers-attack-ukraine.
37 Merlo, "How an Entire Nation Became Russia's Test Lab for Cyberwar."
38 Brandon Valeriano and Ryan Maness, "The Coming Cyberpeace," *Foreign Affairs*, May 13, 2015, www.foreignaffairs.com/articles/2015-05-13/coming-cyberpeace.
39 Erik Gartzke, "The Myth of Cyberwar: Bringing War in Cyberspace Back Down to Earth," *International Security* 38/2 (2013): 42–3.
40 Gartzke, "The Myth of Cyberwar," 57.
41 Martin C. Libicki, *Cyberdeterrence and Cyberwar* (Santa Monica, CA: RAND, 2009), 25; Rid, "Cyber War Will Not Take Place," 16.
42 Gartzke, "The Myth of Cyberwar," 46–7.
43 For a similar argument, see Betz, "The Mystique of 'Cyberwar'," 63–4.
44 Gartzke, "The Myth of Cyberwar," 49; Lindsay, "Stuxnet and the Limits of Cyber Warfare," 404.
45 Ronald J. Deibert, Rafal Rohozinski and Masashi Crete-Nishihata, "Cyclones in Cyberspace: Information Shaping and Denial in the 2008 Russia–Georgia War," *Security Dialogue* 43/1 (2012): 18.
46 Lindsay, "Stuxnet and the Limits of Cyber Warfare," 371.
47 Lionel Beehner, Liam Collins, Steve Ferenzi, Robert Person and Aaron Brantly, *A Contemporary Battlefield Assessment*. West Point, NY: Modern War Institute, March 20, 2018.
48 John Arquilla, "Cyberwar Is Already Upon Us," *Foreign Policy* 192 (2012): 84–5.
49 Sarah P. White, *Understanding Cyberwarfare: Lessons from the Russia–Georgia War* (West Point, NY: Modern War Institute, 2018), 6–8.
50 Peter Dombrowski and Chris C. Demchak, "Cyber War, Cybered Conflict, and the Maritime Domain," *Naval War College Review* 67/2 (2014): 73.
51 US Army War College, "Strategic Cyberspace Operations Guide," June 1, 2016, 15; US Joint Chiefs of Staff, Joint Publication 3-0, "Joint Operations," Washington, DC, January 17, 2017, GL-8.
52 James E. Cartwright, "Memorandum: Joint Terminology for Cyberspace

Operations," November 2010, 3–6; United States Army War College, "Strategic Cyberspace Operations Guide," 17.
53 Valeriano and Maness, *Cyber War versus Cyber Realities*, 32.
54 Brantly, Cal and Winkelstein, *Defending the Borderland*, 40.
55 United States Army Training and Doctrine Command, "Multi-Domain Battle: Evolution of Combined Arms for the 21st Century, 2025–2040," December 2017, i.

7 Non-state threats: From cybercrime to terrorism

1 Federal Bureau of Investigation, "Willie Sutton," www.fbi.gov/history/famous-cases/willie-sutton.
2 James Lewis, *Economic Impact of Cybercrime: No Slowing Down* (Washington, DC: McAfee, 2018).
3 Lewis, *Economic Impact of Cybercrime*.
4 Thomas J. Holt, George W. Burruss and Adam M. Bossler, *Policing Cybercrime and Cyberterror* (Durham: Carolina Academic Press, 2015), 8–9.
5 Justin Jouvenal, "Hackers Tried to Change Grades at Virginia High School, Police Say," *Washington Post*, April 4, 2018, www.washingtonpost.com/local/public-safety/hackers-tried-to-change-grades-at-virginia-high-school-police-say/2018/04/03/924ecf82-3765-11e8-acd5-35eac230e514_story.html.
6 Claes Bell, "Typosquatting: Identity Theft Built on Spelling Errors," *Bankrate*, August 15, 2015, www.bankrate.com/finance/credit/typosquatting-identity-theft.aspx.
7 Shu et al., "Breaking the Target."
8 Brett Hawkins, "Case Study: The Home Depot Data Breach," *SANS Institute*, January 2015, www.sans.org/reading-room/whitepapers/breaches/case-study-home-depot-data-breach-36367.
9 Goodman, *Future Crimes*.
10 Beehner et al., *A Contemporary Battlefield Assessment*.
11 Brett Stone-Gross, Marco Cova, Bob Gilbert, Richard Kemmerer, Christopher Kruegel and Giovanni Vigna, "Analysis of a Botnet Tracker," *IEEE Security & Privacy* 9/1 (1,710): 64–72.
12 Shayan Eskandari, Andreas Leoutsarakos, Troy Mursch and Jeremy Clark, "A First Look at Browser-Based Cryptojacking," *arXiv* (March 2018), https://arxiv.org/pdf/1803.02887.
13 John Leyden, "Polish Teen Derails Tram after Hacking Train Network," *Register*, January 11, 2008, at www.theregister.co.uk/2008/01/11/tram_hack.
14 Sameer Hinduja and Justin W. Patchin, "Bullying, Cyberbullying, and Suicide," *Archives of Suicide Research* 14 (2010): 206–21.
15 James H. Price and Jagdish Khubchandani, "Adolescent Homicides, Suicides, and the Role of Firearms: A Narrative Review," *American Journal of Health Education* 48/2 (2017): 67–79.

16 Justin W. Patchin, "Summary of Our Cyberbullying Research (2004–2016)," Cyberbullying Research Center, November 26, 2016, https://cyberbullying.org/summary-of-our-cyberbullying-research.
17 Robert D'Ovidio and James Doyle, "Study on Cyberstalking: Understanding Investigative Hurdles," *FBI Law Enforcement Bulletin* 72/3 (2003): 10–17.
18 Brian H. Spitzberg and Gregory Hoobler, "Cyberstalking and the Technologies of Interpersonal Terrorism," *New Media and Society* 4/1 (2002): 67–88.
19 Lauren Walker, "Three Family Members Received Life Sentences for the First-Ever Cyberstalking-to-Death Conviction," *Newsweek*, February 26, 2016, www.newsweek.com/family-receives-life-prison-first-ever-cyberstalking-conviction-430833.
20 US District Court, Southern District of New York, *United States of America v. Ross William Ulbricht*, Indictment, February 4, 2014.
21 Kim Zetter, "How the Feds Took Down the Silk Road Drug Wonderland," *Wired*, November 18, 2013, www.wired.com/2013/11/silk-road.
22 Kyle Soska and Nicolas Christin, "Measuring the Longitudinal Evolution of the Online Anonymous Marketplace Ecosystem," *Proceedings of USENIX Security Symposium*, August 12–14, 2015, Washington, DC.
23 Holt, Burruss and Bossler, *Policing Cybercrime and Terror*.
24 Federal Bureau of Investigation, "The Scourge of Child Pornography: Working to Stop the Sexual Exploitation of Children," April 25, 2017, www.fbi.gov/news/stories/the-scourge-of-child-pornography.
25 Federal Bureau of Investigation, "The Scourge of Child Pornography."
26 Federal Bureau of Investigation, "The Scourge of Child Pornography."
27 Lizzie Dearden, "Sadistic Paedophile Jailed for 32 Years after Blackmail Campaign on the Dark Web," *Independent*, February 20, 2018, 18–19.
28 Dearden, "'Sadistic paedophile jailed."
29 Luke Goode, "Anonymous and the Political Ethos of Hacktivism," *Popular Communication* 13/1 (2015): 74–86.
30 Marco Deseriis, "Hacktivism: On the Use of Botnets in Cyberattacks," *Theory, Culture & Society* 34/4 (2017): 131–52.
31 Cross-site scripting is a type of computer security vulnerability typically found in web applications. XSS enables attackers to inject client-side scripts into web pages viewed by other users.
32 SQL injection is a code injection technique, used to attack data-driven applications, in which nefarious SQL statements are inserted into an entry field for execution (e.g. to dump the database contents to the attacker).
33 Parmy Olson, *We Are Anonymous: Inside the Hacker World of LulzSec, Anonymous, and the Global Cyber Insurgency* (New York: Back Bay Books, 2013).
34 Olson, *We Are Anonymous*.
35 Burcu S. Bakioğlu, "The Gray Zone: Networks of Piracy, Control, and Resistance," *The Information Society* 32/1 (2015): 40–50.

36 Keely Lockhard and Myles Burke, "Video: #OpISIS: Why Anonymous Has Declared an Online War Against Isil – in 90 Seconds – Telegraph," *Telegraph*, December 11, 2015, www.telegraph.co.uk/news/worldnews/islamic-state/12003242/OpISIS-Why-Anonymous-has-declared-an-online-war-against-Isil-in-90-seconds.html.
37 Emerson T. Brooking, "Anonymous vs. the Islamic State," *Foreign Policy*, November 13, 2015, https://foreignpolicy.com/2015/11/13/anonymous-hackers-islamic-state-isis-chan-online-war.
38 Alexander Klimburg, "Mobilising Cyber Power," *Survival* 53/1 (2011): 41–60.
39 Beehner et al., *A Contemporary Battlefield Assessment*.
40 Gabriel Weimann, *Terrorism in Cyberspace: The Next Generation* (New York: Columbia University Press, 2015), 6.
41 Bruce Hoffman, *Inside Terrorism* (New York: Columbia University Press, 2006), 2.
42 Helene Cooper, "U.S. Military Social Media Feeds Are Seized by ISIS Sympathizers," *New York Times*, January 13, 2015, A4.
43 Cooper, "U.S. Military Social Media Feeds Are Seized by ISIS Sympathizers."
44 David C. Gompert and Martin C. Libicki, "Decoding the Breach: The Truth About the CENTCOM Hack," *The RAND Blog*, February 3, 2015, www.rand.org/blog/2015/02/decoding-the-breach-the-truth-about-the-centcom-hack.html.
45 John Scott-Railton and Seth Hardy, "Malware Attacks Targeting Syrian ISIS Critics," Citizen Lab, December 18, 2014, https://citizenlab.ca/2014/12/malware-attack-targeting-syrian-isis-critics.
46 RFSID, "Cyber Caliphate: ISIS Plays Offense on the Web," *Recorded Future*, April 2, 2015, www.recordedfuture.com/cyber-caliphate-analysis.
47 RFSID, "Cyber Caliphate."
48 Editor, "UK Jihadist 'Killed in Drone Strike,'" *BBC News*, August 27, 2015, www.bbc.co.uk/news/uk-34078900.
49 Christopher Heffelfinger, "The Risks Posed by Jihadist Hackers," *CTC Sentinel* 6/7 (2013): 1–5.
50 Jytte Klausen, "Tweeting the Jihad: Social Media Networks of Western Foreign Fighters in Syria and Iraq," *Studies in Conflict & Terrorism* 38/1 (2014): 1–22; Gabriel Weimann, "Cyberterrorism: The Sum of All Fears?" *Studies in Conflict & Terrorism* 28/2 (2005): 129–49.
51 J. M. Berger and Jonathon Morgan, *The ISIS Twitter Census: Defining and Describing the Population of ISIS Supporters on Twitter* (Washington, DC: Center for Middle East Policy at Brookings, 2015).
52 Brantly, "Innovation and Adaptation in Jihadist Digital Security."
53 Aaron F. Brantly, "Financing Terror Bit by Bit," *CTC Sentinel* 7/10 (2014): 1–5; Joshua Baron, Angela O'Mahony, David Manheim and Cynthia Dion-Schwarz, *National Security Implications of Virtual Currency* (Santa Monica, CA: RAND, 2015).
54 Sanger, *The Perfect Weapon*.

55 Sanger, *The Perfect Weapon*.
56 Hsinchun Chen et al., "Uncovering the Dark Web: A Case Study of Jihad on the Web," *Journal of the American Society for Information Science and Technology* 59/8 (2008): 1347–59; Gabriel Weimann, *Going Darker? The Challenge of Dark Net Terrorism* (Washington, DC: Wilson Center, 2018).
57 Jon R. Lindsay, "The Impact of China on Cybersecurity: Fiction and Friction," *International Security* 39/3 (2015): 7–47.
58 Soldatov and Borogan, *The Red Web*.

8 Organizing deterrence and defense in cyberspace

1 Ben Buchanan, "Cyber Deterrence Isn't MAD; It's Mosaic," *Georgetown Journal of International Affairs* 4 (2018): 130–40.
2 Office of the President of the United States, "National Strategy for Global Supply Chain Security," Washington, DC, 2012.
3 Andy Greenberg, "A Critical Intel Flaw Breaks Basic Security for Most Computers," *Wired*, January 3, 2018, www.wired.com/story/critical-intel-flaw-breaks-basic-security-for-most-computers.
4 Chris Bing, "Mayhem, the Tech Behind the DARPA Grand Challenge Winner, Now Used by the Pentagon – CyberScoop," *Cyberscoop*, August 11, 2017, www.cyberscoop.com/mayhem-darpa-cyber-grand-challenge-dod-voltron.
5 Alexander L. George and Richard Smoke, *Deterrence in American Foreign Policy: Theory and Practice* (New York: Columbia University Press, 1974), 11.
6 Aaron F. Brantly, "The Cyber Deterrence Problem," in *Proceedings of the 10th International Conference on Cyber Conflict, NATO Cyber Defense Center of Excellence* (Tallinn: IEEE, 2018), 31–54.
7 Thomas Rid and Ben Buchanan, "Attributing Cyber Attacks," *Journal of Strategic Studies* 38/1–2 (2015): 4–37.
8 Jon R. Lindsay, "Tipping the Scales: The Attribution Problem and the Feasibility of Deterrence Against Cyberattack," *Journal of Cybersecurity* 1/1 (2015): 53–67.
9 Will Goodman, "Cyber Deterrence: Tougher in Theory than in Practice?" *Strategic Studies Quarterly* 4/3 (2010): 102–35; Valeriano and Maness, *Cyber War Versus Cyber Realities*.
10 Ponemon Institute, "2017 Cost of Data Breach Study," Research Report, June 2017.
11 Ponemon Institute, "2017 Cost of Data Breach Study."
12 Lindsay, "Tipping the Scales," 58.
13 Martin C. Libicki, *Cyberspace in Peace and War* (Annapolis: Naval Institute Press, 2016).
14 Schmitt and Vihul, *Tallinn Manual 2.0*.
15 Valeriano and Maness, *Cyber War Versus Cyber Realities*.
16 Josh Rogin, "NSA Chief: Cybercrime Constitutes the 'Greatest

Transfer of Wealth in History'," *Foreign Policy*, July 9, 2012, https://foreignpolicy.com/2012/07/09/nsa-chief-cybercrime-constitutes-the-greatest-transfer-of-wealth-in-history.
17 Nathan Thornburgh, "The Invasion of the Chinese Cyberspies (and the Man Who Tried to Stop Them)," *Time*, September 5, 2005.
18 Jon R. Lindsay and Tai Ming Cheung, "From Exploitation to Innovation: Acquisition, Absorption, and Application," in *China and Cybersecurity*, ed. Lindsay, Cheung and Reveron, 51–86.
19 Inkster, *China's Cyber Power*.
20 Rogin, "NSA Chief."
21 Mandiant Threat Intelligence Center, "APT1."
22 Ellen Nakashima, "U.S. Developing Sanctions against China over Cyberthefts," *Washington Post*, August 30, 2015, www.washingtonpost.com/world/national-security/administration-developing-sanctions-against-china-over-cyberespionage/2015/08/30/9b2910aa-480b-11e5-8ab4-c73967a143d3_story.html.
23 Sanger, *The Perfect Weapon*.
24 FireEye, "Redline Drawn: China Recalculates Its Use of Cyber Espionage," 2016, www.fireeye.com/blog/threat-research/2016/06/red-line-drawn-china-espionage.html.
25 Gartzke and Lindsay, "Weaving Tangled Webs."
26 Rebecca Slayton, "What Is the Cyber Offense–Defense Balance? Conceptions, Causes, and Assessment," *International Security* 41/3 (2017): 72–109.
27 Joseph Berger, "A Dam, Small and Unsung, is Caught Up in an Iranian Hacking Case," *New York Times*, March 25, 2016, www.nytimes.com/2016/03/26/nyregion/rye-brook-dam-caught-in-computer-hacking-case.html.
28 Kim Zetter, "A Cyberattack Has Caused Confirmed Physical Damage for the Second Time Ever," *Wired*, January 8, 2015, www.wired.com/2015/01/german-steel-mill-hack-destruction.
29 Steve Morgan, "2018 Cybersecurity Market Report," *Cybersecurity Ventures*, February 17, 2018, https://cybersecurityventures.com/cybersecurity-market-report.
30 Morgan, "2018 Cybersecurity Market Report."

9 Cybersecurity and democracy

1 Ronald J. Deibert and Rafal Rohozinski, "Liberation vs. Control: The Future of Cyberspace," *Journal of Democracy* 21/4 (2010): 48.
2 Chung-pin Lee, Kaiju Chang and Frances Stokes Berry, "Testing the Development and Diffusion of E-government and E-democracy: A Global Perspective," *Public Administration Review* 71/3 (2011): 444–5.
3 Donald F. Norris, "E-Government 2020: Plus ça change, plus c'est la meme chose," *Public Administration Review* 70/1 (2010): 180.

4 Michael Margolis, "E-Government and Democracy," in Russel J. Dalton and Hans-Dieter Klingemann (eds.), *The Oxford Handbook of Political Behavior* (Oxford University Press, 2009 online access).
5 See, for example, the Church Committee report: US Senate, Select Committee to Study Governmental Operations with Respect to Intelligence Activities, "Intelligence Activities and the Rights of Americans," Book II, April 26, 1976.
6 This can be tested at home by accessing the website whatismyipaddress.com.
7 National Security Agency, "PRISM/US-984XN Overview," April 2013, www.washingtonpost.com/wp-srv/special/politics/prism-collection-documents/?noredirect=on.
8 See, for example, Zygmunt Bauman, Didier Bigo, Paulo Esteves, et al., "After Snowden: Rethinking the Impact of Surveillance," *International Political Sociology* 8/2 (2014): 122.
9 Singer and Friedman, *Cybersecurity and Cyberwar*, 34.
10 Matt Burgess, "That Yahoo Data Breach Actually Hit Three Billion Accounts," *Wired*, October 4, 2017, www.wired.co.uk/article/hacks-data-breaches-2017.
11 For a summary on GDPR, see Michael Nadeau, "General Data Protection Regulation (GDPR): What You Need to Know to Stay Compliant," CSO Online, April 23, 2018, www.csoonline.com/article/3202771/data-protection/general-data-protection-regulation-gdpr-requirements-deadlines-and-facts.html.
12 Larry Diamond, "Liberation Technology," *Journal of Democracy* 21/3 (2010): 70.
13 Tom Sorell, "Human Rights and Hacktivism: The Cases of Wikileaks and Anonymous," *Journal of Human Rights Practice* 7/3 (2015): 393.
14 Diamond, "Liberation Technology," 73–5.
15 Diamond, "Liberation Technology," 69–70.
16 Thomas Rid and Daniel Moore, "Cryptopolitik and the Darknet," *Survival* 58/1 (2016): 17.
17 Tetyana Bohdanova, "Unexpected Revolution: The Role of Social Media in Ukraine's Euromaidan Uprising," *European View* 13/1 (2014): 136.
18 Lena Surzhko-Harned and Andrew J. Zahuranec, "Framing the Revolution: The Role of Social Media in Ukraine's Euromaidan Movement," *Nationalities Papers* 45/5 (2017): 758–9.
19 Olga Onuch, "EuroMaidan Protests in Ukraine: Social Media versus Social Networks," *Problems of Post-Communism* 62/4 (2015): 233.
20 Bohdanova, "Unexpected Revolution," 139–40; Megan MacDuffee Metzger and Joshua A. Tucker, "Social Media and EuroMaidan: A Review Essay," *Slavic Review* 76/1 (2017): 187–91.
21 White House, "International Strategy for Cyberspace. Prosperity, Security, and Openness in a Networked World," May 2011, 23–4.
22 Hillary Rodham Clinton, "Internet Freedom," speech delivered at Newseum, Washington DC, January 21, 2010, https://foreignpolicy.com/2010/01/21/internet-freedom.

23 Singer and Friedman, *Cybersecurity and Cyberwar*, 106.
24 Sanja Kelly, Mai Tuong, Adrian Shahba and Madeline Earp, "Silencing the Messenger: Communications Apps under Pressure," in Freedom House, *Freedom on the Net 2016*, 2, https://freedomhouse.org/sites/default/files/FOTN_2016_Full_Report.pdf.
25 Singer and Friedman, *Cybersecurity and Cyberwar*, 108.
26 Brantly, "The Cyber Losers," 142–3.
27 Deibert and Rohozinski, "Liberation vs. Control," 50.
28 Diamond, "Liberation Technology," 80.
29 Diamond, "Liberation Technology," 71.
30 Brantly, "The Cyber Losers," 142.
31 Nick Hopkins and Jake Morris, "UK Firm's Surveillance Kit 'Used to Crush Uganda Opposition'," *BBC News*, October 15, 2015, www.bbc.co.uk/news/uk-34529237; Morgan Marquis-Boire and Bill Marczak, "From Bahrain with Love: FinFisher's Spy Kit Exposed?" Citizen Lab, July 25, 2012, https://citizenlab.ca/2012/07/from-bahrain-with-love-finfishers-spy-kit-exposed.
32 Deibert and Rohozinski, "Liberation vs. Control," 47.
33 Deibert and Rohozinski, "Liberation vs. Control," 54–5.
34 Ronald Deibert and Rafal Rohozinski, "Tracking GhostNet: Investigating a Cyber Espionage Network," *Information Warfare Monitor*, March 29, 2009, 17–45.
35 Deibert and Rohozinski, "Tracking GhostNet," 41.
36 Deibert and Rohozinski, "Tracking GhostNet," 46.
37 Deibert and Rohozinski, "Tracking GhostNet," 48.
38 See, for example, the security planners developed by the Citizen Lab at https://securityplanner.org, and the EFF at https://ssd.eff.org/en.
39 Brantly, "The Cyber Losers," 153.
40 Ellen Nakashima and Barton Gellman, "As Encryption Spreads, U.S. Grapples with Clash between Privacy, Security," *Washington Post*, April 10, 2015.
41 Rid and Moore, "Cryptopolitik and the Darknet," 7. On terrorist use of digital security tools, see Brantly, "Innovation and Adaptation in Jihadist Digital Security," 92–3.
42 Rid and Moore, "Cryptopolitik and the Darknet," 9.
43 Gregory T. Nojeim, "Cybersecurity and Freedom on the Internet," *Journal of National Security Law & Policy* 4/1 (2010): 120.
44 For a summary, see: Editor, "Breaking Down Apple's iPhone Fight With the U.S. Government," *New York Times*, March 21, 2016, www.nytimes.com/interactive/2016/03/03/technology/apple-iphone-fbi-fight-explained.html.
45 David Shammah, "Gov't contract a strong sign FBI used Israeli tech to crack San Bernardino iPhone," *Times of Israel*, April 4, 2016, www.timesofisrael.com/fbi-contract-a-strong-sign-fbi-used-israeli-tech-to-crack-san-bernardino-iphone.
46 Rid and Moore, "Cryptopolitik and the Darknet," 9.

10 The futures of cybersecurity

1. Center for Long-Term Cybersecurity, *Cybersecurity Futures 2020* (San Francisco: University of California–Berkeley, 2016), 2–3.
2. See, for example, Jason Healey, "The Five Futures of Cyber Conflict and Cooperation," Atlantic Council Issue Brief, 2011. For a synthesis of existing scenarios, see Meredydd Williams et al., "Future Scenarios and Challenges for Security and Privacy," paper presented at the IEEE International Forum on Research and Technologies for Society and Industry Leveraging a better tomorrow (2016), https://ieeexplore.ieee.org/document/7740625.
3. Roey Tzezana, "High-probability and Wild-card Scenarios for Future Crimes and Terror Attacks Using the Internet of Things," *Foresight* 19/1 (2017): 1.
4. Leonie Maria Tanczer, Ine Steenmans, Miles Elsden, Jason Blackstock and Madeline Carr, "Emerging Risks in the IoT Ecosystem: Who's Afraid of the Big Bad Smart Fridge?" paper presented at Living in the Internet of Things: Cybersecurity of the IoT Conference, London, 2018, https://ieeexplore.ieee.org/document/8379720.
5. Tzezana, "High-probability and Wild-card Scenarios," 2.
6. Edward Skoudis, "Evolutionary Trends in Cyberspace," 160–1.
7. Jeremy Hsu, "The Strava Heat Map and the End of Secrets," *Wired*, January 29, 2018, www.wired.com/story/strava-heat-map-military-bases-fitness-trackers-privacy.
8. Spencer Ackerman and Sam Thielman, "US Intelligence Chief: We Might Use the Internet of Things to Spy on You," *Guardian*, February 9, 2016.
9. Singer and Friedman, *Cybersecurity and Cyberwar*, 251–2.
10. Center for Long-Term Cybersecurity, *Cybersecurity Futures 2020*, 6.
11. Tanczer et al., "Emerging Risks in the IoT Ecosystem," 1.
12. Aaron F. Brantly, "When Everything Becomes Intelligence: Machine Learning and the Connected World," *Intelligence and National Security* 33/4 (2018): 562.
13. IBM, "What Is Big Data?" www-01.ibm.com/software/in/data/bigdata.
14. John Gantz and David Reinsel, "The Digital Universe Decade – Are You Ready?" IDC, May 2010, 1, www.emc.com/collateral/analyst-reports/idc-digital-universe-are-you-ready.pdf.
15. Andrea De Mauro, Marco Greco and Michele Grimaldi, "What Is Big Data? A Consensual Definition and a Review of Key Research Topics," in *American Institute of Physics Conference Proceedings*, ed. Georgios Giannakopoulos, Damianos P. Sakas and Daphne Kyriaki-Manessi, 1644/1 (2015): 103.
16. Brantly, "When Everything Becomes Intelligence," 566; Damien Van Puyvelde, Stephen Coulthart and Shahriar Hossain, "Beyond the Buzzword: Big Data and National Security Decision-Making," *International Affairs* 93/6 (2017): 1397.

17 Webroot, *Game Changers: AI and Machine Learning in Cybersecurity* (Broomfield, CO: Webroot, 2017), 2, www.webroot.com/us/en/about/press-room/releases/cybercriminals-using-ai-in-attacks?sc=70161000000TRru&rc=8200.
18 Van Puyvelde, Coulthart and Hossain, "Beyond the Buzzword," 1404.
19 Benoit Dupont, "Cybersecurity Futures: How Can We Regulate Emergent Risks?" *Technology Innovation Management Review* (2013): 10.
20 Tanczer et al., "Emerging Risks in the IoT Ecosystem," 4–6.
21 Kristian Lum and William Isaac, "To Predict and Serve?" *Significance* 13/5 (2016): 14–19.
22 Jennifer L. Collinger, B. Wodlinger, J. E. Downey, et al., "High-performance Neuroprosthetic Control by an Individual with Tetraplegia," *Lancet* 381 (2013): 557–64; Dupont, "Cybersecurity Futures," 8.
23 Center for Long-Term Cybersecurity, *Cybersecurity Futures 2020*, 7.
24 Internet Society, *Paths to Our Digital Future*, 2017, Executive Summary, https://future.internetsociety.org/introduction/executive-summary.
25 Amitai Etzioni and Oren Etzioni, "Designing AI Systems that Obey Our Laws and Values," *Communications of the ACM* 59/9 (2016): 29–31.
26 Tanczer et al., "Emerging Risks in the IoT Ecosystem," 4–5.
27 Brantly, "When Everything Becomes Intelligence," 569.
28 Williams et al., "Future Scenarios and Challenges for Security and Privacy."
29 Dupont, "Cybersecurity Futures," 9.
30 Internet Society, *Paths to Our Digital Future*.
31 Alec Ross, "Want Job Security? Try Online Security," *Wired*, April 25, 2016, www.wired.co.uk/article/job-security-cybersecurity-alec-ross.
32 Internet Society, *Paths to Our Digital Future*.

Bibliography

Abbate, Janet, *Inventing the Internet* (Cambridge, MA: MIT Press, 2000).
Adamsky, Dmitry, "From Moscow with Coercion: Russian Deterrence Theory and Strategic Culture," *Journal of Strategic Studies* 41/1–2 (2018): 33–66.
Anderson, Julie, "The Chekist Takeover of the Russian State," *International Journal of Intelligence and CounterIntelligence* 19/2 (2006): 237–88.
Arquilla, John, "Cyberwar Is Already Upon Us," *Foreign Policy* 192 (2012): 84-5.
Arquilla, John, and David F. Ronfeldt, *Cyberwar is Coming!* (Santa Monica, CA: RAND, 1992).
Arquilla, John, and David Ronfeldt, "Cyber War is Coming!" *Comparative Strategy* 12/2 (1993): 141–65.
Austin, Greg, *Cyber Policy in China* (New York: Polity, 2014).
Bakioğlu, Burcu S., "The Gray Zone: Networks of Piracy, Control, and Resistance," *The Information Society* 32/1 (2015): 40–50.
Baron, Joshua, Angela O'Mahony, David Manheim and Cynthia Dion-Schwarz, *National Security Implications of Virtual Currency* (Santa Monica, CA: RAND, 2015).
Bauman, Zygmunt, Didier Bigo, Paulo Esteves, et al., "After Snowden: Rethinking the Impact of Surveillance," *International Political Sociology* 8/2 (2014): 121–44.
Beehner, Lionel, Liam Collins, Steve Ferenzi, Robert Person and Aaron Brantly, *A Contemporary Battlefield Assessment* (West Point, NY: Modern War Institute, March 20, 2018).
Berger, J. M., and Jonathon Morgan, *The ISIS Twitter Census: Defining and Describing the Population of ISIS Supporters on Twitter* (Washington, DC: Center for Middle East Policy at Brookings, 2015).
Betz, David, "The Mystique of 'Cyberwar' and the Strategic Latency of Networked Social Movements," *Strategic Insights* 10 (2011): 61–77.

Bizeul, David, "Russian Business Network Study," 2007, www.bizeul.org/files/RBN_study.pdf.

Bohdanova, Tetyana, "Unexpected Revolution: The Role of Social Media in Ukraine's Euromaidan Uprising," *European View* 13/1 (2014): 133–42.

Braman, Sandra, "The Interpenetration of Technical and Legal Decision-Making for the Internet," *Information, Communication & Society* 13/3 (2010): 309–24.

Brantly, Aaron F., "Financing Terror Bit by Bit," *CTC Sentinel* 7/10 (2014): 1–5.

Brantly, Aaron F., "Innovation and Adaptation in Jihadist Digital Security," *Survival* 59/1 (2017): 79–102.

Brantly, Aaron F., "Public Health and Epidemiological Approaches to National Cybersecurity: A Baseline Comparison," in *US National Cybersecurity*, ed. Van Puyvelde and Brantly, 91–109.

Brantly, Aaron F., "The Cyber Deterrence Problem," in *Proceedings of the 10th International Conference on Cyber Conflict, NATO Cyber Defense Center of Excellence* (Tallinn: IEEE, 2018), 31–54.

Brantly, Aaron F., "The Cyber Losers," *Democracy and Security* 10/2 (2014): 132–55.

Brantly, Aaron F., *The Decision to Attack: Military and Intelligence Cyber Decision-Making* (Athens: University of Georgia Press, 2016).

Brantly, Aaron F., "The Most Governed Ungoverned Space: Legal and Policy Constraints on Military Operations in Cyberspace," *SAIS Review of International Affairs* 36/2 (2016): 29–39.

Brantly, Aaron F., "The Violence of Hacking: State Violence and Cyberspace," *Cyber Defense Review* 2/1 (2017): 1–19.

Brantly, Aaron F., "When Everything Becomes Intelligence: Machine Learning and the Connected World," *Intelligence and National Security* 33/4 (2018): 562–73.

Brantly, Aaron F., Nerea M. Cal and Devlin P. Winkelstein, *Defending the Borderland: Ukrainian Military Experiences with IO, Cyber, and EW* (West Point, NY: US Army Cyber Institute, 2017).

Brooking, Emerson T., "Anonymous vs. the Islamic State," *Foreign Policy*, November 13, 2015, https://foreignpolicy.com/2015/11/13/anonymous-hackers-islamic-state-isis-chan-online-war.

Brown, Gary, and Christopher D. Yung, "Evaluating the US–China Cybersecurity Agreement, Part 1: The US Approach to Cyberspace," *Diplomat*, January 19, 2017, https://thediplomat.com/2017/01/evaluating-the-us-china-cybersecurity-agreement-part-1-the-us-approach-to-cyberspace.

Buchanan, Ben, "Cyber Deterrence Isn't MAD; It's Mosaic," *Georgetown Journal of International Affairs* 4 (2018): 130–40.

Calleja, Alejandro, and Juan Caballero, *A Look Into 30 Years of Malware Development from a Software Metrics Perspective* (Cham: Springer, 2016).

Campbell-Kelly, Martin, William Aspray, Nathan Ensmenger and Jeffrey R. Yost, *Computer: A History of the Information Machine* (New York: HarperCollins, 2017).

Cartwright, James E., "Memorandum: Joint Terminology for Cyberspace Operations," November 2010.
Center for Long-Term Cybersecurity, *Cybersecurity Futures 2020* (San Francisco: University of California–Berkeley, 2016).
Cerf, Vinton G., and Robert E. Kahn, "A Protocol for Packet Network Intercommunication," *Data Communications of the IEEE Communications Society* 22/5 (1974): 1–13.
Ceruzzi, Paul E., *Computing: A Concise History* (Cambridge, MA: MIT Press, 2012).
Chen, Hsinchun, et al., "Uncovering the Dark Web: A Case Study of Jihad on the Web," *Journal of the American Society for Information Science and Technology* 59/8 (2008): 1347–59.
Clarke, Richard A., and Robert K. Knake, *Cyber War: The Next Threat to National Security and What to Do About It* (New York: Ecco, 2010).
Clausewitz, Karl, *On War* (New York: Random House, 1943).
Cohen, Eliot, "Changes and Transformation in Military Affairs," *Journal of Strategic Studies* 27/3 (2004): 395–407.
Collinger, Jennifer L., B. Wodlinger, J. E. Downey et al., "High-performance Neuroprosthetic Control by an Individual with Tetraplegia," *Lancet* 381 (2013): 557–64.
Conti, Greg, and David Raymond, *On Cyber: Towards an Operational Art for Cyber Conflict* (n.p.: Kopidion Press, 2017).
Council of Europe, *Convention on Cybercrime*, Budapest, November 23, 2001, www.coe.int/en/web/conventions/full-list/-/conventions/rms/0900001680081561.
D'Ovidio, Robert, and James Doyle, "Study on Cyberstalking: Understanding Investigative Hurdles," *FBI Law Enforcement Bulletin* 72/3 (2003): 10–17.
De Mauro, Andrea, Marco Greco and Michele Grimaldi, "What Is Big Data? A Consensual Definition and a Review of Key Research Topics," in *American Institute of Physics Conference Proceedings,* ed. Georgios Giannakopoulos, Damianos P. Sakas and Daphne Kyriaki-Manessi, 1644/1 (2015): 97–104.
Deibert, Ronald J., *Black Code: Surveillance, Privacy, and the Dark Side of the Internet* (Toronto: McClelland & Stewart, 2013).
Deibert, Ronald J., and Rafal Rohozinski, "Liberation vs. Control: The Future of Cyberspace," *Journal of Democracy* 21/4 (2010): 43–57.
Deibert, Ronald J., and Rafal Rohozinski, "Tracking GhostNet: Investigating a Cyber Espionage Network," *Information Warfare Monitor*, March 29, 2009, 17–45.
Deibert, Ronald J., Rafal Rohozinski and Masashi Crete-Nishihata, "Cyclones in Cyberspace: Information Shaping and Denial in the 2008 Russia Georgia War," *Security Dialogue* 43/1 (2012): 3–24.
Demchak, Chris, *Wars of Disruption and Resilience: Cybered Conflict, Power, and National Security* (Athens: University of Georgia Press, 2011).
Demchak, Chris, and Peter Dombrowski, "Cyber Westphalia: Asserting

State Prerogatives in Cyberspace," *Georgetown Journal of International Affairs* (2013): 29–38.

Demchak, Chris, and Peter Dombrowski, "Rise of a Cybered Westphalian Age," *Strategic Studies Quarterly* 5/1 (2011): 32–61.

DeNardis, Laura, *Protocol Politics: The Globalization of Internet Governance* (Cambridge, MA: MIT Press, 2009).

DeNardis, Laura, *The Global War for Internet Governance* (New Haven, CT: Yale University Press, 2014).

Deseriis, Marco, "Hacktivism: On the Use of Botnets in Cyberattacks," *Theory, Culture & Society* 34/4 (2017): 131–52.

Diamond, Larry, "Liberation Technology," *Journal of Democracy* 21/3 (2010): 69–83.

Dinniss, Heather Harrison, *Cyber Warfare and the Laws of War* (New York: Cambridge University Press, 2012).

DiNucci, Darcy, "Fragmented Future," *Print* 53/4 (1999): 32, 221–2.

Dombrowski, Peter, and Chris C. Demchak, "Cyber War, Cybered Conflict, and the Maritime Domain," *Naval War College Review* 67/2 (2014): 71–96.

Dunn Cavelty, Myriam, *Cyber-Security and Threat Politics: US Efforts to Secure the Information Age* (London: Routledge 2008).

Dupont, Benoit, "Cybersecurity Futures: How Can We Regulate Emergent Risks?" *Technology Innovation Management Review* (2013): 6–11.

Durairajan, Ramakrishnan, Paul Barford, Joel Sommers and Walter Willinger, *InterTubes* (New York: ACM Press, 2015).

Etzioni, Amitai, and Oren Etzioni, "Designing AI Systems that Obey Our Laws and Values," *Communications of the ACM* 59/9 (2016): 29–31.

Ferris, John, "A New American Way of War? C4ISR, Intelligence and Information Operations in Operation 'Iraqi Freedom': A Provisional Assessment," *Intelligence and National Security* 81/3 (2003): 155–74.

Fireye, "Redline Drawn: China Recalculates Its Use of Cyber Espionage," June 20, 2016.

Folsom, Thomas C., "Defining Cyberspace (Finding Real Virtue in the Place of Virtual Reality)," *Tulane Journal of Technology and Intellectual Property* 9/1 (2007): 75–121.

Gartzke, Erik, "The Myth of Cyberwar: Bringing War in Cyberspace Back Down to Earth," *International Security* 38/2 (2013): 41–73.

Gartzke, Erik, and Jon R. Lindsay, "Weaving Tangled Webs: Offense, Defense, and Deception in Cyberspace," *Security Studies* 24/2 (2015): 316–48.

George, Alexander L., and Richard Smoke, *Deterrence in American Foreign Policy: Theory and Practice* (New York: Columbia University Press, 1974).

Gibson, William, *Neuromancer* (New York: Ace Books, 1984).

Goode, Luke, "Anonymous and the Political Ethos of Hacktivism," *Popular Communication* 13/1 (2015): 74–86.

Goodman, Marc, *Future Crimes: Everything Is Connected, Everyone Is Vulnerable and What We Can Do About It* (New York: Doubleday, 2015).

Goodman, Will, "Cyber Deterrence: Tougher in Theory than in Practice?" *Strategic Studies Quarterly* 4/3 (2010): 102–35.

Gray, Colin, *Another Bloody Century: Future Warfare* (London: Orion Books, 2006).

Gvodsev, Nicholas, "The Bear Goes Digital: Russia and Its Cyber Capabilities," in *Cyberspace and National Security*, ed. Reveron, 173–89.

Haddad, Saïd, "Le Cyberespace ou la construction d'un 'champ de confrontation à part entière,'" in *La Cyberdéfense. Politique de l'espace numérique*, ed. Amaël Cattaruzza, Didier Danet and Stéphane Taillat (Paris: Armand Collin, 2018), 44–51.

Hafner, Katie, and Matthew Lyon, *Where Wizards Stay Up Late: The Origins of the Internet* (New York: Simon & Schuster, 1996).

Hanson, Fergus, *Revolution @State: The Spread of EDiplomacy* (Sydney: Lowy Institute for International Affairs, 2012).

Harnett, Eric, "Welcome to Hyperwar," *Bulletin of the Atomic Scientists* 48/7 (1992): 14–21.

Healey, Jason, *A Fierce Domain: Conflict in Cyberspace, 1986 to 2012* (Arlington, VA: Cyber Conflict Studies Association, 2013).

Healey, Jason, "The Five Futures of Cyber Conflict and Cooperation," Atlantic Council Issue Brief, 2011.

Heffelfinger, Christopher, "The Risks Posed by Jihadist Hackers," *CTC Sentinel* 6/7 (2013): 1–5.

Hinduja, Sameer, and Justin W. Patchin, "Bullying, Cyberbullying, and Suicide," *Archives of Suicide Research* 14 (2010): 206–21.

Holt, Thomas J., George W. Burruss and Adam M. Bossler, *Policing Cybercrime and Cyberterror* (Durham: Carolina Academic Press, 2015).

Inkster, Nigel, *China's Cyber Power* (Abingdon: Routledge, 2016).

Inkster, Nigel, "The Chinese Intelligence Agencies: Evolution and Empowerment," in *China and Cybersecurity*, ed. Lindsay, Cheung and Reveron, 29–50.

Internet Society, *Paths to Our Digital Future*, 2017, Executive Summary, https://future.internetsociety.org/introduction/executive-summary.

Jarmon, Jack, and Pano Yannakogeorgos, *The Cyber Threat and Globalization: The Impact on U.S. National and International Security* (New York: Rowman and Littlefield, 2018).

Jasper, Scott, "U.S. Cyber Threat Intelligence Sharing Frameworks," *International Journal of Intelligence and CounterIntelligence* 30/1 (2016): 53–65.

Jeangène Vilmer, Jean-Baptiste, "Successfully Countering Russian Electoral Interference: 15 Lessons Learned from the Macron Leaks," *CSIS Brief*, 2018.

Jianwei, Zhuge, Gu Lion, Duan Haixin and Taylor Roberts, "Investigating the Chinese Online Underground Economy," in *China and Cybersecurity*, ed. Lindsay, Cheung and Reveron, 87–120.

Johnston, Alastair Iain, "Thinking about Strategic Culture," *International Security* 19/4 (1995): 32–64.

Johnston, Jessica, *Technological Turf Wars: A Case Study of the Computer Antivirus Industry* (Philadelphia: Temple University Press, 2009).

Junio, Timothy J., "How Probable Is Cyber War? Bringing IR Theory Back In to the Cyber Conflict Debate," *Journal of Strategic Studies* 36/1 (2013): 125–33.

Kaplan, Fred M., *Dark Territory: The Secret History of Cyber War* (New York: Simon & Schuster, 2016).

Kello, Lucas, *The Virtual Weapon and International Order* (New Haven, CT: Yale University Press, 2017).

Kelly, Sanja, Mai Tuong, Adrian Shahba and Madeline Earp, "Silencing the Messenger: Communications Apps under Pressure," in Freedom House, *Freedom on the Net*, 2016.

Keohane, Robert O., and Joseph S. Nye, *Power and Interdependence: World Politics in Transition* (Boston: Little, Brown, 1977).

King, Gary, Jennifer Pan and Margaret E. Roberts, "How Censorship in China Allows Government Criticism but Silences Collective Expression," *American Political Science Review* 107/2 (2013): 326–43.

Klausen, Jytte, "Tweeting the Jihad: Social Media Networks of Western Foreign Fighters in Syria and Iraq," *Studies in Conflict & Terrorism* 38/1 (2014): 1–22.

Klimburg, Alexander, "Mobilising Cyber Power," *Survival* 53/1 (2011): 41–60.

Klimburg, Alexander, *The Darkening: The War for Cyberspace* (New York: Penguin Books, 2017).

Kock, Ned, "E-Collaboration and E-Commerce in Virtual Worlds," *International Journal of E-Collaboration* 4/3 (2008): 1–13.

Koh, Harold Hongju, "International Law in Cyberspace," Keynote Address at the US Cyber Command Inter-Agency Legal Conference, Ft. Meade, MD, September 18, 2002.

Kramer, Franklin D., "Cyberpower and National Security: Policy Recommendations for a Strategic Framework," in *Cyberpower and National Security*, ed. Kramer, Starr and Wentz, 3–23.

Kramer, Franklin D., Stuart H. Starr, Larry K. Wentz (eds.), *Cyberpower and National Security* (Washington, DC: National Defense University, 2009).

Kuehl, Daniel T., "From Cyberspace to Cyberpower: Defining the Problem," in *Cyberpower and National Security*, ed. Kramer, Starr and Wentz, 24–42.

Kurbalija, Jovan, *An Introduction to Internet Governance*, 7th edn. (Geneva: DiploFoundation, 2016).

Lee, Chung-pin, Kaiju Chang, and Frances Stokes Berry, "Testing the Development and Diffusion of E-government and E-democracy: A Global Perspective," *Public Administration Review* 71/3 (2011): 444–54.

Leiner, Barry M., et al., "The Past and Future History of the Internet," *Communications of the ACM* 40/2 (1997): 102–8.

Levy, Steven, *Hackers: Heroes of the Computer Revolution* (Sebastopol, CA: O'Reilly Media, 2010).

Lewis, James, *Economic Impact of Cybercrime: No Slowing Down* (Washington, DC: McAfee, 2018).
Libicki, Martin C., *Cyberdeterrence and Cyberwar* (Santa Monica, CA: RAND, 2009).
Libicki, Martin C., *Cyberspace in Peace and War* (Annapolis: Naval Institute Press, 2016).
Libicki, Martin C., "Why Cyber War Will Not and Should Not Have Its Grand Strategist," *Strategic Studies Quarterly* 8/1 (2014): 23–39.
Lin, Herbert, "Operational Considerations in Cyber Attack and Cyber Exploitation," in *Cyberspace and National Security*, ed. Reveron, 37–56.
Lindsay, Jon R., "Introduction. China and Cybersecurity: Controversy and Context," in *China and Cybersecurity*, ed. Lindsay, Cheung and Reveron, 1–26.
Lindsay, Jon R., "Stuxnet and the Limits of Cyber Warfare," *Security Studies* 22/3 (2013): 365–404.
Lindsay, Jon R., "The Impact of China on Cybersecurity: Fiction and Friction," *International Security* 39/3 (2015): 7–47.
Lindsay, Jon R., "Tipping the Scales: The Attribution Problem and the Feasibility of Deterrence Against Cyberattack," *Journal of Cybersecurity* 1/1 (2015): 53–67.
Lindsay, Jon R., and Tai Ming Cheung, "From Exploitation to Innovation: Acquisition, Absorption, and Application," in *China and Cybersecurity*, ed. Lindsay, Cheung and Reveron, 51–86.
Lindsay, Jon R., Tai Ming Cheung and Derek S. Reveron (eds.), *China and Cybersecurity: Espionage, Strategy, and Politics in the Digital Domain* (Oxford University Press, 2015).
Lindsay, Jon R., and Derek S. Reveron, "Conclusion: The Rise of China and the Future of Cybersecurity," in *China and Cybersecurity*, ed. Lindsay, Cheung and Reveron, 333–54.
Lockheed Martin, "The Cyber Kill Chain," www.lockheedmartin.com/en-us/capabilities/cyber/cyber-kill-chain.html.
Lotrionte, Catherine, "A Better Defense: Examining the United States' New Norms-Based Approach to Cyber Deterrence," *Georgetown Journal of International Affairs* (2016): 75–88.
Lum, Kristian, and William Isaac, "To Predict and Serve?" *Significance* 13/5 (2016): 14–19.
MacDuffee Metzger, Megan, and Joshua A. Tucker, "Social Media and EuroMaidan: A Review Essay," *Slavic Review* 76/1 (2017): 187–91.
Madsen, Wayne, "Intelligence Agency Threats to Computer Security," *International Journal of Intelligence and CounterIntelligence* 6/4 (1993): 413–88.
Mandiant Threat Intelligence Center, "APT1 Exposing One of China's Cyber Espionage Units," www.fireeye.com/content/dam/fireeye-www/services/pdfs/mandiant-apt1-report.pdf.
Manjikian, Mary McEvoy, "From Global Village to Virtual Battlespace: The Colonizing of the Internet and the Extension of Realpolitik," *International Studies Quarterly* 54/2 (2010): 381–401.

Marczak, Bill, and John Scott-Railton, "Keep Calm and (Don't) Enable Macros: A New Threat Actor Targets UAE Dissidents – the Citizen Lab," Citizen Lab, May 29, 2016, https://citizenlab.ca/2016/05/stealth-falcon.

Margolis, Michael, "E-Government and Democracy," in Russel J. Dalton and Hans-Dieter Klingemann (eds.), *The Oxford Handbook of Political Behavior* (Oxford University Press, 2009 online).

Marquis-Boire, Morgan, and Bill Marczak, "From Bahrain with Love: FinFisher's Spy Kit Exposed?" Citizen Lab, July 25, 2012, https://citizenlab.ca/2012/07/from-bahrain-with-love-finfishers-spy-kit-exposed.

Mazanec, Brian, "The Outlook for Constraining International Norms for Offensive Cyber Operations", in *US National Cybersecurity*, ed. Van Puyvelde and Brantly, 40–54.

McGraw, Gary, "Cyber War Is Inevitable (Unless We Build Security In)," *Journal of Strategic Studies* 36/1 (2013): 109–19.

Medvedev, Sergey, "Data Protection in Russian Federation: Overview," *Thomson Reuters Practical Law*, December 1, 2017, uk.practicallaw.thomsonreuters.com/2-502-2227.

Mowery, David C., and Timothy Simcoe, "Is the Internet a US Invention? An Economic and Technological History of Computer Networking," *Research Policy* 31 (2002): 1369–87.

Mueller, Milton, *Networks and States: The Global Politics of Internet Governance* (Cambridge, MA: MIT Press, 2010).

Mueller, Milton, *Will the Internet Fragment? Sovereignty, Globalization and Cyberspace* (Malden, MA: Polity, 2017).

Murray, Andrew, *Information Technology Law: The Law and Society* (Oxford University Press, 2016).

Myers, Brad A., "A Brief History of Human–Computer Interaction Technology," *ACM Interactions* (1998): 44–54.

National Audit Office, "Investigation: WannaCry Cyber Attack and the NHS," October 27, 2017, www.nao.org.uk/report/investigation-wannacry-cyber-attack-and-the-nhs.

National Security Agency, "PRISM/US-984XN Overview," April 2013, www.washingtonpost.com/wp-srv/special/politics/prism-collection-documents/?noredirect=on.

NATO Cooperative Cyber Defence Centre of Excellence, "Cyber Security Strategy Documents," October 18, 2018, https://ccdcoe.org/cyber-security-strategy-documents.html.

NATO Cooperative Cyber Defence Centre of Excellence, "National Cyber Security Organisation," https://ccdcoe.org/national-cyber-security-organisation.html.

Naugle, Matthew G., *Network Protocols* (New York: McGraw-Hill Professional, 1999).

Netmundial, "NetMundial Multistakeholder Statement," Sao Paulo, Brazil, April 24, 2014, http://netmundial.br/netmundial-multistakeholder-statement.

Nojeim, Gregory T., "Cybersecurity and Freedom on the Internet," *Journal of National Security Law & Policy* 4/1 (2010): 119–37.

Norris, Donald F., "E-Government 2020: Plus ça change, plus c'est la meme chose," *Public Administration Review* 70/1 (2010): 180–1.

Nye, Joseph S., "Get Smart: Combining Hard and Soft Power," *Foreign Affairs* 88/4 (2009): 160–3.

Nye, Joseph S., "Hard, Soft, and Smart Power," in *The Oxford Handbook of Modern Diplomacy*, ed. Andrew F. Cooper, Jorge Heine and Ramesh Thakur (Oxford University Press, 2013 online).

Office of the Director of National Intelligence, Background to "Assessing Russian Activities and Intentions in Recent US Elections: The Analytic Process and Cyber Incident Attribution," January 6, 2017.

Office of the President of the United States, "National Strategy for Global Supply Chain Security," Washington, DC, 2012.

Olson, Parmy, *We Are Anonymous: Inside the Hacker World of LulzSec, Anonymous, and the Global Cyber Insurgency* (New York: Back Bay Books, 2013).

Onuch, Olga, "EuroMaidan Protests in Ukraine: Social Media versus Social Networks," *Problems of Post-Communism* 62/4 (2015): 217–35.

Patchin, Justin W., "Summary of Our Cyberbullying Research (2004-2016)," Cyberbullying Research Center, November 26, 2016, https://cyberbullying.org/summary-of-our-cyberbullying-research.

Philipson, Graeme, "A Short History of Software," in *Management, Labour Process and Software Development: Reality Bites*, ed. Rowena Barrett (New York: Routledge, 2005), 13–44.

Ponemon Institute, "2017 Cost of Data Breach Study," Research Report, June 2017.

Price, James H., and Jagdish Khubchandani, "Adolescent Homicides, Suicides, and the Role of Firearms: A Narrative Review," *American Journal of Health Education* 48/2 (2017): 67–79.

Raymond, Mark, and Laura DeNardis, "Multistakeholderism: Anatomy of an Inchoate Global Institution," *International Theory* 7/3 (2015): 572–616.

Reveron, Derek S. (ed.), *Cyberspace and National Security: Threats, Opportunities, and Power in a Virtual World* (Washington, DC: Georgetown University Press, 2012).

Reveron, Derek S., "An Introduction to National Security and Cyberspace," in *Cyberspace and National Security*, ed. Reveron, 3–19.

Rid, Thomas, "Cyber War Will Not Take Place," *Journal of Strategic Studies* 35/1 (2012): 5-32.

Rid, Thomas, *Cyber War Will Not Take Place* (London: Hurst, 2013).

Rid, Thomas, *Rise of the Machines: A Cybernetic History* (London: Scribe, 2016).

Rid, Thomas, and Ben Buchanan, "Attributing Cyber Attacks," *Journal of Strategic Studies* 38/1–2 (2015): 4–37.

Rid, Thomas, and Daniel Moore, "Cryptopolitik and the Darknet," *Survival* 58/1 (2016): 7–38.

Roberts, Lawrence G., "The Evolution of Packet Switching," *Proceedings of the IEEE* 66/11 (1978): 1307–13.

Rogin, Josh, "NSA Chief: Cybercrime Constitutes the 'Greatest Transfer of Wealth in History,'" *Foreign Policy*, July 9, 2012, https://foreignpolicy.com/2012/07/09/nsa-chief-cybercrime-constitutes-the-greatest-transfer-of-wealth-in-history.

Rollins, John, "U.S.–China Cyber Agreement," *CRS Insight*, October 16, 2016, https://fas.org/sgp/crs/row/IN10376.pdf.

Ross, Ron, Michael McEvilley and Janey Carrier Oren, *Systems Security Engineering* (Gaithersburg, MD: National Institute of Standards and Technology, 2016).

Rumsfeld, Donald, "Transforming the Military," *Foreign Affairs* 81/3 (2002): 20–32.

Ryan, Camille, and Jamie M. Lewis, *Computer and Internet Use in the United States: 2015* (Washington, DC: US Census Bureau, 2017).

Sanger, David E., *The Perfect Weapon: War, Sabotage, and Fear in the Cyber Age* (New York: Crown Publishers, 2018).

Schmitt, Michael N., "Classification of Cyber Conflict," *Journal of Conflict & Security Law* 17/2 (2012): 245–60.

Schmitt, Michael N., *Tallinn Manual on the International Law Applicable to Cyber Warfare: Prepared by the International Group of Experts at the Invitation of the NATO Cooperative Cyber Defence Centre of Excellence* (Cambridge University Press, 2013).

Schmitt, Michael N., and Liis Vihul, *Tallinn Manual 2.0 on the International Law Applicable to Cyber Operations* (Cambridge University Press, 2017).

Scott-Railton, John, and Seth Hardy, "Malware Attacks Targeting Syrian ISIS Critics," Citizen Lab, December 18, 2014, https://citizenlab.ca/2014/12/malware-attack-targeting-syrian-isis-critics.

Searle, Loyd, "The Bombsight War: Nordern vs. Sperry," *IEEE Spectrum* (1989): 60–4.

Segal, Adam, "Holding the Multistakeholder Line at the ITU," Council on Foreign Relations, October 21, 2014, www.cfr.org/report/holding-multistakeholder-line-itu.

Shadow Server Foundation, "AS40989 RBN as RBusiness Network," www.shadowserver.org/wiki/uploads/Information/RBN-AS40989.pdf.

Sheldon, John, "The Rise of Cyberpower," in *Strategy in the Contemporary World*, ed. John Baylis, James J. Wirtz and Colin S. Gray (Oxford University Press, 2013), 303–19.

Sheldon, Robert, and Joe McReynolds, "Civil–Military Integration and Cybersecurity: A Study of Chinese Information Warfare Militias," in *China and Cybersecurity*, ed. Lindsay, Cheung and Reveron, 188–222.

Shu, Xiaokui, Ke Tian, Andrew Ciambrone and Danfeng Yao, "Breaking the Target: An Analysis of Target Data Breach and Lessons Learned," *arXiv*, January 2017, 1–10, https://arxiv.org/pdf/1701.04940.

Singer, Peter W., and Allan Friedman, *Cybersecurity and Cyberwar: What Everyone Needs to Know* (Oxford University Press, 2014).

Skoudis, Edward, "Evolutionary Trends in Cyberspace," in *Cyberpower and National Security*, ed. Kramer, Starr and Wentz, 147–70.

Slayton, Rebecca, "What Is the Cyber Offense–Defense Balance? Conceptions, Causes, and Assessment," *International Security* 41/3 (2017): 72–109.

Soldatov, Andrei, and Irina Borogan, *The Red Web: The Struggle Between Russia's Digital Dictators and the New Online Revolutionaries* (New York: Public Affairs, 2015).

Sorell, Tom, "Human Rights and Hacktivism: The Cases of Wikileaks and Anonymous," *Journal of Human Rights Practice* 7/3 (2015): 391–410.

Soska, Kyle, and Nicolas Christin, "Measuring the Longitudinal Evolution of the Online Anonymous Marketplace Ecosystem," *Proceedings of USENIX Security Symposium*, August 12–14, 2015, Washington, DC.

Spitzberg, Brian H., and Gregory Hoobler, "Cyberstalking and the Technologies of Interpersonal Terrorism," *New Media and Society* 4/1 (2002): 67–88.

Staeder, Tracy, "Why Russia Is Building Its Own Internet," *IEEE Spectrum*, January 17, 2018, https://spectrum.ieee.org/tech-talk/telecom/internet/could-russia-really-build-its-own-alternate-internet.

Stolberg, Alan G., "Crafting National Interests in the 21st Century," in *U.S. Army War College Guide to National Security Issues*, vol. II: *National Security Policy and Strategy*, ed. J. Boone Bartholomees Jr. (Carlisle, PA: Strategic Studies Institute, 2012), 13–25.

Stoll, Clifford, "Stalking the Wily Hacker," *Communications of the ACM* 31/5 (1988): 484–97.

Stoll, Clifford, *The Cuckoo's Egg: Tracking a Spy Through the Maze of Computer Espionage* (New York: Doubleday, 1989).

Stone, John, "Cyber War Will Take Place!" *Journal of Strategic Studies* 36/1 (2013): 101–8.

Stone-Gross, Brett, Marco Cova, Bob Gilbert, Richard Kemmerer, Christopher Kruegel and Giovanni Vigna, "Analysis of a Botnet Tracker," *IEEE Security & Privacy* 9/1 (2011): 64–72.

Stone-Gross, Brett, Ryan Abman, Richard A. Kemmerer, Christopher Kruegel, Douglas G. Steigerwald and Giovanni Vigna, "The Underground Economy of Fake Antivirus Software," in *Economics of Information Security and Privacy III*, ed. Bruce Schneier (New York: Springer, 2013), 55–78.

Surzhko-Harned, Lena, and Andrew J. Zahuranec, "Framing the Revolution: The Role of Social Media in Ukraine's Euromaidan Movement," *Nationalities Papers* 45/5 (2017): 758–79.

Symantec, "Cybercrime Time-Line," www.symantec.com/region/sg/homecomputing/library/cybercrime.html.

Symantec, "Norton Cyber Security Insights Report Global Results 2017," www.symantec.com/content/dam/symantec/docs/about/2017-ncsir-global-results-en.pdf.

Syverson, Paul, "A Peel of Onion," *Proceedings of the 27th Annual Computer Security Applications Conference ACM* (2011): 123–37.

Tanczer, Leonie Maria, Ine Steenmans, Miles Elsden, Jason Blackstock and Madeline Carr, "Emerging Risks in the IoT Ecosystem: Who's Afraid of the Big Bad Smart Fridge?" paper presented at Living in the Internet of

Things: Cybersecurity of the IoT Conference, London, 2018, https://ieeexplore.ieee.org/document/8379720.

Thomas, Timothy L., "Nation-State Cyber Strategies: Examples from China and Russia," in *Cyberpower and National Security*, ed. Kramer, Starr and Wentz, 468–75.

Thomas, Timothy L., "Russian Reflexive Control, Theory and the Military," *Journal of Slavic Military Studies* 17/2 (2004): 237–56.

Tzezana, Roey, "High-probability and Wild-card Scenarios for Future Crimes and Terror Attacks Using the Internet of Things," *Foresight* 19/1 (2017): 1–14.

UK Government, "National Cyber Security Strategy 2016 to 2021," November 2016, www.gov.uk/government/publications/national-cyber-security-strategy-2016-to-2021.

US Army Training and Doctrine Command, "Multi-Domain Battle: Evolution of Combined Arms for the 21st Century, 2025–2040," December 2017, www.arcic.army.mil/App_Documents/Multi-Domain-Battle-Evolution-of-Combined-Arms.pdf.

US Army War College, "Strategic Cyberspace Operations Guide," June 1, 2016, archive.org/details/USAWCStrategicCyberOpsGuide.

US Cyber Command, "Achieve and Maintain Cyberspace Superiority: Command Vision for US Cyber Command," 2018, www.hsdl.org/?view&did=812923.

US Department of Defense, "The DoD Cyber Strategy," April 2015, http://archive.defense.gov/home/features/2015/0415_cyber-strategy/final_2015_dod_cyber_strategy_for_web.pdf.

US Government, "Improvement of Technical Management of Internet Names and Addresses; Proposed Rule," in *Federal Register*, vol. LXIII (Washington, DC: Office of the Federal Register, 1998).

US Government, "National Military Strategy for Cyberspace Operations," December 2006, www.hsdl.org/?view&did=35693.

US House of Representatives, Committee on Science, Space, and Technology Subcommittee on Technology and Competitiveness, Hearing: Computer Security, Statement of Winn Schwartau, 102nd Congress, 1st sess., June 27, 1991.

US Joint Chiefs of Staff, Joint Publication 3-0, "Joint Operations," Washington, DC, January 17, 2017.

US Joint Chiefs of Staff, Joint Publication 3-12 (R), "Cyberspace Operations," Washington, DC, 2013.

Vacca, W. Alexander, "Military Culture and Cyber Security," *Survival* 53/6 (2011): 159–76.

Valeriano, Brandon, Benjamin Jensen and Ryan C. Maness, *Cyber Strategy: The Evolving Character of Power and Coercion* (Oxford University Press, 2018).

Valeriano, Brandon, and Ryan C. Maness, *Cyber War versus Cyber Realities: Cyber Conflict in the International System* (New York: Oxford University Press, 2015).

Valeriano, Brandon, and Ryan C. Maness, "The Coming Cyberpeace," *Foreign*

Affairs, May 13, 2015, www.foreignaffairs.com/articles/2015-05-13/coming-cyberpeace.

Valeriano, Brandon, and Ryan Maness, "The Fog of CyberWar," *Foreign Affairs*, November 21, 2012, www.foreignaffairs.com/articles/2012-11-21/fog-cyberwar.

Van Puyvelde, Damien, "From Information to Cybersecurity: Bridging the Public–Private Divide," in *US National Cybersecurity*, ed. Van Puyvelde and Brantly, 177–94.

Van Puyvelde, Damien, and Aaron F. Brantly (eds.), *US National Cybersecurity: International Politics, Concepts and Organization* (New York: Routledge, 2017).

Van Puyvelde, Damien, Stephen Coulthart and Shahriar Hossain, "Beyond the Buzzword: Big Data and National Security Decision-Making," *International Affairs* 93/6 (2017): 1397–1416.

Warner, Michael, "Cybersecurity: A Pre-history," *Intelligence and National Security* 27/5 (2012): 781–99.

Warner, Michael, "Intelligence in Cyber – and Cyber in Intelligence," in *Understanding Cyber Conflict*, ed. George Perkovich and Ariel E. Levite (Washington, DC: Georgetown University Press, 2018), 17–29.

Webroot, *Game Changers: AI and Machine Learning in Cybersecurity* (Broomfield, CO: Webroot, 2017).

Weimann, Gabriel, "Cyberterrorism: The Sum of All Fears?" *Studies in Conflict & Terrorism* 28/2 (2005): 129–49.

Weimann, Gabriel, *Going Darker? The Challenge of Dark Net Terrorism* (Washington, DC: Wilson Center, 2018).

Weimann, Gabriel, *Terrorism in Cyberspace: The Next Generation* (New York: Columbia University Press, 2015).

Wendt, Alexander, "Anarchy Is What States Make of It," *International Organization* 46/2 (1992): 391–425.

White House, "International Strategy for Cyberspace: Prosperity, Security, and Openness in a Networked World," May 2011, https://obamawhitehouse.archives.gov/sites/default/files/rss_viewer/international_strategy_for_cyberspace.pdf.

White House, National Security Decision Directive 145, "National Policy on Telecommunications and Automated Information Systems Security (U)," September 17, 1984, https://fas.org/irp/offdocs/nsdd145.htm.

White House, Presidential Decision Directive/NSC-63, "Critical Infrastructure Protection," May 22, 1998, https://fas.org/irp/offdocs/pdd/pdd-63.htm.

White House, "Presidential Policy Directive 41 – United States Cyber Incident Coordination," July 26, 2016, https://obamawhitehouse.archives.gov/the-press-office/2016/07/26/presidential-policy-directive-united-states-cyber-incident.

White House, "The National Strategy to Secure Cyberspace," 2003, https://georgewbush-whitehouse.archives.gov/pcipb.

White, Sarah P., *Understanding Cyberwarfare: Lessons from the Russia–Georgia War* (West Point, NY: Modern War Institute, 2018).

Wiener, Norbert, *Cybernetics: Or, Control and Communication in the Animal and the Machine* (New York: MIT Press, 1961).
Williams, Meredydd, et al., ""Future Scenarios and Challenges for Security and Privacy," paper presented at the IEEE International Forum on Research and Technologies for Society and Industry, Leveraging a better tomorrow (2016), https://ieeexplore.ieee.org/document/7740625.
Wirtz, James J., "Cyber War and Strategic Culture: The Russian Integration of Cyber Power into Grand Strategy," in *Cyber War in Perspective: Russian Aggression against Ukraine*, ed. Kenneth Geers (Tallinn: NATO Cooperative Cyber Defence Centre of Excellence, 2015), 29–37.
Wolfers, Arnold, "National Security as an Ambiguous Symbol," *Political Science Quarterly* 67/4 (1952): 481–502.
Zaman, R. Uz, "Strategic Culture: A 'Cultural' Understanding of War," *Comparative Strategy* 28/1 (2009): 68–88.
Zatko, Peiter Mudge, "If You Don't Like the Game, Hack the Playbook," presentation at DARPA Cyber Colloquium, November 7, 2011, Arlington, VA.
Zetter, Kim, *Countdown to Zero Day: Stuxnet and the Launch of the World's First Digital Weapon* (New York: Broadway Books, 2014).

Index

3G technology 30
4Chan 114
12P 39, 112
@Jenn Abrams 38

Abbate, Janet 43
ABC *see* Atanasoff–Berry Computer
Abkhazia 64
Accenture 37
Advanced Persistent Threat (APT) 21, 63, 65–6, 81, 89
Advanced Research Projects Agency (ARPA) 11, 12, 18, 42
Afghanistan 92, 134
African Union (AU) 88
Agence Nationale de Sécurité des Systèmes d'Information (ANSSI) 85
AI *see* Artificial Intelligence
Aiplex Software 115
Airbnb 69
Al-Qaeda 119, 120, 134
Alibaba 15
Amazon.com 15, 47, 53
Android 59, 125
Anonymous 114–15

ANSSI *see* Agence Nationale de Sécurité des Systèmes d'Information
anti-virus programs 63–4, 127
Apollo missions 25
Apple 149–50
Apple II 10
APT *see* Advanced Persistent Threat
Arab Spring 139, 143–4
ARCYBER *see* US Army Cyber Command
Armenia 29, 30
ARPA *see* Advanced Research Projects Agency
ARPANET 11, 13, 14, 17, 25, 32, 34, 41–2, 43, 44
Arquilla, John 93, 94, 101
Artificial Intelligence (AI) 25, 79, 129, 153, 155–6
ASEAN *see* Association of Southeast Asian Nations
Ashley Madison breach 37
ASL19 39
Association of Southeast Asian Nations (ASEAN) 88–9
AT&T 17, 19

Index

Atanasoff, John Vincent 7
Atanasoff–Berry Computer (ABC) 7–8
Atlantic Council, Washington DC 152–3
AU *see* African Union
Aurora Generator test 19–20
Australia 142
Auto-ISAC (automotive sector) 129
Aviation-ISAC 129

Babbage, Charles 7
Bahrain 146
Baran, Paul 32
Barlow, John Perry 47
BBC 19
BBN Technologies 44
Belarus 96
Belgium 21
Bell Laboratories 8
Berkeley, University of 156–7
Berry, Clifford 7
BGP *see* Border Gateway Protocol
big data 155–6
bitcoin 107, 110, 119
Black Mirror (TV series, 2011 onwards) 157
BlackEnergy 99
Blair, Tony 118
Border Gateway Protocol (BGP) 47, 64
botnets 51, 110, 114, 130, 154
bots 38, 71, 120
Brantly, Aaron F. 146–7
Brazil 50
British Phonographic Industry 115
British Telecom 19
Buckshot Yankee 68
Budapest Convention *see* Convention on Cybercrime (2001)
bugs 37–8, 62, 127

C2 *see* command and control
CA *see* Certificate Authority
Canada 21, 64, 142
Captain Zap 19
Cavelty, Myriam Dunn 98
CCD COE *see* Cooperative Cyber Defense Center of Excellence
CENTCOM *see* US Central Command
Center for Long-Term Cybersecurity, University of Berkeley 156–7
Center for Strategic and International Studies (CSIS) 20–1
Centers for Disease Control and Prevention 20
Central Asia 106
Central Intelligence Agency (CIA) 57, 134
Central Processing Unit (CPU) 29, 124, 126
Cerf, Vinton 11, 44
CERN *see* European Council for Nuclear Research
CERT *see* Computer Emergency Response Team
Certificate Authority (CA) 52
Ceruzzi, Paul E. 13
Charlie Hebdo 115
China 51, 76, 79–82, 87, 89, 100, 120, 121, 135–6, 145
Chinese General Staff Department 418th Research Institute 82
Chrome 46
Church of Scientology 114
CIA *see* Central Intelligence Agency
Citizen Lab (University of Toronto) 118, 147
Clarke, Richard 94
Clausewitz, Carl von 97
Clinton, Bill 45, 86, 148
Clinton, Hillary 49, 84, 145
CNN 20
Codenomicon 36
Cold War 78
Colossus 8

command and control (C2) 70, 71, 102, 117
Commandement de cyberdéfense (France) 101–2
Computer Emergency Response Team (CERT) 18
Computer Misuse Act (UK, 1988) 19
computers
  convergence between computing / networked communication 10–11, 13–14
  development/access 6–7
  history of 7–10
  and mobile computing 25
  spread of personal computers 13–14
Computing–Tabulating Recording Company 43
Confidentiality, Integrity and Availability (CIA) 123
Convention on Cybercrime (2001) (Budapest Convention) 54, 121
Cooperative Cyber Defense Centre of Excellence (CCD COE) 54–5
CPU *see* Central Processing Unit
Craigslist 15
Crocker, Steve 41–2
Cross-site scripting (XSS) 114, 115, 116, 117
Cruise, Tom 114
cryptocurrencies 107, 110, 112, 119
CryptoLocker 71, 72
CSIS *see* Center for Strategic and International Studies
Cuba 58
Cyber Caliphate 118, 119
cyber capabilities
  arsenal of possibilities 59–63
  core areas 57–8
  criminal 64–5
  definition 57
  developing 63–4, 146
  effects/characteristics 71–4

historical strategy examples/ analogies 58–9
offensive/defensive actions 62–3
state 65–71
vs. kinetic capabilities 73
as a weapon 74
cyber conflict 98–100
Cyber Kill Chain 66, 67–71
"cyber Pearl Harbor" 95
cyber power 77–9
  holistic approach 82–6
  imbalance in 147
  information control 79–82
  pro-active 86–9
Cyber Statecraft Initiative (Atlantic Council) 152–3
cyber technologies 143–6
cyber theft 108–11
cyber violence 111–12
cyber war 71
  approach of 93–5
  and cyber conflict 98–100
  debates/arguments concerning 91, 103
  lethality of attacks 95–6
  military operations 101–3
  as taking place / not taking place 95–8
  war in the fifth domain 91–2
Cyber War (Clarke and Knake) 94
cyberattacks 3, 16, 39
  as acts of war 97–8
  anonymous nature of 99
  attributes 57–8
  challenges to deterrence 133–4
  and China 80–1
  Cyber Kill Chain 66, 67–71
  defensive measures/solutions 126–33, 137
  fake anti-virus programs 63–4
  growing concerns over 20
  growth of 94–5
  indirect effects 72

lethality of 95–6
leveraging 101
military implications 17–18
moderate views on 98–9
NATO countermeasures 54–5
non-state actors 106–22
origins of 20–2, 36–7
potential motives 99
psychological effects 137
retaliatory responses 134–5
and Russia 64–5, 83–6, 94, 99, 100, 101
spectrum of activities 96–7
state-on-state 83–6, 89–90
tactical/operational levels 102–4
as threat to national security 92
and the US 86–8
see also malware; named viruses
cyberbullying 111, 112
cybercrime 3, 54, 63, 105–6
bullying/stalking 111–12
deception, fraud, extortion 107–8
definitions of 106–7
development of 64–5
economic impact 113
fraud/extortion 108
hacktivists 114–16
illicit marketplaces 112
increase in 121–2
non-state actor/s 120–2
proliferation/impact of 106
sexual crimes 112–13
terrorism 105–6, 116–20
theft 108–11
trespassing 107
violence 111–12
cyberespionage 146
Cyberpower and National Security (Kramer et al.) 78
cybersecurity
background 1–4
challenges 123
defense/deterrence 123–4

and democracy 139–43
encryption 148–9
futures of 152–9
global issue 20–2
government/policy decisions 140–1
government conversation on 24–5
spyware 146
threats/incidents 16–22
see also national security/strategy
cyberspace
definition / core concepts 2, 26–8, 56
development/proliferation into communities 3–4
etymological roots 25
logical-network layer 32, 34–8
manipulation in 39
military operations 101–3
persona layer 38–9
physical-network layer 27, 28–32
science-fiction writers on 25–6
significance 2–3
technical value 40
threats/opportunities 6–7
Cyberspace Operations Center 130
cyberstalking 111–12
cyberterrorists 105–6, 116–20
cybertrespassing 107
"Cyberwar is Coming!" (Arquilla and Ronfeldt) 93
cybotage 96–7
CYCLADES 11

Daily Beast 38
DARPA *see* Defense Advanced Research Projects Agency
Davies, Donald 32
DCLeaks.com 84
DDoS *see* Distributed Denial of Service
Declaration of the Independence of Cyberspace 46–7
Defense Advanced Research Projects Agency (DARPA) 18, 129

Defense Information Systems Agency (DISA) 61
defense/deterrence 123–4
  anti-virus/firewalls 127
  by denial 124–31
  by punishment 131–5
  costs/benefits 123–4
  hardware/software 124–6
  host-based measures 127–8, 129
  individual protection 126–7
  information sharing 129–31
  multiple approaches 127–8
  network measures 128–9
  organizational agreements 129–30
  painful reality 136–7
  patch management 127–8
  risks/rewards 123–4
Deibert, Ronald 140
Demchak, Chris 89, 102
democracy
  civil liberties 146–7
  encryption / cyber (in)security 148–9
  imbalance of power 147
  liberation technology 143–6
  protection of information 148
  and security 139–43
Democratic National Committee (DNC) 84, 133
DeNardis, Laura 47, 51
denial of service (DOS) 19, 114
Der Spiegel 142
deterrence *see* defense/deterrence
DHCP *see* Dynamic Host Configuration Protocol
Dhondup Wangchen 147
DHS *see* US Department of Homeland Security
Diamond, Larry 143, 146
DIB-ISAC (defense industrial base) 129
diplomacy, information, military and economic capabilities (DIME) 77

DISA *see* Defense Information Systems Agency
Distributed Denial of Service (DDoS) 31, 64, 83, 96, 110, 114, 115, 116
DNC *see* Democratic National Committee
DNS *see* Domain Name Service
DoD *see* US Department of Defense
Domain Name System (DNS) 34, 35, 36, 49, 69
Dombrowski, Peter 89, 102
DOS *see* denial of service
Dubai 49
Duke Energy 128
Dupont, Benoit 156
Dynamic Host Configuration Protocol (DHCP) 34

E-ISAC (electricity sector) 129
East Asia 106
eBay 15
EFF *see* Electronic Frontier Foundation
Egypt 146
Electronic Frontier Foundation (EFF) 39, 147, 148
Electronic Numerator, Integrator, Analyzer and Computer (ENIAC) 8
electronics 26–7
ELIGIBLE RECEIVER 18
ENIAC *see* Electronic Numerator, Integrator, Analyzer and Computer
Estonia 54, 86, 94, 110, 115
Ethereum 110
EuroMaidan 139, 144
Europe 63, 106, 142, 143
European Agency for Network and Information Security 130
European Council for Nuclear Research (CERN) 14

Index

Facebook 15, 35, 53, 80, 119, 141, 144
Fairfax County, Virginia 107
FALCON cable 31
Falder, Matthew 112
FBI *see* Federal Bureau of Investigation
Federal Bureau of Investigation (FBI) 17, 69, 111, 112, 135, 149–50
  Internet Crime Complaint Center 106
Federal Computer Fraud and Abuse Act (US, 1986) 19
Federal Security Service (Russia) (FSB) 82, 85
fiber-optic lines 29, 30–1
File Transfer Protocol (FTP) 34
FinFisher 146
FireEye 65
FireFox 46
firmware 36–7
"Five Eyes" community 142
Flame 63
France 21, 84–5, 88
Freenet 39
FS-ISAC (financial services) 129, 130
FSB *see* Federal Security Service (Russia)
FTP *see* File Transfer Protocol

Gartzke, Erik 74, 100
Gates, Bill 19
General Data Protection Regulation (GDPR) 47–8, 143
General Staff Main Intelligence Directorate (Russia) 65, 84
Georgia, Republic of 29, 64, 83, 100, 110, 115
GhostNet 147–8
Gibson, William 13–14, 27
  Neuromancer 25–6
GitHub 69
Google 53

Google Earth 119
Google Maps 80
governance
  challenges 41
  contentious/difficult issue 42
  Internet as complicated mess 55
  laws/norms of cyberspace 54–5
  major Internet entities 52
  and multistakeholderism 51
  origins/development 41–2
  political, social, economic 46–53
  technical 43–6
Graphical Processing Unit (GPU) 124
Graphical User Interface (GUI) 125
Great Firewall of China 80, 120, 145
Green Revolution (Iran) 49
GRU *see* General Staff Main Intelligence Directorate (Russia)
Guardian 142
Guardian Project 148
Guccifer 2.0 84
GUI *see* Graphical User Interface
Gvodsev, Nikolas 86

hackers, hacking 17–19, 24, 25, 36, 37, 43, 60, 62, 64, 65, 68, 69, 70–1, 74, 108–9, 117–19
Hacking Team 66
hacktivists 105, 114–16, 120, 121
Hafner, Katie 43
"Halal" Internet (Iran) 46
Healey, Jason 152–3
Heartbleed bug 36
Hess, Markus 70
Hoffman, Bruce 117
Hollerith, Herman 7
Home Depot 37, 109
Homer, *Iliad* 58
Host Technical Liaisons 44
HTML *see* Hypertext Markup Language
HTTP *see* Hypertext Transfer Protocol

Hussain, Junaid 118
Hypertext Markup Language (HTML) 61
Hypertext Transfer Protocol (HTTP) 14–15, 34

IAB *see* Internet Architecture Board
IAEA *see* International Atomic Energy Agency
IANA *see* Internet Assigned Numbers Authority
IBM *see* International Business Machines
ICANN *see* Internet Corporation for Assigned Names and Numbers
Idaho National Laboratory 19–20
IDPSs *see* intrusion detection and prevention systems
IDSs *see* intrusion detection systems
IETF *see* Internet Engineering Task Force
IGF *see* Internet Governance Forum
IMPs *see* Interface Message Processors
India 21
Information Sharing and Analysis Centers (ISACs) 129, 130
Information Sharing and Analysis Organizations (ISAOs) 130
Intel chips 126
Interface Message Processors (IMPs) 34, 42, 44
International Atomic Energy Agency (IAEA) 68
International Business Machines (IBM) 8, 10, 25, 43, 61
International Covenant on Civil and Political Rights (1966) 141
International Federation of the Phonographic Industry 115
International Strategy for Cyberspace (2011) (United States) 87, 145
International Telecommunications Regulations (ITRs) 49

International Telecommunications Union (ITU) 48, 49, 51
Internet 30
  cyber threats/incidents 16–22
  data on browsing habits 141–2
  governance issues 43–5, 47–53
  government interventions 145–6
  "Halal" (Iran) 46
  importance of 49
  as "liberation technology" 139
  misappropriation/misuse of IP addresses / domain names 47–8
  net neutrality 53
  as political tool 49–50
  privacy on 143
  reductions in freedom 145–6
  spread of 14–15
  technical functions 45–6
Internet Architecture Board (IAB) 45, 52
Internet Assigned Numbers Authority (IANA) 44, 46
Internet Corporation for Assigned Names and Numbers (ICANN) 35, 45, 46, 48–52
Internet Engineering Task Force (IETF) 36, 42, 45, 52
Internet Exchange Points (IXPs) 52, 130
Internet Explorer 15, 46
Internet Governance Forum (IGF) 48, 49, 52
Internet Network Operators' Groups (NOGs) 51, 52
Internet Protocol (IP) 11, 13, 34, 38, 44, 47, 141, 155
Internet Research Agency, St. Petersburg (Russia) 38
Internet Research Task Force (IRTF) 45, 52
Internet Service Providers (ISPs) 14, 30, 35, 51, 52, 64, 80, 83, 89, 130

Internet Society (ISOC) 45, 52, 158
Internet of Things (IoT) 90, 153–5
intrusion detection and prevention systems (IDPSs) 70, 128
intrusion detection systems (IDSs) 128–9
intrusion prevention systems (IPS) 128, 129
iOS 59, 125
IoT *see* Internet of Things
IP *see* Internet Protocol
iPhones 25
IPS *see* intrusion prevention systems
IPv4 Address 36
Iran 51, 68, 69, 89, 96–7
Iraq 68, 92, 117
IRTF *see* Internet Research Task Force
ISACs *see* Information Sharing and Analysis Centers
ISAOs *see* Information Sharing and Analysis Organizations
Islamic State in Iraq and Syria (ISIS) 115, 117, 118, 119
ISOC *see* Internet Society
ISPs *see* Internet Service Providers
Israel 21
ITRs *see* International Telecommunications Regulations
ITU *see* International Telecommunications Union
IXPs *see* Internet Exchange Points

Japan 21, 58
Jensen, Benjamin 81, 88
Jiang Zemin 79
Jobs, Steve 10
Joint Task Force (JTF) Ares 120

Kahn, Robert 44
Kello, Lucas 74
Kennedy, John F. 58

KGB *see* Soviet Committee for State Security
Khan, Robert 11
King, Gary 80
Klimburg, Alex 115
KLOC 62
Knake, Robert 94
Kramer, Franklin 78
Kuehl, Daniel 26–8, 77

Lashkar-e-Taiba (LeT) 119
Lawrence Berkeley National Laboratory 17, 70
Laws of War 55
Leiner, Barry 13
LeT *see* Lashkar-e-Taiba
Liang Qiao 79, 135
liberation technology 143–6
Lin, Herbert 72
Lindsay, Jon 74, 133
LinkedIn 15
Linux 59, 69, 125
Live Free or Die Hard (film, 2007) 111
Lizard Squad 118
Lockheed Martin 66
Lodz, Poland 111
LOIC *see* Low Orbit Ion Cannon
Lorenz cipher 8
Love Bug ("ILOVEYOU") 20
Low Orbit Ion Cannon (LOIC) 114
LTE technology 30
Lyon, Mark 43

Mac OS 59, 69, 125
McAfee 106
McArthur, General Douglas 58
McGraw, Gary 94
Macron, Emmanuel 85
malware (malicious software) 3, 17–18, 20, 37
   complexity/sophistication of 61–2
   cyber extortion 107–8

Cyber Kill Chain model 66–71
  development of 64, 65, 66
  diffusion of 66
  lifespan 63
  polymorphic sample 61
  production/distribution of 66
malware (malicious software) features
  Entry Point Obfuscator (EPO) 60
  metamorphic 60
  multi-part 60
  multi-partite 60
  polymorphic 60
  resident 60
  stealth 60
malware (malicious software) types 59
  backdoor 59
  bot 59
  exploit 59
  HackTool 59
  Rootkit 59
  spyware/adware 59
  trojan 19, 59, 62, 99
  virus 60, 62
  worm 17–18, 19, 20, 60, 62
Mandiant reports 21, 65–6, 136
Maness, Ryan C. 81, 88, 97, 98, 100
Manning, Chelsea 115
Mao Tse Tung (Mao Zedong) 82
Mark I project 11
Massachusetts Institute of Technology (MIT) 43
Matusiewicz family 111
Mayhem 129
Media Access Control (MAC) address 38
Meltdown 126
Metasplit 65
Microsoft 19, 37, 62, 68, 127
MILNET 14, 17, 25
Minitel 46
Mirai DDoS 69
MIT *see* Massachusetts Institute of Technology

Mitnick, Kevin 69
MITRE Corporation 17
MLAT *see* multilateral legal assistance
Model Railroad Club 43
Moore, Daniel 149
Morris worm 17–18
Mosaic 15
Motion Picture Association of America (MPAA) 115
multilateral legal assistance (MLAT) 121
Mumbai, India 119
MVD *see* Russian Ministry of Internal Affairs

Nakasone, Paul 88
Napster 146
NASA *see* National Aeronautics and Space Administration
Natanz nuclear facility (Iran) 69, 96–7
National Aeronautics and Space Administration (NASA) 18
National Center for Missing and Exploited Children (NCMEC) 112
National Cybersecurity and Communications Integration Center (NCCIC) 87
National Cybersecurity Strategy 88
National Democratic Institute 39
National Health Service (NHS) 62
National Physical Laboratory (NPL) 11, 32
National Science Foundation (NSF) 42, 44
national security/strategy
  China example (controlling information) 79–82
  common lenses/challenges 89–90
  as complex endeavor 76
  government investment 140–1
  maintaining 77–9

Index

need for 76
non-state actors 120–2
objective/subjective understanding of 77
   Russia's holistic approach 82–6
   US as pro-active cyber power 86–9
   see also cybersecurity
National Security Decision Directive (NSDD) 24
National Telecommunications and Information Administration (NTIA) 45, 48
NATO *see* North Atlantic Treaty Organization
Naval Research Laboratories 39
NCCIC *see* National Cybersecurity and Communications Integration Center
NCMEC *see* National Center for Missing and Exploited Children
Netflix 69
Netherlands 85
NetMundial 50
Netscape 15
Network Measurement Group 44
Network Solutions Inc. (NSI) 44–5
networked communication 10–11, 13–14
New York Times 18–19, 20
New Yorker 38
New Zealand 142
NGOs *see* non-governmental organizations
NHS *see* National Health Service
Nigerian Prince email scam 107
Nimitz, Admiral Chester 58
NIPRnet *see* Non-Classified Internet Protocol Router Network
NIST *see* US National Institute of Standards and Technology
nodes 28–9
NOGs *see* Internet Network Operators' Groups

Non-Classified Internet Protocol Router Network (NIPRnet) 126
non-governmental organizations (NGOs) 44, 46, 49, 53, 147
NORSAR 14
North Atlantic Treaty Organization (NATO) 3, 54, 55, 86, 92, 94, 130
North Korea 62, 72, 134
Norton, Vice Admiral Nancy A. 61
NPL *see* National Physical Laboratory
NSA *see* US National Security Agency
NSF *see* National Science Foundation; US National Science Foundation
NSFNET 14, 25
NSI *see* Network Solutions Inc.
NTIA *see* National Telecommunications and Information Administration
Nye, Joseph 77

Obama, Barack 118, 136
Oliver, John 53
"Olympic Games" 97
The Onion Router (Tor) 39, 65, 87, 112, 145
Open Systems Interconnection Model (OSI Model) 35
Open Technology Institute 39
OpenSSL 36
Operation Avenge Assange 115
Operation Orchard 94
Operation Payback 115
OPISIS 115
Orbot 39
Orwell, George, *Nineteen Eighty-Four* 142
OSI Model *see* Open Systems Interconnection Model

Pacific 106

packet switching 32–4
Pakistan 146
Panetta, Leon 95
Paris 119
Patch Tuesday 127–8
Paths to Our Digital Future (ISOC report) 158
Pentagon 17
People's Liberation Army (PLA) 65, 82, 102, 135
personally identifiable information (PII) 66, 109
Pirate Bay, The 115, 146
PLA *see* People's Liberation Army
Postel, Jon 44
PPD *see* US Presidential Policy Directive 20
PRISM 142
Psiphon 39
Putin, Vladimir 84

RAND Corporation 32, 93
ransomware 63, 107–8
Raymond, Mark 51
RBN *see* Russian Business Network
Reagan, Ronald 17, 24
Recording Industry Association of America (RIAA) 115
Reddit 69
Regional Internet Registries (RIRs) 52
Renren Network 15
Reporters Without Borders 39, 147
Request for Comment (RFC) 41–2, 43, 44, 45
RIAA *see* Recording Industry Association of America
Rid, Thomas 74, 95–7, 149
RIRs *see* Regional Internet Registries
Rohozinski, Rafal 140
Ronfeldt, David 93, 101
router 29, 30
RUNET 83, 85
Russia 51, 63, 65, 76, 79, 82–6, 87, 89, 94, 99, 100, 120–1, 133, 145
Russian Business Network (RBN) 64–8, 71, 86
Russian Foreign Intelligence Service (SVR) 65, 85
Russian Ministry of Internal Affairs (MVD) 85
Russo-Georgian war (2008) 101

Safari 46
Samson, Peter 43
San Bernardino 149, 150
San Francisco Municipal Transportation Agency 108
SCADA systems 19
Schmitt, Michael 92
SDL *see* security development lifecycle
Second Life 39
Second World War 6, 8, 10, 25, 58, 94, 155
security development lifecycle (SDL) 125
server 27, 29, 30, 35, 48, 70, 94, 109, 114, 147-8
Shadow Brokers 62, 73
Sheldon, John 77, 98
signals intelligence (SIGINT) 82, 85
Silk Road 112
Simple Mail Transfer Protocol (SMTP) 34
Singapore 130, 142
SMTP *see* Simple Mail Transfer Protocol
Snowden, Edward 50, 142
social media 15, 35, 47, 49, 53, 69, 80, 115, 118, 119, 141, 143, 144
software 36–7
SOLAR SUNRISE 18
South Africa 21
South Korea 88
South Ossetia 64

Soviet Committee for State Security (KGB) 17, 70, 71, 82
Soviet Union 58, 82
spade-hacker 29, 30
Special Forces 134
Spectre 126
spyware 59, 118, 146
SQL injection 114, 115, 116, 117
Stanford University 11
Starr, Stuart 78
Steiner, Peter 38
Stoll, Clifford 17, 70–1
Stone, John 97
Storybox 84, 98, 101
Stuxnet 96–7, 99
Sun Zhigang 143
Sutton, Will 105
SVR *see* Russian Foreign Intelligence Service
Syria 92, 94, 117
System for Operative Investigative Activities (Soviet Union) 82

Tactical Technology Collective 39
Tails Boum 39
Taiwan 21
Taliban 134
Tallinn 55, 94
Target Corporation 37, 108–9
TCP *see* Transmission Control Protocol
teaMpOison 118
Tech of the Islamic State 110
Telcos 51
Tenenbaum, Ehud 18
terrorism 105–6, 116–20
Time magazine 135
Titan Rain 81, 135
TLDs *see* Top-Level Domains
TLS/SSL *see* Transit Layer Security / Secure Socket Layer
Tomlinson, Ray 13
Top-Level Domains (TLDs) 47, 49

Toronto, University of 118, 147
Transit Layer Security / Secure Socket Layer (TLS/SSL) 34
Transmission Control Protocol (TCP) 11, 13, 34, 44
Trump, Donald 53, 88
Twitter 15, 49, 53, 69, 115, 118, 119, 143, 144

UCL *see* University College London
Uganda 146
UK Joint Forces Cyber Group 101
UK National Cyber Security Centre 88
Ukraine 63, 69, 83, 98, 99, 144
Ulbricht, William ("Dread Pirate Roberts") 112
UN GGE *see* United Nations Governmental Group of Experts
Uniform Resource Locator (URL) 15, 47
Unit 61938 65–6, 68, 70, 71, 82, 136
United Arab Emirates 21
United Kingdom 6, 8, 19, 21, 32, 62, 85, 88, 101, 142, 146
United Nations 48, 89
United Nations Governmental Group of Experts (UN GGE) 54
United States 6, 8, 21, 63, 85, 86–9, 100, 142
Universal Declaration of Human Rights (1948) 141
University of California–Los Angeles 11
University College London (UCL) 14
Unrestricted Warfare (Liang Qiao and Wang Xiansui) 79, 135
URL *see* Uniform Resource Locator
US Army 126
  Cyber Command (ARCYBER) 120
US Army Counterintelligence 135
US Central Command (CENTCOM) 118

US Cyber Command (USCYBERCOM) 16, 87–8, 101
US Department of Commerce 45
US Department of Defense (DoD) 2, 6, 9, 11, 13, 18, 26, 35, 44, 61, 135
  Joint Publication 3-12 27
US Department of Homeland Security (DHS) 87
US Department of Justice 87, 136
US Library of Congress 66
US National Defense University 26
US National Institute of Standards and Technology (NIST) 37, 127
US National Science Foundation (NSF) 14
US National Security Agency (NSA) 17, 18, 50, 73, 142
US "National Strategy on Global Supply Chain Management" (2012) 125
US "National Strategy to Secure Cyberspace" (2003) 20
US Presidential Policy Directive 20 (PPD-20) 88
US Senate 20
USCYBERCOM *see* US Cyber Command
User Datagram Protocol (UDP) 34

Valeriano, Brandon 81, 88, 97, 98, 99–100
Virtual Private Networks (VPN) 65
VirusBlokAda 96
viruses 19
VKontakte 15, 83
VPN *see* Virtual Private Networks

W3C *see* World Wide Web Consortium
Wang Xiansui 79, 135

WannaCry 62, 108
WarGames at Camp David (film, 1983) 24, 107
Warner, Michael 16, 18
Washington Post 142
Web 2.0 15
websites 35
Wentz, Larry 78
Westworld (TV series, 2016 onwards) 157
Wi-Fi 15, 30
Wiener, Norbert, *Cybernetics: Or, Control and Communication in the Animal and the Machine* 25
Wikileaks 115
Willis, Bruce 111
Windows 59, 63, 125, 128
Windows Defender 127
Working Group on Internet Governance 48
World Summit on the Information Society (WSIS) (2003–5) 41, 48
World of Warcraft 39
World Wide Web (WWW) 14–16, 19, 46, 139–40
World Wide Web Consortium (W3C) 46, 52
Wozniak, Steve 10
WSIS *see* World Summit on the Information Society
WWW *see* World Wide Web

Xi Jinping 136
XKeyscore 142
XSS *see* Cross-site scripting

Yandex 83
Yanukovych, Viktor 99
YouTube 47, 118, 143

Zotob worm 20